Home
Was Never
Like This

Published by
Yardley Enterprises
P.O. Box 1335
Evergreen, CO 80437-1335

Copyright © 2002 by Charles A. Turnbo

For information about this publication contact:
Charles A. Turnbo
303-674-3989
caturnbo@aol.com
www.scriptart.com/Yardley.html

Printed in the United States of America.

Library of Congress Control Number: 2002110783

ISBN 0-9717439-0-8

Home Was Never Like This

The Yardley Diaries
A World War II American POW Perspective
Colonel Doyle R. Yardley
Edited by Charles A. Turnbo

4/1/2006

Thank you for letting us share this story with you!

Respectfully -
Charles Turnbo
700 Ashley Ct.
Salado, TX. 76571
USA!

Contents

Dedication

Col. Doyle R. Yardley's account of his experiences in World War II is dedicated to all the men and women of the U.S. Military who serve to keep our Country free.

This is dedicated to the early parachutists of the U.S. Army who introduced a radical new military strategy during World War II.

This is further dedicated to the brave soldiers of the 509th Parachute Infantry Battalion, a predecessor unit of the Army Special Forces. Most of this unit did not survive the behind-the-enemy-lines special mission in Southern Italy. Your heroism will live forever.

This book is also dedicated to all the soldiers who were confined in World War II POW camps, especially one of the most infamous, Oflag 64. In spite of enormous hardships, your spirit and unity were never broken! This account of your survival is a tribute to the American combat soldier. Your courage and your sacrifice, on behalf of all Americans, will never be forgotten.

Charles A. Turnbo, Editor

Acknowledgments

Special thanks go to my Uncle, Colonel Doyle R. Yardley, for recording his World War II experiences in these handwritten diaries.

Thank you to Nita Yardley Gauntt and Peggy Yardley Turnbo, his two sisters who encouraged me to put Uncle Doyle's experiences into book format.

To my wife, Beverly, and to Aunt Nita, who spent hundreds of hours doing technical proofreading and editing of the manuscript, I give tremendous thanks.

Thank you to my niece Kenna Lang, who through her studies of World War II prison camps interested me once again in publishing this work.

For taking the diaries from pencil-written format to book, a heartfelt thanks goes to Jan Fallon, ScriptArt, and to her husband Chuck for additional proofreading.

We thank those who have given us technical direction and assistance in the printing and distribution of this work.

Finally, thank you to those who read Colonel Yardley's account and by purchasing the book help us produce it.

Charles A. Turnbo, Editor
P.O. Box 1335
Evergreen, Colorado 80437-1335

"Home Was Never Like This"
The Yardley Diaries

Prologue

As a boy, I looked forward to spending time at my grandparent's farm in Erath County, Texas. My grandparents were always glad to have their oldest grandson come to visit and there was much to do to keep me busy. One hot summer day, I found a small storage closet located on the farmhouse porch with a military footlocker in it. I was thrilled to discover all kinds of military clothing, patches, and souvenirs.

Grandma sat down with me and told me that it all belonged to my Uncle Doyle, her oldest son, who had died several years earlier. She told me that Uncle Doyle was a paratrooper in the Army and that he was a German prisoner of war (POW) during World War II. She let me wear his beige-colored hat and I played soldier wearing his medals and ribbons. As a young child, I came to appreciate Uncle Doyle and his legacy.

Several years afterwards, my grandparents both passed away. Back at the farm, I came across all of Doyle's military items I had earlier discovered, still stored in the large metal footlocker labeled "Col. Yardley." Looking through the footlocker, I found something I had missed before, a cache of small student notebooks filled with penciled entries, each neatly dated, detailing his military experiences during World War II.

These diaries cover from 1942-1945, three of his five years in military service. Doyle kept daily records with details of his assignments, his contacts with fellow soldiers, and his combat and POW experiences.

Early Days

Doyle R. Yardley was born April 21, 1913, on a small farm near Lingleville, Texas, where his parents, Al and Emma Yardley raised Doyle and his two sisters, Electra Pauline, or "Peggy," born in 1917, and Juanita, or "Nita," born in 1927. One other sibling, Herschel, was born in 1915 but died at the age of twelve.

As a farm boy, Doyle learned the intricate workings of raising crops and farm animals. He attended school in Dublin, Texas, graduating from high school there. He then attended John Tarleton College in Stephenville and later, Texas A & M at College Station. He was active in the ROTC at A & M and did very well academically, graduating on June 5, 1937.

After college, Doyle moved to the Rio Grande Valley and became a vocational agriculture teacher in the small community of Raymondville, Texas. He purchased a farm and practiced his trade while teaching in the local school system.

On August 29, 1940, Doyle married Eva Mae Brownfield. The marriage was performed by Willacy County Justice of the Peace, M. Brownfield (from Marriage License, Willacy County, Texas). An undated Houston Chronicle newspaper clipping entitled "Col. From Raymondville Writes from Prisoner Camp" mentioned his marriage and subsequent entry into the U.S. Army: "Col. Yardley married Eva Mae Brownfield, daughter of the Mallie Brownfields in Raymondville, shortly before joining the service as a reserve officer."

U.S. Army

According to an Army Certificate found in his footlocker, Doyle R. Yardley, 0356190, Infantry, served in the U.S. Army from November 19, 1940 to February 4, 1946, ultimately achieving the rank of Colonel.

He was involved in the Invasion of North Africa on November 8, 1942, and in the Invasion of Italy on September 14th, 1943. He commanded the first parachute battalion to attack the enemy in Europe (509th Parachute Infantry Battalion). Doyle's service records and diary chronicle his military experiences, including these accounts:

"On September 15, 1943, five days after the Invasion of Italy at Salerno, Lt. Gen. Mark W. Clark ordered Yardley's paratroopers to drop forty miles behind the German lines!"

"It was on this mission that Lt. Col. Yardley received a bullet wound in the hip and was taken prisoner a few minutes later."

"The Germans sent him in a box car to the infamous concentration camp, Oflag 64, Szubin, Poland, where he spent almost 16 months."

"While in the prison camp, Yardley organized and trained a group of officers to dig a tunnel to escape from the German camp. The tunnel was almost completed when the Russians broke across Poland in 1945, at which time the Germans forced everybody to march out of the camp for Germany."

Col. Yardley's diary tells of his ultimate escape from the Germans in this January 1945 entry:

"At 4:00 A.M. on January 21, we were marched out of Oflag 64-Z. The temperature was fifteen degrees below zero. During two days of marching, many Americans escaped from the guards. At midnight of January 23, I slipped by my guards, and once more became a free man. For three days, I stayed with a Polish family until the Russians captured Rogozno."

His diary and other official records chronicle the next few weeks following Col. Yardley's escape. He joined up with the Russian 5th Army's Invasion into Germany until they reached Driesen, Germany. He saw the Russians battle and kill Germans for 21 days. Col. Yardley was then sent to the rear lines to Warsaw, Poland, and from there he was sent down through the Ukraine to Odessa, Russia. On March 7, 1945, he sailed from Odessa, passing through the Basparous, at Istanbul, Turkey, then to Port Said, Egypt. On April 2, he flew to the U.S. via Naples, the Azore Islands, Newfoundland, to his U.S. destination of Washington, D.C.

From diary notes handwritten in pencil, Col. Yardley comments on his observations of the Third Reich and calls one entry, "German Slavery":

"While in Poland and Russia, I learned of many Nazi atrocities. I saw a human soap factory at Turek, on the Vanta River, Poland. The flesh from the bodies of Poles had been melted and made into soap. I was given a bar

of this soap and it has a German stamp mark on it."
(This reminder of the horrendous inhumanity of war
was carried with him and deposited in his footlocker,
where it remains to this day.)

Doyle's diaries reveal a great deal about his life and
the lives of hundreds of others involved in or affected by
the war. He left us a detailed account of military life and
the events that altered history during the 1940's. Col.
Doyle R. Yardley, Commanding Officer of the 509th
Parachute Infantry Battalion and German Prisoner of
War, entitled his diary, *"Home Was Never Like This."* I
hope this glimpse into his thoughts and experiences will
be enlightening.

Charles A. Turnbo

Diary One

Doyle R. Yardley

"Home Was Never Like This"

By Col. Doyle R. Yardley

Introduction

Home was never like this - as far as the GI was concerned, in Great Britain, French North Africa, Sicily and Italy. This diary covers my experiences as a prisoner of war, for seventeen months, under the Germans, and as an escapee with our Allies, the Russians and Poles. The diary was buried when I left Oflag 64, and was secured from the "hide" by Lt. Lou Otterbien, who carried it until I met up with him in Rembertow, Poland, February 1945, after being with the Russians, who so kindly allowed me to keep it.

I have sandwiched into this diary, copies of "The Oflag 64 Item," our little camp paper, which of course, was well "Gepruft" (censored) by a Nazi, Willy Kricks, who incidentally owned the printing press; that is to say, he once stole it from the Poles. The "Items" are cherished souvenirs. Not many officers got out of "Deutschland" with them.

My old battalion, the 509th Parachute Infantry Battalion (not a part of an airborne division), saw all these places. This was the first American parachute battalion to attack the enemy and to make the longest airborne flight to invade the enemy in history, from Lands End, England to Oran, Algeria, French North Africa, on November 8, 1942. Fifteen days later the battalion dropped in to southern Tunisia, near Gafsa. We were the only American troops within at least two hundred miles; however, we had French friends in Tunisia whom we calculated would help us - and who did.

But this is getting away from what I wanted to say, or write about. I hope to put down in black and white, in true, simple and frank language what the officers and men of the battalion thought and did while overseas, in or out of combat. How they acted, their gripes, their bitches, their complaints. And how, as typical Americans, they always found something funny to do - in spite of hardships and handicaps.

There is one thing characteristic about all American GIs: by their nature and ingenuity they know how to entertain themselves better than any other race in the world. I write with assuredness, and I have seen many peoples and many armies in many lands. No other is like the American GI. Perhaps that is a 'trite' statement, for you know that already.

I shall call this manuscript, *"Home Was Never Like This."* Part two of my manuscript carries on with the Yank as a prisoner of war, under our wonderful "pals" the Germans, in a POW camp in Poland.

I was wounded and captured September 15, 1943, on the Invasion of Italy, when my old battalion dropped at midnight at Avellino, Italy some forty miles north of Salerno and behind Jerry (German) lines. Part two also covers true observations and reflections of the Russian soldier - both men and women - during January, February and March 1945. I was with the Ruskies (Russians) during this period, after having escaped from the German clutches on January 23, 1945.

Dedication

To all the boys of the old 509th Parachute Infantry Battalion, to those four hundred and eighty who made the supreme sacrifice on foreign soils, to the boys and girls in our armed forces at home and abroad - God bless them all!

Acknowledgment

To the British, French, Arabs, Sicilians and Italians, whose countries we tread, cussed, condemned and contaminated.

Chapter One
May 1942

It was during the closing days of May 1942 that the 509th got orders to "go over." Lt. Col. Edson D. Raff commanded the battalion. I was his executive officer, second in command. All were happy (except the few who went AWOL). Everything was "hush-hush" - yet all the wives and sweethearts knew we were leaving. The area (Ft. Bragg, N.C.) was full of weeping women; some of the boys were touched just as much.

Airborne Command ordered Raff to give a "show-down" inspection to see how well we were prepared. Maj. Bassett from Command Headquarters conducted the inspection. Finding things not to his liking, he told Raff that the inspection "stunk." Raff retorted, "You're a damn liar! My battalion is the best." You see, Raff was a Lt. Col. and Bassett was only a Major - and both were West Point graduates! After Bassett left, Raff said, "You, know, Yardley, somebody ought to spell his name right - Major B-a-s-t-a-r-d."

Raff is a little squirt about five feet five with more temper than a wet hen! The boys of the outfit called him "Little Caesar" which Raff knew and liked - if you ask me! But you had to admire and respect him, if for no other reason than for his guts and front.

Anyway, Command saw fit to send me to the New York Port of Embarkation to fully supply and equip the battalion. So, on or about the last day of May 1942, the unit boarded H.M.S. Queen Elizabeth, Britain's second biggest ship, with about 15,000 others. They were mostly 8th Air Force personnel. There were eighty Army nurses on board, and did the nurses, God bless 'em, have a field day! Unless you wore eagles or General's stars, you hardly had a Chinaman's chance!

The Queen Elizabeth was under the administrative control of a South African by the name of Col. O'Brien-Trigue, whom I shall never forget. The daily ration was "stinko," if you compared it to the good food we were used to in the States! We ate mutton until the boys got the "blates." On about the third day at sea, things broke loose. An American Sergeant, working down in the Queen's kitchen discovered that Col. O'Brien-Trigue and the ship's crew were "bashing" good old American ice cream, fresh vegetables and Hereford steaks! The Chef, who was Australian, and the Sgt. went to blows! Good for the Sgt. as this brought about a slight improvement in the messing.

It was discovered after about three days at sea that there were anti-aircraft guns on the "bloody old ship" and none of the guns were armed. Col. Murtog, U.S. Air Corps, and "Defense Officer" had been "plastered to the gills," and naturally didn't know about the guns! Finally, we learned that out of the 15,000 human beings on board our paratroopers were the only ones who knew how to fire guns. What happened? The paratroopers became the victims from then on, and we lived up on the top deck, in the snow and ice, manning the rusty old British guns. There wasn't much bitching, though, because the paratroopers knew the "pencil-pushers," as the boys called them, never had fired guns anyway. Besides, these "pencil-pushers" didn't have nice shiny paratroop boots!

While the battle with the ice and snow went on up deck, the battle for the nurses went on downstairs. Capt. Doc Carlos Alden, who always did "other things" more than "doctoring," was the only paratrooper who managed a date. When the Doc was not exploring the Queen's interiors, he was usually found giving first aid of some sort to his nurse friend. When Little Caesar would yell, "Maj. Yardley, where in hell is Doc Alden?" I would say, "I don't know, Sir, but I'll try to find him," as though I didn't have the slightest idea! Why I took the rap for that man . . . but I always did.

Since the Queen plowed through the water, zigzagging all the way at about 35 knots, there was little to fear from Jerry submarine attacks. An attack from the air was more probable.

On the morning of the fifth day out at sea, Raff got permission to warm up the guns to see if they worked. After all, the things might *not* work. The GIs thought this was a brilliant idea, too, since they had been standing by the guns for two days without even firing them! So warm the guns up, we did. While Commanding Officer Raff and I were making the rounds, we came upon a gun, a GI, and an Air Corps Colonel - which and whom we had not seen before. Lt. Col. Raff asked the Colonel what the hell he was doing fooling with the gun, anyway. The Colonel, a bit nonplussed, replied, "I'm showing this soldier how it works." Raff said, "Well, keep your gawd-damn hands off. My soldier knows more about this gun than all your gang put together!" (Incidentally, the soldier looked puzzled; I laughed up my sleeve. Raff's feathers re-ruffled and the Colonel decided he wasn't wanted and left.)

All was quiet until about dawn the next morning. A paratrooper who decided the Queen's people needed a little excitement, "accidentally" let his Bofer gun warm itself up to the tune of a few dozen rounds! Without expounding too much on the subject, you guessed it; the Captain of the ship sounded the alarm! Everybody afloat, including the eighty nurses and Doc Alden, thought Jerry Stukas were attacking. After a brief spell, the atmosphere calmed down a bit, but everybody was still scared stiff - except the soldier who knew about the "accident." The Captain accosted Raff, who pretended to be quite angry with one Pvt. Huff (confidentially, Raff and Huff were in their glory). The soldier knew he couldn't be reduced in rank because he was a buck private already. If they made him KP that would be better than the cold deck anyway. Besides, down in the kitchen he might get a bite of Col. O'Brien-Trigue's ice cream!

The Battalion in England

On or about June 4, 1942, the old Queen skirted around the shores of Ireland and glided down the Irish Channel to anchor not far out from Glasgow, Scotland.

"Holy-Flaw, is this Greenland?" the boys asked. You see it was 11:30 P.M. - and it was still daylight. No Yank is interested in anybody's geography except the geography of his home state. So how could you expect him to remember that at one time or another he had read that Scotland was quite a ways north, and that its summer nights were short ones?

What a relief it was to be off the sea and on good old sod once more! The Scotch Highlander's bagpipe band, its members dressed in gaudy kilts that looked like circus dresses to the GI, played us into the staging area. Beautiful, quaint, rolling Scotland, with all its thatch-roofed houses, was nice to see while rolling along on a train, but I wouldn't want to live there.

Orders were orders and it was a secret just where we were to stop in England. Only the Commanding Officer (C.O.), the conductor and I were supposed to know where we were going to live for the next few months. We knew it had to be west of London, for we had already passed through London - even though the "bloody" old city was so smoky and foggy one would hardly know it.

The jolly old conductor talked for hours and told us about everything - except where we were going. He really knew his bit of history, especially of the quaint old manor houses and castles. Take it from me rather than from the conductor - some of the old manor houses really had a history; so did the old dukes and lords who had lived in them, loved in them, and died in them.

According to the old timer, the royal and divine bloods were really the playboys of their day. He pointed out one castle to the C.O. and me, where one old king was supposed to have chopped off the head of his queen because she (the queen) had caught him (the king) fiddlin' around with a beautiful chambermaid! I wish I could remember history, and then I could tell you who they were, but you probably know already.

"God Save The King" and "Star Spangled Banner"

Finally, in the beautiful village of Hungerford, Berkshire, England, the train came to an abrupt English halt - and practically everybody landed on the floor on his bottom. "I'll say, old chap," I asked, "Are we he-ah?"

"Righto, righto - exactly," was the conductor's reply, and off down the aisle he went humming and singing some crazy song which none of us could understand. You see his English accent sounded as funny to us as ours, perhaps, did to him.

We looked out the windows and saw that the entire village and countryside must have turned out. There were also British troops - fine looking fellows, they were. When GIs whistle, you know what that means, too: pretty girls. Even Private Shin, the Chinaman from New York, and Private Kukec, Raff's orderly, whistled!

"Wow - look at that!" cried the boys in the rear. The battalion detrained. Raff yelled, "Maj. Yardley, hurry up and line 'em up. Here comes a British General!" "Yes, Sir," I said and saluted. I lined the battalion up and gave the boys a quick look-over. Their parachute boots shined like a Hollywood chandelier. That's one the boys could be counted on to do without orders: shining their boots.

Most of the party was British Airborne officers: Maj. Gen. F.A.M. Browning; M.C., British First Airborne Division Commander; Lt. Cols. Oppenheim and Smith-Pigot; and a host of aides accompanying the General approached. Incidentally, Gen. Browning is the husband of Daphne du Maurier, the English novelist, who wrote *Rebecca, Frenchman's Creek,* et al.

This ceremony was soon concluded - Raff was very proud - and the R.A.S.C. band played "God Save The King", and "The Star Spangled Banner." As we marched away from the station, the band played "Hold That Tiger." There we were, marching along the line of English lassies. Every paratrooper had his pants well tucked in his boots. We were "hot stuff" - we thought! After all, Col. "Little Caesar" had told us that we were "the best damned outfit in the U. S. Army." Raff always said, "You gotta have esprit de corps" - and we had it, I think.

Two-miles from Hungerford is the picturesque little village of Chilton Foliat; this was to be our new home for almost six months even though we didn't know it at the time. Lady J. T. Ward, who was an American before she married into British nobility, owned Chilton Foliat Lodge. Her father was Ambassador W. Reed, New York City. Lady Ward was a little princess to us.

"What, No Flushing Toilets and Running Water?"

This was what the GIs asked when they moved into the Nessen Huts (each hut would contain twelve soldiers, comfortably, according to the British.) The GI's disgusted description of the situation: no crappers, no windows, no water, and no nothing! "If you Joes want runnin' water, well, run to the tower after it; if you want your crapper flushed, well, take it to the creek and flush it. See? Simple isn't it?" Yes, we had a lot to get used to and to learn, as we later found out. Seven months in pup tents later on, brought back dreams of those "oh so wonderful cozy Nessen Huts at Chilton Foliat." Home was never like this . . .

"Damn Those Officers!" Cried the GIs!

All the officers were billeted in one wing of Lady Ward's manor houses and did the Joes squawk! (Personally, I don't blame them. We had running water and inside toilets.)

For the first three days British R.A.S.C. troops cooked and served all the meals, so that our cooks could learn how to cook mutton and boil tea, and serve it - English fashion. (You see we were on British – not American rations.) The first meal in the Lodge was a "cutter." Gen. Browning and some of his officers were our guests, mind you, one meal in seven courses! Why? I don't to my name know; I could have eaten it all in one course, saved a lot of time, and still been hungry. All the rattling of the dozens of dishes certainly didn't satisfy the old tummy. However, we tried to look "frightfully satisfied" for Little Caesar had told us to.

After "dinnah" we had "teah" (tea) in Lady Ward's fine parlor. General Browning and Raff delivered a little pep talk. We had to take notice because some of the British fellows had something we didn't - previous combat experience. After a while Raff gave me the gawd-awfulist look I ever saw. I asked myself, "What's wrong now?" Pretty soon I knew. Some of the young officers had their feet "cooked" upon Lady Ward's fine old furniture all the time Gen. Browning was talking. I knew there would be "hell to pay" when the guests departed. I prepared myself. Pretty soon they left and in came Raff with venom in his very eyes.

"Yardley, teach them gawd-damned dumb hillbilly officers some manners!" "Yes, Sir," I said and saluted. The fellows didn't do it again - to my knowledge.

English Spoken But Not Always Understood

Among other things to learn was this strange language called British English. However, we learned "straight-away" that the British fellows were "jolly fine" people, even if they "khan't" say "can't" and even if they "dhance" when we dance; even if "petrol" means gasoline; "laid-on" means planned; "tuppence-hapney" is two and a half pence; NAAFI is a PX; even if they do use "righto," "frightful," "terrible," and "right you are" too much. After all don't we overwork "OK?" And who would know what a "screw-ball" or a "hep-cap" is except a Yank?

"Yardley, you will be my social secretary in addition to being my Exec," said Raff. That is what Little Caesar told me when he began to get too much publicity for his own good. Of course I didn't like it, but I said, "Yes, Sir," and saluted. That's the Army thing to do.

I'm telling you the honest to gawd's truth when I say this social business went on without a let-up for four solid weeks. Everybody in the whole community was inviting everybody in the battalion to all sorts of social doings; dances, teas, receptions, bicycle rides, parties - and the vice versa. There was plenty of good will on both sides, and the officers and men of the 509 were plenty willing.

Oh, Those Pretty Parachute Patches!

As seems to be SOP (Standard Operating Procedure) with the Army, it puts out an order to correct a wrong, or prevent one, before a wrong has been done. But usually the wrong has already been done, anyway. Well, it seems that the 509 so did. Soon after we arrived in England, an order came down from E.T.O.U.S.A. (Eisenhower's headquarters) saying, "It has been reported that some of your boys have been seen wearing parachute patches on their caps" and, "they will cease this practice immediately" for "the Germans must not know that paratroopers are in England" - or something to that effect! The GI reaction in plain words: "Hell! Tell E.T.O. that we're usin' psychological warfare and besides, we have been seen in so many places in England already, that Hitler spies think there are a million of us here!

Take away a paratrooper's patch and he's plenty hurt, because who will know that he is a graduate of Ft. Benning's Glamour School? The boys were allowed to continue stuffing the pant legs in the boots, and morale didn't drop too much.

Chilton Foliat Aircraft Factory and Its Gals

Adjacent to Lady Ward's Lodge was a little factory that made taps and bolts for "Spitfires." Practically all of its workers were pretty young English lassies. So far as I was concerned it was a "worry factory." It's hard to mix blonds, bolts, taps, boots and paratroops, if the final results are to be "Spitfire" and combat soldiers. Not only did the GIs like to visit the factory but also so did the officers. One Doc Alden, whose hometown is Buffalo, New York, could always be found here "doctoring" everything but soldiers. Two of the GIs later married two of the factory's pretty blonds: Pfc. Leo W. Martin to Miss Barbra Russel, Hungerford, Berks, England; and Private James Keachum to an Admiral's daughter, Miss Gladys Rigley, Reading, Berks, England. The net results of the association with the factory, as far as I could ascertain, were two marriages, four babies, and broken hearts on both sides when the boys moved out!

Chapter Two
June 1942

Hungerford Hospitality

In spite of the many infractions of minor civil laws by the boys, it didn't seem to affect the local hospitality in the local towns of Hungerford, Chilton Foliat, Tottertown, Inkpen and Kintbury. Inspector Rogers, Hungerford Police Department, handled all cases of infraction with deference and tact. The infractions ranged from "swiping" vegetables and fruit, riding bicycles on the wrong side of the road, giving bicycles to daughters of anxious mothers (there was a thriving black market for bicycles), and cracking up a few telephone booths (kiosks, in England).

In Hungerford there was the Corn Exchange, duly remodeled with waxed floors for weekly dances. The boys of the battalion will long remember the lively dances at the Corn Exchange - where eager girls learned how to jitterbug and do the Rumba, and where all the old folks for miles around came to see "these crazy American antics." Leading jitterbuggers were Lt. Bill Sherman, Sgt. McCook, T-5 Jones and T-5 Pardieck. Incidentally, it was during one of these dances in June 1942 that the paratroopers heard the first air raid alarm in Hungerford. The music stopped, and everybody stopped in his or her tracks. Inspector Rogers came rushing in and wanted to know the trouble. "Is Jerry over tonight?" asked some GI. Suddenly the sound came again: it emanated from the lips of one Private Suarez, Alabama - GI and the battalion clown. Inspector Rogers wanted to arrest Suarez, but Suarez talked him out of it. This soldier could imitate anybody or anything capable of making a sound.

There was the Hungerford Common (public park), a playground for church functions, picnics, parties and promenades - though not on the scale of Hyde Park, London. Best of all, according to the boys, there were no

automobiles to disturb the pastoral atmosphere. Old
and young alike enjoyed the strolls through the
Hungerford Common.

And there was the ancient old Bear Hotel
(pronounced BAER), where many an English Nobleman
had resided while fishing for trout in the River Kenner.
Gen. Sir Allen Cunningham, Commander of the Middle
East Forces until Rommel caused a shake-up in the
British command, had resided here during June 1942.
The Bear Hotel served as the only nice meeting place
(drink place) for British and American officers and their
friends. Old Mrs. Cadd, "cinchy" owner of the place,
knew this situation and charged prices accordingly.
There were three prices: a price for Mrs. Cadd's friends,
a price for the British, and a price for the Americans! I
managed to get along with the old girl all right: I had
taken her for a jeep ride through the streets of
Hungerford one day. But Raff and Mrs. Cadd were
bitter enemies. Raff had once cussed her out for
over-charging some of the officers for the stale English
beer! There were always a lot of married women who
spent most of their time at the Bear. American and
British officers were equally generous in their attention
to the women. The women loved, among other things,
the American cigarettes and free Port.

In spite of the many other "spirits" manifested
locally, there was the fine old religious spirit. I loved to
attend the English church services. Most of the churches
were very old and typically old English. Through the
village Catholic and Protestant churches the
paratroopers made fine impressions and gained many
new friends. One officer and several men became new
converts of religion while in England. The Catholics
were always the most devout churchgoers.

One could not select a more beautiful part of
England to visit than Wiltshire and Berkshire counties.
It's Old England, every acre of it, with its rolling hills,
scattered forests, and narrow winding roads, its
picturesque villages with old-fashioned pubs, its old
English manor houses and palaces of the vanishing
"class." Its pastoral quiet is beautiful, yet almost

melancholy. If you would like this atmosphere and ever visit England, then you must see Wiltshire and Berkshire. From Hungerford, London it is less than seventy miles to the east. Wantage is to the north, Swindon and Oxford to the northwest, and Tidworth and Andover to the South.

Yank Invasion of London – 1942

Since most of the officers and many of the men of the outfit had visited London, opportunity came my way and I visited the dear old city, June 19-20. Since London covers a lot of ground, I only touched some of the high spots. Our British liaison officer, Capt. John Creiton, accompanied me, along with a number of men of the battalion.

Upon arrival at Paddington Station, a party from the Special Service section of E.T.O. met and directed the men to the Washington Club, which was under the operation of the American Red Cross. Accommodations for the men were good and prices reasonable at the Club. Creiton and I roomed at the Cumberland Hotel, the only hotel that seemed to have a vacant room. The Cumberland and Mayflower were more like a modern American hotel. On the other hand, the Claridge was something entirely different, with its aristocratic atmosphere - and scared most Americans away. (Confidentially, they were not wanted, anyway.)

London - yes, yes - with its fog; its devastated St. Paul and Thames sections; its Hyde Park - full of ack-ack guns, spooning and "necking" boys and girls (their daring unsurpassed!); its old timers strolling around; old maids mortified by lover's antics; religious "fanatics" attracting audiences; playing bands. It was a curious sight.

London, Thoroughly Invaded by Yanks

All the E.T.O. officers, down to the shave tail, had nice hotel rooms or apartments and usually adequate female company! Since the arrival of Americans, prices had already begun to climb. The salary of the American soldier, as compared to that of the British soldier, is one reason why the English lassies went pro-American. That, and the glamour of being with the Yanks. The salary of a paratroop Private was greater than that of a British paratroop Lieutenant.

It was easy for me to understand why the Englishmen cursed the Yankee when the taxi driver passed him up to pick up the Yankee. The taxi driver knew very well where his bread was buttered and that the Yankee would tip him about three times as much as his brother Englishmen! Yankee dollar strikes again.

Piccadilly, like all the other places in London, was a madhouse. So I was really happy to get back to dear old Chilton Foliat. Work was piling up for there were dozens of letters, mostly invitations, to be answered.

Raff thought the boys needed more physical exercise – hence, he ordered Lt. Albert Crosby to build a mock-up (a dummy plane fuselage of a C-47). This was for the purpose of training men how to "remember how to jump out of a plane - as if they didn't know how already."

Raff said, "Yardley, I want you to see that this mock-up is completed within a week!" I said "Yes, Sir!" and passed the order on to Crosby, who passed it on to Cpl. Valdez, who got some help from the boys and the Air Craft Factory and completed the old "ship" in the scheduled time! (The old Army game of "passing the buck," I have you know, seems to work).

Little Caesar, who in the meantime had been sort of sweet on Susan Ward, daughter-in-law of Lady Ward, decided that it would be really cute to name the "ship" in honor of Susan. So for short and because Raff wanted it, the thing was named "SUZY." Little Caesar was in his glory - Susan had complimented him. The same day of the christening Raff was invited up to dinner! (Why I didn't think of it first is beyond me.)

For several days I could see Raff walking across the pasute, with a tennis racket in hand, to Suzy Ward's tennis court, where the two would play for an hour or two. Susan wore very loud red shorts that could be seen for several hundred yards. Little Caesar didn't know it, but the officers - hidden behind the fence bushes, were roaring with laughter! Raff thought he was a lady's man, but he wouldn't have had the officers know it for the world. I think the reddest thing I have ever seen - redder than Suzy's pants - was when Susan, dressed up ready to play tennis, walked into the officer's lounge one afternoon to get Raff to play tennis. Raff's face was the reddest thing I had ever seen.

"Are you ready to play, Edson?" asked Susan. She was as pretty as a movie star. Raff swallowed, and said "Ah, yes," and walked out with his face flashing like a stoplight! The officers in the lounge were bursting their sides and trying to hold back the laughter until Raff got outside. The little Colonel wouldn't have had this to happen for the world. He was an important figure in England for what he was and not because Susan Ward thought so. He was the only American parachute Colonel in England, because just a day or so ago the press had said so. It's a strange thing, this, for Raff was easy to get along with until Susan went down to St. Mawes, near Plymouth, to relax. We would have paid her well if she would only have remained at Chilton Foliat. It was worth anything just to have Raff in a good mood. So, for a couple of weeks, Raff worked us day and night. He would send me out with the battalion in the daytime, and have me answer letters for him during the night. You see I was still his social secretary, in addition to being second in command of the outfit.

The Marquis of Salisbury Predicts!

One evening I fell heir to a social function, which I thought would be a bore but which actually turned out to be a most interesting evening. I attended a dance given by British officers in the famous Tottenham Castle, hereditary home of Lord Ailsbury, the sixth in line of the Ailsbury tree to occupy this 210-room mansion, in the heart of the Savernack Forest. I spent most of the evening talking with the kindly old Marquis. The conversation ended in discussing genetics, races, and racial problems. He made this unusual statement: "You Americans are making a big mistake by not intermarrying with the colored race. Mixing and fusion of bloods of different races breeds a stronger race and precludes social discrimination. The English are becoming a degenerate race because there has been no admixture of bloods for generations." That came from an English Nobleman, the Marquis of Salisbury.

Training during the latter part of June and during July developed progressively. Raff had said something was "brewing" and we trained accordingly. Some of the exercises were with the British Airborne Division on the expansive Salisbury Plains, the only part of England that might resemble the Plains of Texas. Training around our own campsite was very much restricted. If the boys got off the road, they were usually in someone's cabbage patch. Then, too, the men very often forgot to close the gates; consequently, the owner's cattle and sheep went visiting and the battalion Commander got a letter of protest the next day. The local British Army officers would mark our maps with various colored pencils, to show the restricted areas, but that didn't do much good at night. The men didn't have flashlight batteries, and you couldn't tell the color of a map at night without a light!

Until C-47s arrived at the nearby airport of Ramsbury, we concentrated on physical training - as usual. Lt. Crosby and some of the men built a very unique "obstacle course" patterned after the British Assault Course. (The local press even thought it was pretty clever.) The officers and men were drilled through this so many times that they had begun to bet one another they could go through it blind-folded!

Littlecote

The closest unrestricted training area was the famous Littlecote Estate. There is an interesting book titled, *Littlecote*. Littlecote, two miles west of Chilton Foliat, with its ancient manor house, forest and pasture, has an amazing history.

The original Littlecote had its beginning about the year 1220. Ancient armor inside the house is black with age. In the 1700's the aristocratic Darrell family owned the estate until a family tragedy caused a change in the ownership.

One room of the house is called the "haunted room." Even today servants refuse to enter the room. So the story goes, young John Darrell had relations with his sister, who later had his baby; John Darrell killed the baby in the room that became known as the "haunted room." A shrewd lawyer by the name of Pampom vindicated young Darrell. As a reward Pampom gained title to the estate. Littlecote remained in the hands of the Pampoms until recently, when Sir Frank Wills, British tobacco king, bought the estate. Mrs. Lyliah Wills, daughter-in-law, occupied a small portion of the mansion. As a wartime emergency, British troops were quartered in the part not occupied by the family. Before the war, Sir Frank employed twenty men to care for the gardens; now there are two gardeners, according to Lyliah.

June 30

Miss Dora Morris, manager of the Chilton N.A.A.F.I. canteen, invited me to dine with her and guests from London. Among the guests was Lady Margaret North, native of South Africa, and Mr. Arthur Duckworth, MP (Member of Parliament). The conversation ranged from war politics to divorces. (They both thought Mr. Churchill "rotten.")

I was surprised when Mr. Duckworth asked, "I'll say, old fellow, how easy is it to obtain a divorce in your country?" "Oh, not very hard, why?" I asked. "It must be terribly easy, for last summer my wife and three children went to New York to visit some friends, and before I knew what was going on, she had gotten a divorce and married the 'stinky' band leader Benny Goodman! As far as I am concerned, he can keep my wife but I wish he'd send my three children back to England. I don't want them to become bandleaders!" I felt sorry for the fellow and went home.

Chapter Three
July 1942

July 4

The battalion celebrated the holiday by taking a twenty-three mile hike.

July 5

The rate of exchange, Sterling-Pound-Dollar, has just been announced (Circular from the Chase National Bank). Sterling-Dollar Conversion Table shows:

One pound (20 shillings) .... $ 4.02
Half pound (10 shillings 2.01
Florin (2 shillings) .... .40
Sixpence .... .10
One penny .... .02
Half penny .... .01

July 7

The local "whore lady" of the village has been cohabitating with some of the paratroopers and giving them a present of "bugs." Inspector Rogers locked her up, but the bugs are still on the loose.

At the mess hall today Capt. Creiton made this statement:

"When war broke out, England had a Regular Army of 80,000 officers and men and a total of three ack-ack guns! Last year at this time, the thirty-five men comprising the Chilton Rome Guard were armed with two shotguns and two hay forks." Thank heavens for a few Spitfires and a lot of courage.

There seems to be a growing resentment among the British troops against the upper class. Some say there will be some changes after the war. They do not hesitate to gripe to the Americans about it. This, a typical complaint story, came from Pvt. Robert Windows, Bristol:

"Last year I was driving an ammunition truck when it broke down near a manor house belonging to Sir Frank

34

Wills. This was just outside Bristol. I walked up to one of the houses and knocked at the front door. When a butler answered the knock I asked him if I might use his telephone to call my company to get the truck pulled in. "Certainly not. And next time use the back door!" I walked to another manor house and again knocked on the door. I asked, "Do you have a phone?" "Phooone? Certainly, there's been a phooone in this house for thirty years!" When I asked if I might use it, he replied "Certainly not!" as though I was a dirty pup. This was during the Blitz. It's too bad Jerry didn't drop a few bombs on some of the manor houses!

I just listened since I didn't understand.

July 10

This was payday, the first the battalion has had since coming to England. Payday means boys with money; money means gals and drinks; put all of them together at one time and that spells plenty of trouble. Sensing that there would be a little trouble, Raff decided to spend the weekend down at St. Mawes.

Raff said, "Yardley, I'm going to get a little rest. You're in command of the battalion. You don't know where I am unless an official call comes through for me. In that case, I'll be at Idle Rook Hotel, phone 266 St. Mawes. Don't let any of the officers take gals to their rooms. Lady Ward's house must be respected." I said, "Yes, Sir!" and saluted. "A little rest," I mumbled to myself - not very loudly, and walked away.

Later in the evening I walked down to Hungerford. Considering the amount of money and the number of boys and gals in town, things seemed rather quiet. Inspector Rogers reported that he had just run about twelve soldiers out of the alley where they were serving our old friend, the Chilton "whore lady." The MPs informed me that a drunk had been put to bed and all was quiet.

I decided to retire to my quarters and spend the rest of the evening in the lounge listening to the radio. There is nothing like a quiet evening. But when I got to the lodge, I found the lounge, which I thought would be quiet and peaceful, full of officers and girls! I was thankful that Raff wasn't worrying about his officers too much about that time. I retired to bed so that I wouldn't be an eyewitness to anything.

Sunday evening found Little Caesar back from St. Mawes. I observed the long look on his face and moved out of his way.

Before retiring, Raff called me to his room to layout the week's work - plenty of marching and exercise for the men. I was to go down to Morthoe, North Devonshire to make arrangements for the battalion to move down on about July 20 for three weeks training with British Airborne units. And I could give a party for the officers next Saturday night in Lady Ward's Lodge. Raff said that he planned to be away again next weekend, but that he held me responsible for good conduct of the officers at the party. I assured the C.O. of good conduct.

By Tuesday, word of the coming parachute officer's dance had reached the ears of local lassies and interested mothers. One mother wrote this letter on behalf of her daughter:

Hidden Cottage
Hungerford,
Berks.
Telephone
Hungerford 27

Dear Officer Commanding:
Please forgive my writing, but may I send my daughter, Dianna, Captain in the A.T.S. (similar to our W.A.C.s) who is home on seven days leave, and your dance is

Saturday night! She will come with Miss Shipway, if she may? I hope you don't mind my asking, but I know you will love to do it! I am sorry but I have not seen any of you. Transport is difficult! Please come to see us if you can spare the time, on any day, especially on weekends.

P.M.S. Winifred L.

Raff assured Mrs. W. L. that her daughter would have a good time, and why didn't she come, also!

Looking over the London "DAILY MAIL"

"Marshal Timoshenko's Red Army falling back . . . Germans pouring across the River Don, down the banks with two main thrusts to capture Voroschilovgrad and Voronezh . . . Von Book is unchecked . . . The Royal Navy's guns blast Mersa Matruh . . . 700 shells rain in 15 minutes . . . Rommel bringing up fresh forces in a new thrust against Gen. Auchinleck's 8th Army in El Alamein sector, Libya . . ."

July 17 - To Morthoe and Back

Pvt. Windows, my English driver, and I made an interesting trip to Devonshire, passing through two very interesting old cities, Bath and Bristol.

Bath - Though not generally known, there is a subterranean city and factory - safe from the blitz, near Bath. Thousands of people from Bath and the nearby towns work in this underground city.

Bristol - The city, what is left of it, lies in a valley and on both banks of the River Avon. The destruction of the industrial sections was almost complete. Five churches remained undamaged, the most beautiful being St. Mary Radcliffe.

The Avon Suspension Bridge, the most colorful of bridges, has been the scene of unusual happenings, one of which I shall relate. Office records of the Lord Mayor, Bristol, may verify this story. Private Windows related the story as follows:

"About 1892, a young father threw his two daughters, five and six years, over the 300-foot bridge, with the intent to destroy them. A salmon fisher, passing under the bridge, saw the two girls plunge into the river. He rescued both girls, who suffered slight body injuries! The girls are alive today! In 1941 this same salmon fisher married one of the girls, believe it or not!"

Just up the Avon from Bristol stands the precipitous Clifton ("Death") Gorge, where each year averages of eight unhappy people plunge to a suicidal death.

Bristol is the native city of John Cabot, explorer and discoverer of Newfoundland. The Cabot Tower of Bristol stands in memorial.

Beautiful North Devonshire, with its two popular resort towns of Ilfracombe and Woolacombe, is famous for its strawberries, dairy farms and beaches. Morthoe, on a high hill, overlooks the Bristol Channel. Arrangements were made for the battalion to move down to the area for training.

Upon return to Chilton I reported, "Col. Raff, everything is in order for the battalion to move down to Morthoe, Sir," and saluted. "Well everything's not in order here! Three men A.W.O.L., two men locked up in London for beating up a civilian, one held in Newbury for beating up a Sgt. of Company B, 205th Quartermaster Battalion, one charged for kicking over a telephone booth in Hungerford. Now get all this mess cleared up - or you don't have a party Saturday night," barked Raff - as though I could help it.

"Yes, Sir," I said and saluted. What else could I do in the Army?

About 9:30 P.M. I walked down to old Lady Cadd's Bear Hotel and bought a beer. I shocked the old lady and her whole "staff" something "frightful" when I asked for a little salt to go in the beer. (I didn't tell her that the salt was to kill the taste!) "Salt! Salt in your beer? How terrible!" she said.

Here are some British-American synonyms:

"Pub" .... a public bar
"Inquires, please?" ..... Information, please?
"Petrol" .... Gasoline
"Programme" .... Program
"Tyre" .... Tire
"Scheme" .... Exercise
"Radiogram" .... Radio phonograph
"G.P.O". .... General Post Office.
G.P.O. is in charge of the post office, radio,
telephone, and telegraph in England.

Saturday, July 18

"The Stars and Stripes" (Military Newspaper)
announced that Maj. Gen. Mark W. Clark would be in
charge of all ground forces in England.

Saturday P.M.

Dear Diary: I'll close and prepare for the party. The
officers seem happy that Little Caesar is absent!
Capt. Bill Dudley, from Vancouver, Washington, is in
charge of all arrangements for the party.

Sunday After

As chaperon of the party and to uphold my prestige,
I must say that the party was a success - even if some of
the men of the battalion did steal some of the beer and
sandwiches from the kitchen (5th column suspected);
even if there was a surplus of females - old and young;
even if two blonds down from London had to walk back
to the Bear Hotel unescorted; even if the radiogram did
break down; even if Lt. Ralph Whitmore did run off with
Doc Alden's Capt. Dianna of the A.T.S.; even if
Sgt. Tony Viteritto, who was invited to the officer's
party to sing a song, did forget to go home; even if Lt.
Crosby went to sleep and his gal friend was "furious";
even if a table did break down when five officers and
dates got upon it and pretended they were about to bail
out in thin air! (How am I going to explain this to Lady
Ward?) Among other things, Dudley got engaged again.
He was engaged to a girl in North Carolina when we

sailed, he got engaged recently to an American Nurse - near London, I was told, and now, he is engaged to an English A.T. (of the A.T.S.)

Little Caesar just called to inform me that he would meet me with the battalion at the Taunton railway station Monday morning and that we would march from there to Morthoe, a distance of 45 miles.

The battalion moved from Hungerford (where the girls cried because they thought the boys were off to war!) to Taunton by rail. At the Taunton station there was Raff and Casey, his newly acquired dog. Raff marched the boys for two hours without calling a halt. You see, he carried no carbine or pack; therefore, he could march much more easily. The roads were narrow, winding and hard surfaced. I cautioned him, "Sir, don't you think you should slow the pace down and call halts more often?"

"Maj. Yardley, I've been in this man's Army a hellova lot longer than you have, and I have forgotten more about how to march men than you ever knew!"

"Yes, Sir," I said and saluted and mumbled to myself, "We'll see, we'll see, Little Caesar."

By 2:00 P.M. the men's canteens were empty and their "dogs" were aching. Five percent of the men had already fallen out and Raff was raving mad! "Paratroopers! Some tough guys!" he would say. And "I'll show 'em."

By 10:30 P.M., the battalion (less the thirty percent back down the road) had marched 55 miles. Since Raff, too, was about to fall out he yelled, "Yardley, halt the outfit; we'll camp here tonight. Empty the baggage trucks and go back and pick up them damn "goldbricks." Take down their names. I want to give them a special workout when we get to Morthoe."

"Yes, Sir." I said and saluted, telling myself, "I knew it. I knew it."

Morthoe, North Devon

For one long week this outfit trained day and night. The only persons that went visiting were Raff, the C.O.'s prerogative I guess, and Capt. Dudley, the adjutant. ("Ah, ah, now Raff will find another gal, and Dudley will get engaged again.") Sure enough, Dudley met the daughter of the proprietor of the Collinswood Hotel, Ilfracombe. And Dudley, knowing how to tactfully handle the C.O. introduced Raff to a Mrs. Mary Hewland, a former actress - and very attractive. Many things were to come of this meeting, I felt sure. Finally, and feeling right guilty, Raff said, "Yardley, you and ten of the officers and twenty percent of the men may have the afternoon and night off to visit Ilfracombe. I'll stay in tonight."

"Yes, Sir," I said and saluted, and saying not very loudly, "Well, it's about time!"

Lt. Whitmore and I took Raff's car and drove to the town. I knew I couldn't be bored with Whitmore along. (Before the "Guerre," Whitmore had been a Hollywood announcer. He could say more and say less than any man I have ever known. If you wanted to know something and had time to listen, all you had to do was ask Whitmore. He'd tell you, briefly - in a few thousand words! The English girls called him, and fittingly, Lt. "Talkmore.") As Talkmore and I strolled down the streets, we right away saw that the paratroopers were doing all right. Ilfracombe seemed to be swarming with women. By 9:30 P.M. the boys were showing their "likker," so I instructed the MPs to round up the boys and take them home, before things got lively. After all, we didn't want to wear out our welcome before we saw the town.

Ilfracombe is a very picturesque little resort town that just seems to step down from the high bluff to the sea. It is considered England's warmest resort town. I would like to see it again someday, after the war is all over.

July 31

I had to laugh at Little Caesar. During night training the other night, Capt. William Medlin, from South Carolina, had the problem of leading his company from point to point across country with a map and a compass. Medlin got lost and Raff cussed him out.

41

Medlin told Raff he didn't believe anybody could do it the first time without getting lost. Raff called Medlin a boy scout and he would show him how the very next night. The next night Raff took charge of Medlin's company, and within two hours the company was so thoroughly lost that it took First Sgt. Swain three hours to find camp again. Little Caesar blamed the compass! The only one, or thing, that didn't laugh about it was Casey, the dog. (Raff and Casey had become great friends.)

This is aside from the subject, but one must write down a few amusing things or how would the great grandchildren know about it? It was funny to see this couple, Raff and Casey, going down the streets of Ilfracombe: Casey, in his bold dog-like fashion, irrigating all the lamp posts; and Raff is saying; "Now Casey, you aughta be ashamed of yourself! (Confidentially, Casey never missed a post!)

Swing Your Partner

To bring the rigorous training to a conclusion, everyone in the battalion went through the famous British Assault Course (or Weapons School of Confidence) at Woolacombe. The course, with its barbed wire, exploding mines, machine gun fire, steep cliffs, etc., was supposed to be the closest thing to the "real thing:" combat. This bath of fire scared everyone. But it was the type of training we really needed. There were a few burned faces, one broken leg, and a lot of bruises. (Doc Alden got into trouble when he took some pictures of the course. The British said it was a "secret.")

Following the completion of the battle course, the boys were ready to relax a bit. A Capt. Doris Simpson, A.T.S, of Ilfracombe, called up to inform us that her girls were giving a dance just for the American boys.

"Fine! Tell her we'll accept with pleasure, Yardley," Raff said with glee. "Yes, Sir!" I said and over the telephone, "Yes, ma'am, we'll accept with pleasure."

Then she asked if we could spare some young officer to work out the details with her. I suggested Whitmore. This man, with his usual verbosity, could work out the "details" to anything. If he couldn't - he could talk himself clear of any blunder. Talkmore and Miss Simpson worked out the details beautifully. Whitmore was thrilled over the assignment.

The dance was a big success. Everybody had a grand time. You should have seen Little Caesar and Capt. Simpson dancing, even if she was a head taller than he. It wasn't Raff's fault. The Colonel left the dance pretty early, though. I think he must have had a late date with his actress. He left me in charge of Casey, the dog, and he put Whitmore in charge of Capt. Simpson of the A.T.S. No casualties reported, though there might have been a few strained ligaments from jitterbugging.

Chapter Four
August 1942

August 7

Picking up a copy of the London "Daily Mail" in the Morthoe N.A.A.F.I., I read:

"Von Book captures Rostov and drives toward Caspian Sea . . . Rommel now being jabbed by Auchinleck's 8th Army in the narrow corridor of El Alamein."

Col. Fortesque, brother of Lord Fortesque, who owns practically half of Devonshire, toured Raff and me over the Exmoor, where we saw wild ponies and sheep. In a way, the Exmoor is a wild and dreary country, considering it is England. Col. Fortesque directed us to a spot, which is rarely ever seen by human beings. This spot is the very origin of the River Ex, a tiny stream that began its trickling course down the Exmoor. Many stories by poets and novelists have been written about the River Ex.

August 9

The battalion moved back to home base - this time riding instead of walking. The Chilton Foliat and Hungerford people gave us a welcome as though we had been off to war.

Dudley and Private Leonard managed to get engaged before they left Ilfracombe, so I was informed!

"Jumping" Planes Arrive

Word came that fifty-two C-47s arrived at the Ramsbury Airdrome, and Col. Raff went to ascertain when his boys could start jumping out of them. After all the local population would like to see some parachuting. This would help the prestige of the paratroopers, for they hadn't been wearing paratroop boots for nothing.

August 15

Last evening the C.O. attended a benefit banquet in London called "The Anglo-Russian Banquet To Aid War-Stricken Horses!"

Lt. Kurtz decided that the meat in his men's mess should be cooked a little better, so he had the local blacksmith make three frying pans - to the tune of five pounds ($20.10).

Lt. Sherman decided that one barber in the battalion was not sufficient to keep the boys in fresh haircuts, so he rode a bicycle to Lambourn and purchased a complete barber set, to the tune of four pounds ($16.08).

Air Marshal Harris, Chief of the British Bomber Command predicts, "If I could send 1,000 bombers over Germany daily, the war would end by October . . . and if I could send 10,000 bombers over Germany tonight, that country would be out of the war by tomorrow!"

"Coming Generations . . ."

This is a true copy of a letter that arrived at Battalion headquarters August 19:

41 Lewton Rd,
Newbury,
Berks,
August 12, 1942

Dear Officer Commanding,
May I venture to make a request? I am wondering whether it might be possible for one of your officers from the U.S. to come and introduce to us first hand information to problems - racial, educational, political, etc., about home states.

I will explain who (sic) I speak for. We are a London Girls' School, evacuated to Newbury. The Godolphin Latimer School, Hammersaint, W.E. A group from 16 to 19 years, all girls who have done exams; some 40 to 50 of them perhaps, would be glad of

a chance to enlarge their knowledge. We
have heard about New England and
northern United States and would like to
get a picture of differing problems of the
South.

I feel that I am asking a great deal of
you and I know how occupied you are, but I
felt I might approach you in the interest of
coming generations of citizens! If you could
spare someone, perhaps a teacher, but not
necessarily so, to talk to us for about an
hour and allow us to ask questions, we
should be most grateful. In case you think
it is possible, I mention a possible time:
Sunday or any time after Monday. These
are only suggestions and any time
naturally possible could no doubt be found.

I hope you will forgive me for writing at
such length,

> Yours truly,
> Wene Butler

"Yardley, send over an officer," ordered Raff and I
said, "Yes, Sir" and saluted. I sent Lt. Henry Tipton
from Mississippi. He talked to the girls "in the interest
of coming generations of citizens."

August 21

For the first time in England, we staged parachute
drops all around Hungerford. The local gentry and all
their servants were out to see the parachute show.
Casualties: one broken leg, four sprains - Capt. Bill
Schloth broke his leg when he sailed down on Lady
Ward's stables!

Ordinarily one C-47 carries twenty troopers. It
requires about 12 seconds for these troopers to leave the
plane. We usually jumped at an altitude of 400 feet.
From this altitude it required about 27 seconds for the
paratrooper to hit the ground.

Capt. Doc Alden, who as I have said before, stays involved in most anything in order to avoid "doctoring," was given the names of nine men to be taken to the American General Hospital at Tidworth to be reclassified. When the Doc got to the hospital, he only had seven men. He had forgotten to count them before he left the battalion area!

Recently Doc, who makes his second headquarters at the Aircraft Factory in camp, thought he would play a joke on one of the ladies at the factory. Without telling her, he drove her automobile off down the hill and forgot to tell her later that it was a joke - and where he left the car. Four hours later the local Policeman was out looking for the "stolen" car. Doc heard about it and happened to think that he had forgotten to tell her where he drove the car! No arrests were made, but Doc had to do some tall talking.

I didn't mention the incident to Raff as I thought it best that Doc and I worked this problem out between us. Alden didn't leave the area the following weekend.

Whitmore Becomes Social Secretary

Raff designated Whitmore as his social secretary, as per my request. (I never heard of a battalion Commander having a social secretary before; however, Raff has one and the facts were written down in the form of an order by the adjutant.)

Recently, Lt. Talkmore was going to do the men of this outfit a favor by bringing over about twenty-nine girls of the A.T.S. for an enlisted men's dance. Whitmore ended up at the dance and delivered twenty-six girls, He dated the other three! (The men never knew the difference.)

August 23

I have just returned from the home of Sir Alexander Godley, with whom I had Sunday dinner. The old gentleman, very kind and gracious, spent most of the two hours telling me the history of his very fine old house located in a little forest near Hungerford.

According to Sir Alexander Godley, "The 15th century house was formerly occupied by one of the wives of Henry VIII. She was Lady Jane Seymour. Henry VIII spent many romantic week-ends here with Lady Jane - before she was beheaded!"

August 28

More disciplinary headaches: the Hungerford Policeman brought in Private R. P. Culvertson, charging him with three offenses: (1) shooting a pistol in public; (2) resisting arrest; and (3) stealing a bicycle. (If these lads fight the enemy as well as they get into trouble, then Hitler had better look out!)

Just back from the Bear Hotel, where Mrs. Cadd, after I bought a couple of her friends a beer, told me more of the old Hotel's history:

Records show that this hotel was in existence in 1279 as the Bear Inn. In 1540, the Bear was settled to Queen Ann of Cleves by Henry VIII, as part of her dowry, and was later included in the dowry of an unhappy successor, Catherine Howard. During the time of the Civil War, King Charles I had his headquarters in the Bear Inn from November 16 - 19, 1643. Queen Elizabeth visited Hungerford on more than one occasion, and the room in which she slept is still marked at Bear Hotel. The Parish register contains the entry of one of her coachmen, who died here in 1601. In 1688 no less a person than Prince William of Orange stayed at the Bear Inn, on his way to Windsor, and was met by Commissioners of James II. He received them in the Bear Inn bedchamber.

(I didn't buy any more beer: I was tired of the Bear's history.)

August 25 to 30 was a very active period for the paratroopers. We staged day and night drops in preparation for parachute exercises and maneuvers with the British forces in North Ireland. (We had our doubts about the exercises being in North Ireland.)

Whitmore Makes Long Distance Call

"*Tatler*," London's picture magazine, recently featured the family life of the Duke and Duchess of Marlborough in their Blenheim Palace, Oxford, England. There were pictures of the Duke and Duchess and their four children, Lord Blandford, age 16, Lady Sarah, age 20, Lady Caroline, age 18, and Lady Rosemary, age13.

Whitmore was so fascinated with the bust of Lady Sarah that he picked up the telephone and called her at the Blenheim Palace! Before the conversation ended, he and two other officers had an invitation to dinner! Lts. Whitmore and Boettner and I drove to the Palace in a jeep. Raff and Casey, the dog, were using the sedan.

The Palace is about ten miles from Oxford and thirty from Hungerford and is surrounded by forests and lakes in the beautiful countryside. We approached the Palace through a maze of lanes, gardens and gates. At the door the butler conducted us to the sumptuous waiting room of "Her Grace," the Duchess. From the Palace balcony we viewed a most unique garden - beautifully landscaped with purely vegetables! (The flowers and roses had been replaced with vegetables as a wartime emergency!)

Very shortly the entire family entered and we all got acquainted very informally. The Duke and Duchess graciously explained to us the success of their victory garden. The Duke, it seems, had done most of the work himself.

The Duke and Talkmore did most of the talking. He told us how proud he was that Gen. Eisenhower's Headquarters had just notified him that he was to be commissioned a Major and would be a Military Police officer in London. Finally the conversation switched to America. The girls wanted to know all about it, and

Whitmore told them all about it, including Hollywood and the American Parachute School. Little Lord Blandford wanted to know if it were possible to parachute out near the Palace some day, and Whitmore said, "Yes."

We had cocktails and then a lovely dinner of grouse, vegetables, etc., with champagne, Port and coffee in the parlor. (Lord Blandford, in the meantime, had gotten too much champagne and the Duchess sent him to bed - straight away.) Following the coffee, Lady Caroline suggested playing some popular American recording, and maybe dancing a little. "Terrific idea!" exclaimed the Duchess. Whitmore and Lady Sarah amused the rest of us with a jitterbug number! "Terrific, that" exclaimed Lady Caroline.

There was a Mrs. Berry present, and the Duke spent most of his time with her - to the annoyance of the Duchess. This Mrs. Berry was the manager of the local Army canteen. The Duke certainly had an eye on her and the Duchess had her eye on the Duke.

Before the pleasant evening ended and we departed for Chilton Foliat, Whitmore had a date with Lady Sarah for the next Parachute officer's dance. "Her Grace" and Lady Ward were intimate friends and Lady Sarah could stay with Lady Ward. The Duchess said it was quite possible that Lady Sarah might be able to attend. Whitmore had done it once more.

Chapter Five
September 1942

September 1

Al Jolson , Merle Oberon, Patricia Morrison, Allen Jenkins and Frank McHugh and a host of newspaper reporters visited the battalion to view an exhibition parachute drop. The parachutists gave them the necessary thrills. One planeload of troopers dropped from an altitude of 130 feet! As expected more fractured limbs occurred. One man broke his back. I was against this "gratis" drop in the first place, but Raff said it was good publicity. It was . . . for him.

After the drop, Jolson and his gang entertained us with a few stale jokes and songs. Al sang the everlasting "Mammy," and told some jokes. About the only joke that got a hearty laugh was the one about English beer. "As far as I am concerned," joked Al, "you can take this beer and pour it back into the horse!" The local English talent didn't think it funny at all.

September 19

In fifty planes of the 60th Troop Carrier Group, the battalion flew to Nuts Corner, near Belfast, North Ireland to train for a week with British forces. During the flight we passed over the Isle of Man, where German prisoners of war were reportedly being held.

September 21

By early afternoon the British Commander on "our side" gave us a mission: to drop near an important bridge, capture and destroy it. This is all staged, of course.

The Air Corps dropped us on what looked like to them very nice ground. Actually, it was a peat bog. We went up to the belt line in mud! I never saw such mud. By the time we waddled out of the mud and muck, there wasn't much "fight" left in us.

Doc Alden and part of the Machine Gun Platoon, the only ones to hit on fairly dry ground, reached the bridge first! Raff, without Casey, followed in "close support." There must have been a regiment of the "enemy" guarding the bridge. The umpires explained to the troopers that they were outnumbered and that they must stop and play the game fair.

"The hell you say," yelled Raff, so the platoon moved to the bridge! Doc Alden lighted a firecracker, which represented the bomb, and "destroyed" the bridge! The umpires, in order to get along with Raff and to make us feel good, ruled that the bridge had been "destroyed." One platoon of paratroopers against a regiment of the "enemy!" Some joke, if you ask me . . .

Anyway, the press wrote, "The American parachutists did a magnificent job." All I could say that we got out of the exercise was muddy feet.

North Ireland is the only place in the world that is muddier and wetter than England; it's also the only place in the world that has more men with redder faces and women with pinker legs than England.

It rained for five straight days, and the planes were grounded. However, Raff and some of the men managed to see Belfast. Yours truly stayed in out of the rain. My, how it does rain in North Ireland.

Air Vice Marshal Cole-Hamilton, the officer in command of the Nuts Corner area, was extremely nice to us. But I know he must have been very happy when we flew back to England. ("These Americans funny blokes, they.")

Saturday, September 26

To round out the month of September, the men of the battalion were given a party at the Corn Exchange last evening. The funds from the dance were donated to the Hungerford Boy Scouts. A Mr. Nichol was in charge of the party. He reported that it was the finest party yet given at the Corn Exchange. Mr. Nichol's daughter, Gene, was at the time engaged to Lt. John Martin, Eagle Pass, Texas. (Incidentally, a lot of the officers and men were getting engaged about this time.)

Tonight the officers are having a "Prop Blast Party." This is to be our last in England, according to Raff. Lady Sarah Churchill from the Blenheim Palace is to be at the party. Green, Lady Ward's butler, is to be her chaperon, so Whitmore said.

Sunday After

Like the party before, there were more females present than could be accommodated even by inviting a number of British officers. Whitmore, underestimating his capacity, got too much beer and was "advised" to go to his room and sleep it off. Crosby took charge of Lady Sarah. At midnight butler Green got tired of chaperoning Lady Sarah. I assured him that everything would be all right and Green went to bed. When the party ended Crosby and Lady Sarah went walking and walked until almost daylight.

During the month of October, everybody was too busy training to enjoy much nightlife. Secret orders had come down from the E.T.O. Headquarters directing certain things to be done that indicated very clearly that the Invasion date was approaching. A number of men in the battalion were trying their best to get married but there was a thirty-day "cooling off" period, even after applications for marriage license were filed. The engaged were desperate. Even the aid of preachers and padres was solicited to speed the process, but that didn't work. You can't get around Army regulations.

One day Col. Little Caesar assembled all the officers and men for an "important" session. He told us that the Invasion was about to come off and that paratroopers would participate in the initial assault. He told us that we were the best soldiers in the U. S. Army and that a lot of things were expected of us. Raff said that if they did a good job, everyone in the battalion would get "gold parachute wings," even if he had to buy them. This we doubted very much, but that didn't matter anyway as long as we were to be in the show. The British paratroops were to participate in the Invasion, but in a different sector. Maps and models of the Invasion area were delivered to study. All identification as to the location and country was eradicated. Everybody speculated, but few guessed it right.

Chapter Six
October 1942

October 12

Mrs. Franklin D. Roosevelt and the usual number of newspaper reporters visited the battalion. The battalion dropped near the area for her edification and for some more publicity! Mrs. FDR thought the mock-up SUZY was "extraordinary." One of the boys displayed all of his "jumping" equipment. One by one - to make it impressive - the equipment was grounded and ejected from the dozens of pockets. The last "necessary" equipment to be pulled out of the pocket and placed on the ground was a small roll of toilet paper! It was no blushing matter for the paratrooper. There was one other little package left in the pocket that Mrs. Roosevelt never saw.

220 Pounds of Qualified Fat

Battalion Sgt. Maj. and Staff Sgt. Alain Joseph, New York City, was not a qualified parachutist but wanted to be, so that he could jump with us in the coming Invasion of somewhere. So an airplane was made available and Joseph was kicked out of the plane five times in one day - in one of Lady Ward's plowed fields. The only damage that resulted was Lady Ward's field, which Joseph's 220 pounds landed on, bounced over and plowed up some more. Joseph got his parachute wings all right. He deserved two sets of parachute wings in my opinion! Joseph, about five feet six, is known as "Mr. 5 by 5" to the boys in the outfit.

During the month of October it rained just about every day. It was getting very cold. The English weather, very humid, really penetrates. Everybody was ready for something to happen on October 25. The battalion got orders to move immediately to a staging area at Great Torrington, not far from Plymouth. Word leaked out and all the gals and their families called to say goodbye. One Padre and Private Leonard's sweetheart came up from Ilfracombe. The girl was pregnant and the Padre wanted to get them married so that the baby would be legal. In all sympathy, there was nothing we could do about it because of the thirty-day "cooling off" period. Orders were orders. We couldn't call off the war just to make the baby legal. Someone in the battalion got a brilliant idea that a donation should be made to the girl so she could have money to support the baby when it arrived! This would be the 509th Parachute Battalion Baby, practically adopted already.

Raff thought it a good idea and said, "Yardley, call the boys together. Tell them the story and pass around the hat."

"Yes, sir," I said and saluted. "Of all the screw-balled ideas", I said to myself, "a collection for a baby who has not even arrived."

"Mr. 5 by 5" passed the hat and collected 302 Sterling Pounds, or about $1,200.00 - in American equivalent! This project even got wide publicity: The 509 Baby! Someday the baby may sprout wings and become an Anglo-American paratrooper, a by-product of World War II. (Incidentally, if there had been a lot of cases like this one, the battalion would have gone bankrupt!)

Raff informed me to ready the battalion and move it to the staging area; he was going to North Devon on "Special Duty." I knew what kind of "special duty:" duty at the Collinswood Hotel.

"I'll meet you at Great Torrington, October 30, Yardley - and if you have to get in touch with me, call me! Ilfracombe 5. My headquarters will be there."

"Yes, Sir," I said and saluted. Raff didn't know that I knew that "Ilfracombe 5" was the telephone number of the hotel in which his actress resided.

October 26 - In the Black of the Night

In the very early hours in the black of the night, while all the local people were asleep, the battalion marched to the Hungerford station and moved out for Great Torrington. From this place, where would we go? Only two persons in the battalion knew. Excitement and speculation were high.

On the 30th Raff and Casey, the pup, joined the battalion. He had a sheepish look on his face . . . and I wonder why. The very idea of this guy gallivanting with a woman - when his outfit was about to go into action!

On November 4, the battalion moved to the great St. Eval Airdrome, Lands End, England. This had to be the jump-off place for it was the south end of England.

Where would the Invasion be, was the big question on the minds of the GIs as they sat around in little groups playing cards, poker, singing and trying to seem happy. Some joked, some cursed, but some prayed. Catholic mass was held. Protestant services were held. All money was collected and receipts given. Escape pouches, which contained money, water purification tablets, chocolate bars, rubber maps and a small compass were also given. All pouches were sealed and were not to be opened in enemy territory.

Raff and Casey were running around in circles. Raff was yelling and shouting at everybody as if this was the last moment on earth to prepare for the show. One GI asked, "I wonder if Raff is going to take Casey?" "If the C.O. wants a friend, he'd better take him," predicted another.

Everybody was ready.

Chapter Seven
November 1942

November 7, 1942

The 60th Troop Carrier Group commanded by Col. Schofield, Air Corps, staged the planes. Hot coffee was placed in each plane. This was very indicative. The Paratroop and Air Corps officers were assembled and briefed on the Invasion of French North Africa. That was it. The Paratroopers were to drop near Oran, Algeria and capture the Tafaroui Airdrome. (We had rehearsed the problem from a model sent down from London.) Then the men were called together and briefed on the problem. At 5:30 P.M. Raff gave orders for everybody to "take equipment and move to their designated planes."

A Paratrooper Without a Paratroop Suit

To go back a little, before Raff left for Ilfracombe, he had instructed Sgt. "Mr. 5 by 5" to bring his paratroop suit, equipment and carbine. At the last minute Raff, who was all excited, yelled, "Joseph, where is my gawddamn suit?" Joseph remembered having brought it along but someone must have misplaced it. Raff cussed out Joseph and me and sent Joseph looking for the suit and equipment. Poor Joseph looked everywhere but he had no luck. Well, this was the last straw for Raff. There he was the Commander of the first American Paratroop battalion to ever go into combat and he had no paratroop suit! An exchange of clothing was made. Little Caesar ordered Joseph to take off his suit and exchange it for the slacks and shirt. This was a show, and every GI was busting with laughter. Raff weighed about 150 pounds against "Mr. 5 by 5's" 225 (he had gained five pounds since the last weighing.)! They made the funniest two pictures I had seen in a long time: Raff with his suit overlapping and Joseph with only the bottom button of his pants, buttoned!

This was the biggest laugh the battalion had had since Raff and Susan had played tennis together! It was also good for the morale of the battalion: it made the boys laugh! (I never knew for sure, but I believe that some GI hid Raff's uniform.)

Last Minute Message

Just as everybody was about to board planes, Col. William Bentley of the Air Corps, came running down to tell us that a message had come through from E.T.O.U.S.A. stating that the French in Algeria were on our side and that the planes would land at the Airdrome without a fight! Everybody was doubtful, but orders were orders.

"What, no fight?" asked the GIs. They still didn't believe it, and neither did I. We would see. This was a SNAFU (Situation Normal, All Fouled Up) idea, the boys said.

November 7, 1942 - 6:00 P.M.

The order was given to load up. The planes warmed up and sailed into the air - to a "peaceful" land, the Great French North Africa. For eleven hours and for 1,500 miles, forty-eight C-47s, with 610 paratroop officers and men, flew across Spain, the Mediterranean Sea, headed for the Tafaroui Airdrome, Algeria.

Chapter Eight
Invasion of North Africa

In final preparations for the Invasion of French North Africa, United States and British parachutists carried out maneuvers in Scotland, England and North Africa. The date for the Invasion of North Africa approached . . . the battalion was moved to the most southern point of England, Lands End.

For an American without combat experience, these were tense, yet exciting moments. Action was near at hand. Everybody sang songs, some sang battle songs, and some sang folksongs . . . religious services and mass were held.

At 4:00 in the evening of the 7th of November 1942, the battalion parachutists boarded American troop-carrier planes, with complete battle rig. The motors warmed up and we flew from England. Africa was 1,500 miles away. For twelve hours, we flew across Europe and the Mediterranean Sea, toward Tafaroui Airdrome, which is near Oran, Algeria.

At 5:30 in the morning of the 8th of November, the pilots gave the signal to stand up and prepare to descend upon the objective. Most of us were excited and nervous at this moment - believe me!

As we passed over the city of Oran, Algeria, I was standing in the door of the plane. It was light enough to vaguely see the ground. Suddenly, three French fighter planes dived into us, and shot down three planes before we reached our point to descend. Three minutes later, we went sailing down to the ground. Our objective was Tafaroui Airdrome.

At this very moment American Amphibious Armored and Infantry Units were landing at Casablanca, Oran and Algiers.

The parachute mission was to surprise the enemy by capturing the airport and destroying the aircraft before they could get into the air. Some of our men force-landed in Spanish Morocco. They were interned for several months. I landed in the mud of the Sebkra, with part of the battalion.

We organized without much interference and moved on to the objective, along the railroad.

Company "A" was the loading company. Companies "B," "E" and Headquarters Company followed in support. Before the French Legionnaires could go to their firing positions, our snipers and submachine gunners were firing on them. The Legionnaires, who were commanded by Nazis or Nazi sympathizers, were in complete confusion. Some of the pilots did get to their planes. The Legionnaires resisted weakly with machine guns from the buildings of the airbase. Our rifle, mortar and machine gun fire was accurate and effective.

My men got to the buildings of the airbase. The French commandant pulled up the white flag from the operations buildings. The action was over. The first American airborne battle had been won. Our losses were about 90 killed or wounded, 60 missing in action - out of about 810 officers and men. The 60 missing were none other than those who had force-landed in Spanish Morocco and been interned. The French commandant said he had been forced to resist by Nazi orders.

The parachutists took positions of defense around the field. Prisoners were locked in a big barrack. Many of the French wanted to join in the battle with the United States parachutists. One hour later, French Legion Artillery from the hills, to the east, began to bombard the field. Some casualties were inflicted during this barrage. At 9:00 A.M. American tanks approached the Airdrome. Those American tank units destroyed the French Legion Artillery units. By late evening, all units around Oran had surrendered.

This ended the first battle for our parachute battalion. Exactly seventeen days later, the battalion flew and dropped in Southern Tunisia at "Youks Le Bain" near Gafsa, Tunisia.

On this airstrip, there was a battalion of the "French 3rd Zouaves." They recognized our planes as being American, and did not fire. Instead, they helped us to disengage from our parachutes, and kissed our cheeks, and brought us wine. This was the real surprise of our lives. The kind of war I liked.

Five days later, my battalion and a French regiment captured "Faid Pass" near Foriana, from the Germans and Italians. The Italians surrendered easily; however, the Germans fought bitterly. Two weeks later we lost the Pass. The American 1st Armored Division and the 26th Infantry Regiment recaptured the Pass in February 1943. In March 1943, the battalion was moved back to French Morocco to train the French Parachute Regiment of Col. Souvenac in American methods, and in the use of American equipment and aircraft. I enjoyed working with the French, however, I had my difficulties; the French parachutists wanted to jump all the time. They liked this better than learning how to fire our rifles and machine guns. Col. Souvenac was a fine soldier. He had jumped 465 times in exhibitions and in training. However, he had had no previous experience in combat as a parachute officer.

Sicily

As there was an active American Parachute Division in the Invasion of Sicily in July 1943, my battalion played only a minor role in the Invasion. At the time of the Invasion of Italy on September 5, 1943, my battalion was stationed in Licata, Sicily. The landing at Salerno was difficult; though costly, it was successful.

Italy

On the night of September 14, Gen. Mark W. Clark, Commanding General of the American 5th Army, ordered my battalion to drop in the enemy rear areas, thereby intending to create confusion and surprise for the enemy. We had the mission of blocking the Salerno-Avellino Road to prevent the enemy from counter-attacking the British X Corps. This was a difficult mission, but we knew there was a good reason for it.

At midnight of September 14, 1943, my battalion flew from Sicily and dropped from C-47 aircraft at St. Lucia, 5 km. south of Avellino, Italy. The main body of the aircraft dropped its paratroops at the designated "drop zone." However, some pilots dropped my soldiers all over southern Italy. Lt. H. G. Hogan, of Oswego, New York, and his seventeen men were given the green light near Battapaglia, Italy, about 60 km from the objective! One kilometer from the "drop zone," units of the 16th Panzer Grenadiers were securely bivouacked. Some of the paratroops were fired upon in the descent. But I could not ascertain whether or not any of them were hit. Due to the rugged tree-covered terrain there was great confusion in the assembly and reorganization on the spot.

As my men and I descended to the ground between two mountain ranges, the Germans fired on us. There was a full moon. The fighting commenced immediately. Some of my men were killed while hanging in their parachutes in pine trees. As each parachutist dropped with either a rifle, a pistol, or a carbine attached to his body, they were able to protect themselves to a certain extent.

The area where we landed was very thickly settled, and the Italian people rushed out of their homes to greet the "Americans." Two farmers, who had formerly lived in New York, greeted my men.

Upon assembly of part of Headquarters Company, we commenced the march for our objective. After a brief march the scouts were fired upon. They halted for further reconnaissance. I ordered them to detour the firing and the column again moved out. Entirely unaware of the danger, we were sucked into a trap. Instantly, enemy fire broke out from all directions. Discovering that we were in the center of a Panzer bivouac area, a quick conference was called to decide on future action. We made the decision to fight our way out.

Lt. McKinney was ordered to form a section wedge and continue to move forward. Again, machine guns and rifles opened up at close quarters. We retaliated by tossing grenades at the fire points. Suddenly, the Germans threw inferior concussion grenades all around us.

In this nocturnal skirmish, I was wounded in the left hip by a machine pistol bullet. This was as far as I get in the "Liberation of Italy." The time: 2:45 A.M. After the firing ceased, the Germans came out to look for the dead and the wounded. When a German discovered me, he prodded me with the point of his bayonet. The Good Lord must have been with me as the German spared my life. He dragged me to an enemy aid station, where I was given simple first-aid treatment, then taken to a Panzer headquarters. Here, a German Captain who spoke perfect English with an Oxford accent interrogated me. There were two things he wanted to know: What was the mission, and, were any more parachutists to be dropped that night?

After seeing the futility of further questioning, the Captain, quite sociably gave me a drink of whiskey, a cup of ersatz (substitute) coffee and asked many questions about the war, the United States and whom I thought would win the war (of course, he thought the Germans would win).

During the night I was not allowed to communicate with any of my captured paratroops. The next morning, I was allowed to see Lt. Jack Pogue of New Mexico. He had suffered two machine gun wounds and the loss of his left eye. A grenade fragment had penetrated the eyeball, and he seemed to be in great pain.

By 9:30 A.M., I ascertained that several paratroop officers and a number of men had been killed. They included Lt. Cole of San Angelo, Texas, Lt. Gee, Sgt. Cherry and Private Lowhorn, the latter two having been in my plane. Lt. Pogue and I were the only officers captured at this time.

We had caused a diversion and confusion but the cost had been high. All morning American Mustangs (P-51s) dive-bombed and strafed the enemy and not one German plane did I see. I asked the Captain, "Where is the Luftwaffe?" "Ah, but there is Russia, you know," was the laconic reply.

About noon, some paratroops of Luftwaffe, whose job it was to collect the day's extra ration and ammunition, dropped and set up a Browning Automatic Rifle upon a crest opposite the Panzer headquarters and delivered harassing fire. One man of this group was captured. I learned from him that Sgt. Miller of Company "F" had been killed after having killed several Germans with his Tommy gun.

I also learned that some of my men had been killed during the night, while hanging from their parachutes in pine trees.

Just before Lt. Pogue, my men and I were evacuated, some Germans brought in an aerial delivery container with 18 mussette bags (military backpack). The fun came when they began to divide the cigarettes, candy, coffee and K-rations found in the bags! They were astonished at the American supplies, arms and equipment. Everything was "prima" (tops, excellent). One individual, who spoke English, asked if all Americans were this well supplied! You must remember that the Germans had not seen real coffee or genuine cigarettes for years. Their cigarette ration was three ersatz cigarettes per day.

At 4:00 P.M. an ambulance came and the wounded were collected and placed aboard. The ambulance ride was very slow and tiresome. American Mustang dive-bombers and "Lightnings" (American fighter planes) constantly harassed us on the road. Consequently, the drivers took great precautions. Many wrecked vehicles were passed. After riding for approximately one hour, the ambulance came to an abrupt halt under a tree. Instantly, a dive-bomber came for the ambulance, dropped a bomb, strafed the ambulance and climbed away. This all happened before anyone inside the ambulance could do anything about it. The driver and assistant driver, both being slightly wounded, scrambled for cover. Lt. Pogue managed to kick one door open. The plane did not reappear. Fortunately for us, the bomb struck 40 feet away, and the machine guns had cut a pattern on either side of the road.

Twice now I had "sweated out" my life and twice I had come through. Not only the Germans but also Americans feared the wicked little dive-bomber.

Just before sundown, the ambulance arrived at a so-called evacuation hospital at St. Angelo, Italy. It was in an old school and the place was simply filthy. The building was literally packed with wounded, suffering, and dying soldiers. About 12 British and American soldiers were among the lot. Promptly, two Germans (English speaking) "reminded" me how "barbarous" the American pilots were, and what a plutocrat Roosevelt was. My answer was "American planes fly too fast to see the Red Cross on ambulances" and "Roosevelt suited us or we wouldn't have elected him."

During the night, Private Lauer, paratrooper, died.

Chapter Nine
September 1943

September 17

Finally, a dilapidated ambulance was made available, and Lt. Pogue and I were transferred to a hospital at Paranopoli, east of Naples. This place was also overcrowded and filthy. The overworked staff performed operations the best they could under the circumstances. The medical facilities were poor, the quarters were unhealthy and crowded, and the rations were meager. Everyone received the same meals regardless of his physical condition. Breakfast consisted of one slice of bread with a smear of jam and a cup of ersatz coffee. Lunch was soup made from local vegetables, and supper was the same as breakfast with Italian spam or Portuguese salmon on occasion. No plates or cups were available. Our few canteen cups were rotated.

During the daylight hours, we sat by the windows watching fighters and dive-bombers in action. An explosion, then a spiral of smoke indicated a score on some Army vehicle, nevermore to serve the Reich. The civilians were scared to death of the airplanes. And while on the subject of civilians - I observed that nearly all were very poor and certainly looked pathetic. Few wore shoes, and women carried loads balanced on their heads, as do the Arabs. All villages and small towns in southern Italy showed the effects of weathering and age. The streets and alleys were littered with filth and the livestock lived as members of the family. Only in Sicily were conditions more deplorable. Hardly any civilian showed any interest in the Germans.

The second day at Paranopoli hospital, an American officer, Lt. Weineger, a Mustang dive-bomber pilot, was admitted. He was badly burned. The inquisitive Germans thoroughly questioned him about the Mustang. (All troops in this area knew the man, and certainly, the looks of this plane.) During our stay at this hospital, Lt. Pogue received no treatment whatsoever for his blinded eye - not even an eye bath!

September 22

In the early morning, Lt. Pogue, a number of my men, British X Corps men and I were loaded into trucks, with German wounded, and transported to a hospital in Rome. For the trip, each man was issued a ration of several slices of hard rye bread plus one can of salmon and six cigarettes. No dive-bombing or strafing occurred during the trip - to our surprise! I saw only four German medium tanks and very few troops along the way.

Arriving at Rome at 4:30 P.M., the trucks pulled up beside the hospital - a former Fascist headquarters building inside Rome where we remained for two hours. We became a curiosity group to the civilians. The American soldiers had to be reprimanded by me to avoid trouble for whistling at the attractive Italian girls. An "international incident" occurred when a small Italian girl attempted to give one American soldier a cup of ice cream! An infuriated German abruptly slapped the ice cream from her hand and yelled "vaus" (get going!). Many Italian civilians sneered, made faces and stuck out their tongues at us. This scene definitely was not a German staged affair. No, it was a natural expression they had for Americans.

Inside the hospital we were grouped in rooms with straw to sleep on. The place was frightfully filthy. The odors were stifling. Obviously, the Germans had no intention of staying here permanently. Officers were not separated from the men as per International Agreement. In this hospital, I met Maj. Monroe-Fraser, British official of Allied Military Government of Occupied Territory (AMGOT). He had been shot off a motorcycle near Salerno. I curiously queried him. He told me that he had tired of paper work, become fed-up as it were, and borrowed a motorcycle to visit the front lines and rode too bloody far.

Incidentally, Rome and its railway system were not nearly as devastated as we had been led to believe by the radio and press. Only a small section of the railway terminal had been hit. Most devastation had occurred in an apartment house section, near an old cemetery in Rome. Furthermore, the trams (British streetcars) were operating between Naples and Rome. At this time, Rome was supposed to be an open city. It was - except for German service troops.

September 23

About dark, forty of us were placed aboard a hospital train to be evacuated to Germany. By the way, all trains in Italy and Bavaria (southern Germany) are electrically powered. The train was well within the northern half of Italy by sunrise. The further north we went, the more prosperous and wealthy the country seemed. The farms and towns were quite modern. The terrain flattened out in contrast to the rugged south.

The train pulled into Bologna at 2:30 P.M. Here we saw the true effects of concentrated aerial bombardment. For half a mile the entire railway section, including all buildings and factories for two blocks on either side was completely flattened, comparable to the Thames area in London. Boxcars, Pullmans and engines stood on end and only two main tracks had been repaired. It was a sad looking state of affairs. No wonder they capitulated.

The ride through the narrow, torturous Brenner Pass was a cool, pleasant one. Unfortunately, night came too soon. The weather became noticeably colder the further north we went.

Throughout Northern Italy, I saw very little of the Wehrmacht (German Army). None of the Americans or British escaped during the ride; we were vigilantly guarded. I was placed in a compartment with five wounded German soldiers. Not until the Bavarian border was crossed was a separate compartment provided for the British Major and me.

All through Germany and on to Nurnberg my interest was confined to observing and appraising the country, the farms and the people. There is so much forest land in Germany. September is potato-harvesting time, and everybody able to work was digging potatoes, the most important stock food of Germany. They are accordingly served at every meal. The farm work-stock was cattle and oxen, steers and even cows. Seldom did I see a horse. Two tractors were all I saw in southern Germany. The civilians were certainly feeling the pinch of war. Everywhere, I saw fine houses and barns with tall slanting roofs in the country and in the towns - I suppose to protect the houses against the winter snows. Surprising to me, it is so much colder in southern than in northern Germany.

Nurnberg too, had felt the effects of aerial bombardment; for the entire railway terminal and many houses, installations, and factories lay in ruins. Dozens of Polish and Russian prisoners were laboring under heavy guard repairing the railway tracks.

During the trip from Nurnberg and Hammelburg, where we were temporarily confined, a German doctor engaged us in conversation. He seemed to want to admit the forthcoming fate of Germany, always hedging to save his pride. Why was the United States fighting Germany? What would America and Great Britain do with these "Barbarians" (the Russians), if the Allies did win? He preferred to see the Americans and British in Berlin - indeed, yes, preferred to the Russians. The Russians are not human to the Germans and the thought of their ever being in Berlin is terrifying to the Germans.

Our train arrived at the little town of Abelsbach, where I remained at a Reserve Lazaroff (Hospital) for Allied troops. Before quarters were assigned, we received a 4-minute hot shower, turned over our clothes for decontamination, and received a pair of pajamas. Next, we were assigned bunks in a building partially occupied by New Zealand and Australian repatriation selectees. Those men had been captured at Crete, May

1941. At 9:00 P.M., I received my first real meal since being captured on September 15 - food from Red Cross parcels! These precious and coveted gifts!

Until 10:30 P.M. when the lights went out, we spent our time firing questions at each other. A redheaded chap, Alan Pinkerton, of Victoria, Australia, acted as master of ceremonies. "Pinky" was well informed on "inside Germany." He knew all the answers. He thought the war would be over by Christmas! I think he was influenced by the sight of 400 Flying Fortresses flying over the Lazaroff to bomb Nurnberg.

Daylight bombing has had a peculiar effect on the civilians - according to the Kommandos (prisoners of war who work on railroads and farms). Of course, the Kommandos might well surmise this, for they were constantly in contact with the civilian population. During one of the daylight raids on southern Germany, one of the Flying Fortresses made a forced landing near our hospital; the pilot climbed out, backed off and saluted his plane. The inhabitants, very excited, rushed out to the plane with pitchforks, axes and shotguns. A local blacksmith knocked the pilot on the head to make sure that he didn't cause any more trouble. By nightfall, the rumor was abroad that this super-ship was armed with 30, even 40 machine guns!

September 27

I was surprised to find so many nationalities represented here at Abelsbach: Americans, British, Australians, New Zealanders, Serbs, Polish, French, and Russians. All of us received International Red Cross parcels, except the Russians, who never signed the agreements at the International Convention at Geneva. They only received bread, beet jam, soup and ersatz coffee. Furthermore, they were isolated, officers and men together, in an enclosure about 75 yards away and were only allowed near the rest of us when they passed by to get their noon soup. The other prisoners slipped food, clothing and cigarettes to them when they could - as they were so pathetic.

According to Dr. Ingram McDonald, British POW from Edinburgh, the treatment and food had improved considerably during the last six months. One Sergeant. told me, "Two winters ago, the Russians died daily by the hundreds and were buried in mass graves. In many of the Russian work groups the Communist creed binds their loyalty to the Soviet Union and any member who becomes friendly with the Germans is disposed of immediately."

September 28

Today Maj. Monroe-Fraser and I transferred to Stalag XIII C near Hammelburg. This was a camp for non-commissioned officers of mixed nationalities. Under the Articles of the Geneva Convention non-commissioned officers do not work as "Kommandos." Sgt. Maj. W. R. Brown from Australia was the "Man of Confidence" here. He had much freedom of action, and it was his job to distribute the Red Cross food and clothing to this and nearby Stalags, as well as to the many "Kommando" groups. I was given a British battle suit, which is a very warm uniform, and it had become quite cold and rainy here in southern Germany. My only contribution for Sgt. Maj. Brown's hospitality was an old issue of *Readers' Digest,* which was the first magazine other than German that they had received since capture. I had managed to keep this with me ever since I jumped in southern Italy. No magazine or newspapers had gotten by the censors of the mail, so this was considered quite a prize!

Chapter Ten
October 1943

October 1

To be on the move again was a happy feeling, why I don't know. The "postums" (two guards) and I limped five miles to the railway station, as the camp couldn't afford transportation. We took our time and munched on wild apples which grow everywhere in southern Germany.

The railway is the only means of transportation available for the civilian population, and everyone must present his identification card to the ticket agent and to the conductor. Non-citizens cannot ride unless for the benefit of the Reich. Once on the train, Army representatives check the passes of all soldiers to make certain they have a reason for the ride and that there is no "slipping by." Lights flood the tops of trains at most underpasses. This systematic check is a precaution against escaped POWs who might attempt a ride on top of the cars.

The two "postums" found a seat for me in an over-crowded third class car. As a matter of fact, only the Generals and Nazi party leaders ride in first class cars. Civilians and soldiers scrutinized me with much curiosity, as one of the guards, who vaguely resembled Adolf Hitler (having a little wire-mustache) had passed the word around that I was an "Amerikaniche Oberstlufnant" (American Lieutenant Colonel). The public was accustomed to seeing prisoners of war of other nationalities, but not Americans. This guard seemed a pretty good guy and was quite a comedian, for he kept everyone on the train laughing. As a matter of form, he gave everybody the "Heil Hitler" salute, but once he turned to me, and said, "Hitler Kaputt" (Hitler is finished). Being a POW, I made no comment.

Twenty miles from Berlin, the train stopped and "Adolf Jr." informed me that Berlin was being bombed.

I'm sorry we passed through at night. We changed trains at Berlin and had to walk several blocks through the subway to board a train for Posen. I was surprised to see so such traffic and activity, for I had been led to believe that there was nothing left of the Berlin railway system. Not a bomb had touched the terminal, which closely resembles the Pennsylvania Station, New York City. All trams and trains were filled to capacity and then some! Dim lights glowed everywhere and I strained my eyes to see searchlights and flak, but to no avail. I learned later that a suburban district had been bombed earlier in the evening.

Prior to departure from Hammelburg, Sgt. Maj. Brown had given me a Red Cross food parcel, which was a great pleasure on the trip. I had shared some cigarettes with the guards and we obtained some hot water from the locomotive with which to make some coffee. When we arrived at Posen, the guards carried me off to a German Red Cross Canteen, to get some hot ersatz coffee. There were about forty soldiers there. One guard thought it a good idea to make our own coffee with some hot water from the girls in the kitchen. A good idea! So, we made a nice display of Red Cross articles on the table. Coffee, powdered milk, sugar cubes and biscuits were all lined up conspicuously on the table, then the coffee was made. The once familiar aroma was too much for the curious soldiers who crowded around to watch.

First, they could hardly believe it was the real thing, so the guard gave a Sergeant a sip to prove it. Then came the American cigarettes and the Sergeant had a drag from one. He was astonished to discover that a prisoner of war had the luxuries that they had been deprived of for years. None had seen the genuine articles for so long that they believed everyone else was in the same situation. This Red Cross food parcel had as much propaganda value as it had food value!

October 2

After leaving Posen, I noticed a distinct change in the land. Now it was better for farming, being flatter and less wooded. The crops were still potatoes and various foods but more horses were being used. My guards were quite friendly by now, probably due to the cigarettes and coffee. They told me we were now in New Germany, to be exact, the Polish "corridor." Most of the towns had both German and Polish names, but were inhabited mostly by German families transplanted there, or people of German descent.

On this train, there were a number of soldiers bound for the Russian Front. They looked decidedly unhappy! Some of them had distinguished themselves in the Oral Sector and I guessed where they were heading. The stark reality of recent events was more convincing than Herr Gobbel's propaganda and the fear of both Russian fanaticism and the Russian winter had taken strong hold.

At 1:30 P.M. the train pulled into Altburgund where a prisoner of war camp (Offizier-lager, called Oflag 64) was located just outside the little town of Altburgund - 1/2 kilometer away. Before entering camp, I was again searched, for the "umpteenth time," but by now I had nothing left that could be confiscated except a pocketknife - which they allowed me to keep - and my Red Cross food. However, all the cans were punctured for fear I might escape with a convenient escape ration.

Each new prisoner is welcomed at the gate. There's always a friend in the crowd, perhaps someone you've served with at some time. Questions are eagerly asked of each new arrival, most of them unanswerable! After two weeks of constantly moving and being pushed around, I almost welcomed the camp life.

Lt. Col. John Waters, former Commander of an armored tank destroyer unit, assigned me to a room. Maj. M. A. Meacham, Col. Drake's adjutant, issued me four blankets, eating utensils, and other necessities. By this time, a supper of hot water, bread, and the Red Cross parcel was ready. More questions were asked and at last I fell into bed.

October 3

"Appell" (formation for counting prisoners) was held at 8:00 A.M., 12:00 noon and 5:00 P.M. That was the German schedule! Immediately following the morning "Appell," breakfast, consisting of hot water, bread, and the Red Cross parcel, was served. For the noon meal, soup was added to the same menu! It wasn't hard to learn the daily routine.

At 9:30 A.M. I called on the "Camp Senior," Col. Thomas D. Drake, who formerly had commanded the 168th Infantry and had been captured at Sidi Bou Sid, Tunisia, in January 1943.

Oflag 64 had formerly been a prison camp for R.A.F. pilots. Until June, the Americans had been imprisoned at Eichstagg, near Munich, with some British officers. When the Germans decided to separate the Americans and the British, Oflag 64, which is 125 kilometers from Danzig, was selected as a permanent camp for American officers, exclusive of Air Corps officers who were imprisoned in separate camps. As of today, the strength of the camp is 189 officers, 18 American orderlies, 10 British orderlies, and 20 Russians who perform the menial tasks for the German personnel. These Russians considered themselves well off. Comparatively they were, for they ate the leftovers and picked up the cigarette butts. The Germans allowed them to do our laundry and we compensated them with cigarettes and soap.

The Red Cross supplies the food and clothing and the Y.M.C.A. supplies recreational and educational facilities, such as sports equipment, musical instruments, stage decorations, and costumes, text books and novels, and note books. By the courtesy of these two agencies, life is made bearable.

Every officer has the opportunity to participate in volleyball, indoor baseball, horseshoe pitching, table tennis, and hardball. Educational courses in French, Spanish, Italian, and German, as well as Calculus, Art, and Music are now being conducted. We have several men who formerly were professors at home as our instructors. Capt. J. W. Barker had taught German before, and I enrolled in his course and also in Spanish. Once a week the camp puts on a short play and concert. A "sponsor" is chosen for each play from the products in our Red Cross parcels, for example, "Black Beauty Prunes Review," "Corn Products Parade," and "Milko Show." Camp life is frequently reenacted while Lt. Robert Rankin's 12-piece orchestra provides the music, with Jim Marlow as vocalist.

I added some new words to my vocabulary today. I learned that "Kriegy" means a prisoner of war, and when a "Kriegy" learns that "Nix" means most anything, any time of the day, then he has "Kriegyitis!"

October 6

The German radio confirmed the rumor (via a German guard) that Naples had fallen to the Allies. The Germans ("Goons" in camp slang) provide us with music and propaganda by means of a loud speaker in the camp. William Joyce (Lord Haw-Haw) comes on each night at 10:30 P.M. with his analysis of the "News" which we all enjoy but not in the way he supposes. Classical music is the most common type of radio entertainment, and popular music is heard very rarely.

Today a Representative of the Swiss International Committee visited the Oflag. We appreciated his visit because the lights remained on in camp while he was there, and we were able to get on with our studies. The Committeeman confessed to Col. Drake that the Swiss people fully expected an Allied victory in 1945.

Excitement About Dark

Lt. Col. J. H. Van Vliet, Jr., Kansas, Lt. Roy Chappell, Jr., Texas, Lt. William F. Higgins, Colorado and Lt. Frank Aten, Texas, made an unsuccessful attempt to escape. Unfortunately, a guard walking down the street saw them just as the last one crawled through a hole in the barbed-wire fence. All, except Lt. Aten, were sentenced to fourteen days solitary confinement. This being Lt. Aten's fifth attempt to escape, he is being held for decision from Posen headquarters.

Before an officer attempts to escape, he must have a plan and this plan must make sense. Before the SAO (Senior American Officer) will approve a plan, all Red Cross foods to be taken along must be changed from the original state. Chocolate and cheese must be melted to prevent the German authorities from asserting that parcels were being used to aid in escaping.

October 7

The local guards informed us today that the Polish electrician, who had been working in the Oflag, was arrested, tried, and sentenced to be shot, because a pair of wire-cutters found on one of the escaping officers was of the same type used by the electrician! As a matter of fact, the wire-cutters had been smuggled in by one of our own officers. The Germans would not listen. I suppose they wanted to eliminate any doubt. We received no further information on the case nor did we ever see the man again. Your guess is as good as mine.

October 9

At 6:30 A.M., eight new prisoners of war, of the 36th Infantry Division, arrived. They had been captured September 16 on the Salerno beachhead, and had been detained in solitary confinement at Luckenwalde for interrogation by a certain Capt. Williams, who according to the prisoners handled all Americans as convicts. This Capt. Williams, by the way, boasted of having lived in the United States, mostly around Washington Square, New York City. He had returned to Germany in 1938 "to see a sick uncle!"

October 10

Following the morning roll call, the Germans pulled a "show-down inspection" of the barracks in an attempt to uncover contraband equipment. Army and civilian Nazi experts collaborated in the search. Col. Drake obtained permission for American officers to accompany the searchers, since the guards had helped themselves to personal possessions on previous raids.

October 15

I have been a prisoner of war exactly one month today! The time passes very slowly.

Der Angriff, a German newspaper, carries this headline: "Hamburg Raided by American Planes, 120 shot down." The *Volkisher-Beobachter* headlined the Azores deal as "Der Raub Der Azores" ("The Rob of the Azores").

There is a general complaint today in the camp against the peculiar censorship policy of American customs and censor officials. To illustrate, certain types of delicious chocolate candy have been extracted and returned to the senders. In referring to friends in letters, the first name (or all three) has been blotted out. Even personal statements are often eradicated. Via the local "Goons," we learned that camp guards of all POW camps are to be cut one-third to meet the demands of the Russian Front. My guess is that many will suddenly discover that they have weak hearts, lumbago or arthritis. In fact "Unterofficier" Hartl says he is in a bad way, physically.

October 19

Thirty more prisoners of war arrived at 2:30 A.M. today. The majority of these officers were captured in Tunisia in January and February 1943. The 34th Infantry Division was practically annihilated by two Panzer divisions.

In this group is Larry Allen, Naval Correspondent for the Associated Press, formerly with the British Navy. The Italians captured Larry at Tobruk, Lybia. Since early winter 1943, these prisoners have been held at Camp No. 2, Chieti, Italy. When Marshall Bagdelio signed the armistice terms surrendering Italy, the Italian guards informed some 1,500 American and British prisoners of war that they were at liberty to go! Everybody made ready to leave. Colonel William D. Marshall, British Senior Officer, ordered them to remain calm and collected. No one was to be allowed to leave camp. "The Allies will be here in a few days."

Lt. Col. Max Gooler, an American officer who had been a forward observer with the British 8th Army, was the Senior U. S. officer. Five days later the German paratroopers, by order of Air Marshall Erich Student, took charge and declared them prisoners of the Reich. The POWs blamed Colonel Marshall, and you can imagine their indignation at his "Stay Put" order. Whatever the opinion of the POWs was at the time does not mean that Colonel Marshall was in the wrong. He probably had orders.

When the German prison train departed for Germany, some 75 Americans jumped off the train. Lt. Col. Max Gooler was among the first to hit the dirt, saying to his buddies," To hell with the armistice, I'm leaving." Larry Allen followed suit, but was recaptured the following day.

October 20

Thirty-one new prisoners, mostly 36th Infantry Division personnel, arrived today. Lt. Col. G. J. Barron, 142nd Infantry, Waco, Texas, was the Senior Officer of this group. Lt. S. J. Bires, New York City and Lt. H. G. Hogan mentioned previously, both paratroopers of my battalion, were also among the new arrivals. Lt. Col. Barron and several others had met Capt. Williams at the interrogation center at Luckenwalde, Germany. The Commandant at the Luckenwalde, Col. Wilhelm, was a gentleman farmer for ten years near New Orleans, La. His two children were born in the United States. Both Williams and Wilhelm are looking forward to returning to the states after the war, "Provided we are dumb enough to allow them," said Lt. Col. Barron.

October 21

Today I took my first "Parole Walk." Every officer has the opportunity to go on a five-mile walk each week. The group must not exceed 50 officers, who are guarded by two Germans. As extra security, each officer must give his word not to escape. Once this word of honor is broken, there will be no more "Parole Walks." This privilege has not been broken as of this date.

October 22

To afford "Kriegies" propaganda, a loud speaker was installed in my barrack this afternoon. Furthermore, Col. Drake was ordered to designate a field officer in each barrack to make certain that the speakers are not turned off during German news periods. Frankly, we enjoy the irony of the news; however, we are not quite as gullible as the local authorities might think. Mind you, they never make the mistake of switching on CBS, NBC or BBC.

"Goon Jam and Bugs Issued"

Lt. Col. W. M. Oakes, San Antonio, Texas, found a big, juicy worm in the German issue of jam today. It was mounted on a pin and stuck in the bulletin board. There was plenty of leftover jam for everybody. This "exclusive" jam is made from compressed ground stock beets. (There might be a time when it is not left on the table, regardless.)

October 25

Lt. Col. J. H. Van Vliet and Lts. Roy Chappell and Lt. Frank Aten were released from solitary confinement, where they had been serving time for an attempt to escape (see Oct. 6).

"Oberst" (Col.) Schneider, Oflag commandant, had an order read to all prisoners of war: "The act of putting cigarette butts, matches or tin lids in the leavings from the table, is an act of sabotage and will not be tolerated." Apparently, the German pigs don't do so well on cigarette butts!

Rumors filtered in today that Germany now has 60,000 Italian prisners of war. The German press admitted the fall of Melitopol, an important city on the Dnepr.

Eight phonograph sets arrived from the Y.M.C.A., with a few popular, but mostly classical and operatic selections.

There are twelve doctors here, but not an aspirin in camp. We "sweat out" our headaches. Occasionally, aspirin and vitamin pills come in the Red Cross medical parcels. The doctors eat the vitamin pills, and the first come, first served boys get the aspirin.

October 27

Col. Drake made a trip to Posen to discuss repatriation with German officials. While there, he was allowed to visit the British POW Camp where he consulted the British "Man of Confidence." As to be expected, the British Camp was very efficient, internally. Having excellent liaison and representation with the Red Cross, food and clothing is in stock (in surplus). The British "Man of Confidence" stated that the camp now has 5,000 Army uniforms on hand. Our camp, Oflag 64, has zero uniforms in stock. Col. Drake suspects that our representative in Geneva is not sympathetic to our cause. The International Red Cross will not accept Col. Drake's figures of camp strength. The German Commandant must certify to all figures! The British "Man of Confidence's" word and figures are accepted. Furthermore, today Col. Drake got a bill from the German authorities to pay for an emergency telegram (requesting clothing) sent to the I.R.C. (International Red Cross). The I.R.C. had refused to pay the bill. The good news of the day is the German forces have evacuated Dnepropetrovsk on the Dnepr.

October 28

In bloody battles, one sees many horrible, cruel, and blood-curdling things. After the war, many yarns will no doubt be told; however, I think the battle stories, re-enacted with all the gestures and demonstrations, can be classified as reasonably reliable. I am about to write one down which I wish to remember. There were half a dozen witnesses and I believe their story.

On September 12th, a battalion of the 143rd Infantry was counter-attacked near Ebili, Italy, and practically annihilated to the last man by the German 16th Panzer Division. For several hours, tanks engaged in a type of warfare that was hitherto unknown to the members of the battalion. The tanks sought out individual foxholes, approached within a few yards, lowered their cannons and blasted the doughboys out, point blank! Many soldiers were blown to smithereens. A few miraculously escaped death. Cpl. G. E. Oskarson, Granada, Minn. is one of these fellows. About sundown, he was blasted in his foxhole and subsequently packed in by the crushing weight of the tank. When Cpl. Oskarson regained his senses, some 20 hours later, a tank was parked over his foxhole. The tank personnel pulled the tank from over his body and tried to pull him out but succeeded only with the aid of shovels! Paralyzed from the waist down and punctured in many places, the Corporal lived. This moment he is recuperating in our hospital at Oflag 64. He will be a hospital cook.

October 29

German newspapers often play up statements of prominent American and British leaders. The October 26th issue of *Der Angriff* carried this headline: "Ein Langer, LanforWeg, Gowarden Eisenhower und Alexander" (A long, long way, spoke Eisenhower and Alexander). "Dies ist ein harter, bittere and blutiger Krieg." (This is a hard, bitter sad bloody war) quoting from Gen. Eisenhower's speech made from Radio Algiers. I didn't hear it.

October 30

First Sgt. Carn A. Godsey, 168th Infantry, from Pacific Junction, Iowa, arrived at camp today to become the senior non-commissioned officer over the American orderlies. He was captured in Tunisia, February 1943. Newcomers are asked to report on affairs inside Germany. His story goes like this:

"I was held for several months at Stalag 111B, 87 km from Berlin. There were 750 enlisted POWs here, including Americans, British, Poles, Serbs and French. Recently, 15,000 Italian prisoners were brought into this area. The Germans persuaded only 400 to join up with the German Army. The rest were sent to Kommando groups and are now working for the Reich." The following is a story on the treatment and handling of German prisoners of war in Africa and on board ship, bound for the United States, by Lt. F. L. Vaden, 143rd Infantry, from Dallas, Texas. Vaden's company had the assignment of guarding prisoners from the Tunisian battlefront to Newport News, Virginia:

German and Italian prisoners of war were transported from Tunisia to Casa Blanca by rail. Officers were placed in coaches, enlisted men in boxcars, thirty to a car. They were issued American "C" rations. Each car had two 6-gallon cans for water. They were issued ample cigarettes. At every stop they were allowed to refresh themselves. I will admit that at times they were roughed about, especially when the French themselves assisted. One French sergeant., who had escaped from Germany, handled them exactly as he had been treated. All government property was taken away and a receipt given. At Casa Blanca, French Morocco, they were divided into groups of 100, decontaminated, given baths, issued American uniforms complete, and then sent to a compound, which contained 3,000 POWs. Here, they had access to reading rooms, showers and recreation grounds. A German Band, captured intact, visited the compound. They often played their favorite piece, "The Beer Barrel Polka." American "B" rations, plus eggs and bacon were the rations!

Cigarettes, one towel, razor and blades, toothbrush and paste, soap and candy were issued to each man! Officers were separated from the men. A Colonel was allowed a tent to himself and one orderly;

two Lieutenant Colonels to a tent and one
orderly; 4 Majors to a tent and one orderly;
six Captains or Lieutenants to a tent and
one orderly. I was then given the job to
guard 3,000 Italian POWs, aboard a ship,
across the Atlantic. The group included one
German and 150 Italian officers, who ate
at a second setting in the officers' mess.
The men were given three meals a day.
The food, including ice cream every day,
was excellent. A party was given one
Italian Lieutenant Colonel, who had a
birthday. After 7 days we arrived at
Newport News, Va. where the POWs were
turned over to the Army Service forces.
"Considering the treatment up to here you
can imagine the treatment they are
receiving in the States," concludes Vaden.
("We prisoners of war can hardly believe
our ears.")

October 31

It's Halloween but there's not much to say about it -
except that it is six degrees below freezing, the coldest
day of the season. To splurge a little on this day, most of
us ate our American cheese and drank two cups of coffee
for breakfast. (A fancy recipe on the cheese box provided
us a hearty laugh: "Shrimp Rabbit" - 1 green pepper, 2
cups whole shrimp, eggs, etc.)

Chapter Eleven
November 1943

November 1

The extraordinary news of the day was the announcement of the fall of Kremenschug, the last German-held city on the Dnepr River. Dr. Goebbel personally announced its fall. The temperature today is 10 degrees below freezing. Many of the officers are without caps, coats and gloves. The German prisoners of war in the United States are not without adequate clothing, I'd bet my last Reichsmark on it.

November 2

Twelve new prisoners of war, from the 36th Infantry Division, arrived today. They were captured September 12th on the Salerno Front. Lt. Col. Charles H. Jones, Jr., Temple, Texas, is the group senior officer. Incidentally, Jones was one of the eyewitnesses to the packing of Cpl. Oskarson, whom I mentioned under the date October 28. There are now 281 officers in this camp and 37 are from Texas. Barrack 3A was labeled "Hotel Texas." Lt. R. F. Bonomi, Wallace, Idaho, returned from Berlin where he went to edit, voluntarily, the "O.K.", a newspaper, printed by the propaganda ministry in English for American prisoners of war. Dr. Goebbel's assistant agent informed Bonomi that he would "work on the last two pages only." He replied, "I'd rather not accept the job." Each said good-bye, and Bonomi returned to Oflag 64. The Goons announced tonight that we no longer had to do our own laundry. In the future, they would collect it every two weeks but that we must pay for the laundry at the end of the month, with lager money.

November 3

Rumors are filtering in by new arrivals that since the English repatriates (prisoners returned to their homeland) returned home, the German authorities are staging raids on various Oflags and Stalags for contraband articles. It seems that some of the repatriates, in a radio interview, stated that prisoners of war could bribe the German guards to bring in contraband articles for a few cigarettes or a can of coffee. We fully expect a shakedown here. All newspapers today headlined the coal mine strikes involving some 500,000 miners in the United States. This is shower day. We get one shower per week per officer. Lt. Col. Oakes informed us that the vegetables from the POW garden are exhausted. The inmates planted these vegetables in June. The quality of the noonday soup is bound to deteriorate.

November 4

Four hundred pairs of bowling shoes arrived from the Y.M.C.A. We have no bowling equipment, but just the same, they are gratefully appreciated (we can use them as house slippers). In my diary on October 19, I told the story of American prisoners of war in Italy falling into the hands of Air Marshal Eric Student and his paratroopers. Today, his picture appeared in a newspaper. The occasion: awarding medals to German paratroopers for rescuing Mussolini. Larry Allen, the Associated Press correspondent, in his little daily analysis of the news, cut out the picture and substituted the headline, "The man who took 1,500 POWs at Chiete, Italy." This was displayed on our bulletin board! The "Goons" did not protest.

After telling this one, I shall call it a day. Lt. I. C. Erie was tried today for yawning in the face of the German Security Officer, Capt. Zimmerman. His sentence was a reprimand and a warning never to do it again.

November 5

Each month a letter chart, showing the number of letters received and average time in transit, is published and placed on the bulletin board. For the month of October, there were 2,090 letters, with an average time in transit of 99 days. The best time of transit (to date) for any letter is 31 days.

Three Swedish Y.M.C.A. representatives visited camp today. They were, apparently, very fine men. One of them by the name of Henri Johannet was scheduled to visit the United States upon return to Geneva. In my barrack, a gentleman asked how the Y.M.C.A. could better our existence. "How about sending us some popular music, Mr. Johannet, instead of so many long-hair numbers." "Oh! You mean 'hot music?'" "Yes," replied the POW. "It makes me cold to listen to your 'hot music.'" Thus, ran the conversation. Everybody laughed, and the representatives made their exit, joking about "hot" and "long-hair" music.

For a change in the subject, I would like to tell another "mouth-to-ear" story, a Russian one. It is hearsay and I have no concrete proof of its validity. Private Ivan Rapkabokav, Tykomouvwkab, Russia, told the story as follows:

I was captured near Wastonie, Russia in October 1941. 25,000 Russian prisoners of war were being temporarily held in this area. While there, I saw 6,000 prisoners die - 30 daily.

In November, I was sent to Wolstein with a group of 1,200. Only 700 got there alive. The rest died of starvation and sub-zero weather. We were allowed 100 grams of bread a day, and sometimes soup. Flesh was sometimes sliced from the dead and eaten. We were not allowed water to wash our face and hands. Once I was caught washing my face in the snow, and a German Sergeant held my face in the snow for about five minutes. The body fleas were so bad that our bodies were completely covered with infectious sores. I saw people stacked in wagons like logs, taken off, shot and dumped in ditches. In the City of Kiev, 50,000 partisans and communists were either hanged or shot. In Odessa, there were 48,000, in Minsk, 18,000 and in Korkov, 27,000. The Russian did not

89

stammer when he recited these figures. All communist officers, whose identities could be determined, were shot or hanged. Not many officers posed as privates to keep from being shot. (Incidentally, there are five Russian officers in this camp posing as privates.)

The reason the Germans are so nice to us here is due to the presence of the Americans. I would hate to leave here. You must not let the Germans know I have told you this. They would send me away or shoot me.

I would like to interrupt here to say that his story was told in Polish and interpreted by Lt. T. A. Powlaski, who is a prisoner of war in my barrack (3-A). Lt. Powlaski inquired about his future plans upon returning to Russia. He replied, "I do not care to go back to Russia, for all soldiers have to sign an oath to the effect that before surrendering to the Germans, we will take a pistol and blow our heads off."

After hearing this story, I am truly proud of the fact that I will some day return to my own America, instead of to Germany or Russia. Americans are the envy of every nationality. We who have fought in this war will fight at home to keep America, as we knew it before the war. No changes.

November 6

Lt. Col. Charles H. Jones submitted his report to Col. Drake on the recent murder of Lt. Dowling B. Deacon by a German sentry at Lager XVIII A, Spittel, Germany, Austria. The report was typed and posted on the bulletin board for every American officer to read. Extract follows:

On October 10, 1943, Lt. Deacon and Lt. McGaffin, South African Army, were taking their daily exercise by strolling up and down the camp promenade. For some unknown reason, a crazy sentry on duty ordered everyone to go inside the building, threatening the group with his poised rifle. Through curiosity, Lt. Deacon and Lt. McGaffin halted at the fence to ask the sentry what the excitement was all about. The sentry wheeled about, threw his gun on Lt. McGaffin, who immediately threw up his hands in defense. The German, jabbering something about his folks at home having been bombed, threw the rifle on Lt. Deacon, leveled it and cold-bloodedly shot him. The bullet entered his chest, penetrating one of his identification tags, which is in my possession. The next day Lt. Deacon died.

A copy of this was mailed to the Germans, but I am not sure that anything can be done about it.

November 7

Larry Allen, Associated Press Correspondent, made a speech tonight titled "War in the Mediterranean." Larry was the first and only correspondent to ever accompany the Royal Navy up to this time. He told how the Italians had consistently avoided engagement and how the Aircraft Carrier, "Illustrious," had been pounded 7-1/2 hours by 150 Stuka dive bombers and still managed to hobble into the Port of Alexandria. I am sure everyone remembers reading the epic story of the "Illustrious." The story, written by Larry, was headlined in practically every American newspaper.

November 8th (North African Invasion Anniversary)

How well I remember November 8, 1943. We flew 1,500 miles from England and dropped near Oran, Algeria, to participate in the Invasion of French North Africa. Part of the battalion dropped in Morocco and part in Oran, Algeria. Since this date, the German radio and press referred to the Allied victories as one of starvation and subjugation for the civilian population or the "victims." The radio announced that 250 people were dying daily in Naples of starvation.

November 9

Complaints! Protests! Read the true copy of a letter Col. Drake conveyed to Oberst Schneider, the Commandant.

Nov. 9, 1943
An Den Kommandant
Oflag 64

1. Coal

The present amount of coal being issued for heating of occupied rooms in this camp in insufficient.

Request that the following be placed in effect.

A. POW Quartermaster officer be present at weighing of coal in coal yards

B. Coal be issued for,
  1) School room
  2) Theatre
  3) Parcel store
  4) Green house
  5) Chapel
  6) Library

2. Theatre Props

Due to the cancellation of our agreement on the care of stage props, I withdraw my 'word of honor' given in respect to all things connected with the theatre. All the props allotted by the Y.M.C.A. have not been brought into this camp from Montwy.

It is desired that my letter to the "Protecting Power" in reference to the lack of cooperation in our efforts on entertainment, be forwarded.

3. Promenade Walk

The work on the Promenade Walk has been in progress for sometime, but now is at a stand-still.

Request that the necessary material be furnished so that we may finish it before the ground freezes.

4. Shoe Repair

A large consignment of shoe repair material, which we have been waiting for, has arrived from the United States, and has been seized and locked away from us. Article 43 Geneva Convention, clearly states the collective shipments shall be turned over to the prisoner of war representative, who is charged with the reception and the distribution.

Request that this material be inspected by the security officer in conjunction with me, and turned over to us without delay.

  5. Removal of Scrap from the Tailor Shop

Last week a German soldier entered and removed all the scrap cloth left over from altering shirts, ties and etc. from the Tailor Shop. These scraps were being used to patch and repair clothing.

Request that the Tailor Shop be furnished with suitably replacement cloth for the repairing of clothing.

  6. The Y.M.C.A. Piano

The Y.M.C.A. desires that we ship the piano received from Geneva, to the British Man of Confidence, Stalag VIII - C. Sagan. Request earliest date shipping arrangements may be made.

  7. Barracks 3-A and 3-B

  a. The security officer told Lt. Col. Barron that he intended to put 90 officers in 3-B.

  b. Your attention is called to the fact that under German Army Regulations this barrack has floor space for 38; under the minimum U.S. Army Regulations, 44.

I have agreed to overcrowding to the effect of 50%, or 65 men; but as long as empty barracks are available in camp we cannot agree to further overcrowding, which would be a menace to health -- even though it may make the task of security easier.

  c. Article 10 Geneva Convention states that "conditions shall be the same as for depot troops of detaining powers."

  d. This question has continually arisen since the very first day of our arrival here, June 6, 1943. This case was satisfactorily agreed upon when the barracks were opened. I see no reason for it to continually be brought up, unless it is for harassing purposes.

e. At the present time no more POWs can be accommodated in 3B unless the storage space is cleared out. This has been promised, but no action has been taken.

f. Upon the clearing out of the storage space only 16 more POWs can be accommodated; and in event of arrival of more, one of the five empty barracks should be made ready for them.

8. Mistreatment of Officers

a. The order requiring the turning in of laundry bags and Y.M.C.A. wooden suitcases is designed, by your security officer, as harassing action.

This action will leave the officers with no place to store their belongings. It is treatment calculated to provoke, and it is in violation of Article 6 and 21 Geneva Convention.

b. The taking of musette bags from officers after nearly 6 months in this camp can only be construed as unfriendly.

c. The German prisoners of war in the United States are treated like officers and soldiers of our forces, and I am sure my government will view with consternation the treatment to which we are almost daily subjected.

In the case of our orderlies (British) some things in their possession almost 3-1/2 years have been taken. Request that you cancel these latest orders pertaining to officers' and orderlies' personal belongings.

9. Confinement of Officers

Your attention is called to the fact that Lt. Higgens has again been punished by confinement (for attempted escape) for a period greater than 30 days.

This is in violation of Articles 47 and 54 Geneva Convention.

10. Orderlies

a. There are 39 orderlies assigned here, two of whom are absent in the hospital, and four who have passed the repatriation board.

b. Under the reciprocal agreement between the American and German governments, orderlies should be assigned as follows:

1 to a Col.

1 to 2 Lt. Cols.

1 to 4 Majs.

1 to 10 Lts.

    c. Based upon that we should have 40 for our present strength of officers.

    Request the assignment of 7 more orderlies.

Thomas D. Drake
Colonel, U. S. Army
Camp Senior

November 11 - Armistice Day

All prisoners of war expected a real "Second Front" on Nov. 8th (the date of the North African Invasion). It did not happen. Now, Nov. 11th is the day. The moon is full. Stalin had announced that there would be a great Allied Invasion soon. It is now 10:15 P.M. And no news of a Second Front!

November 14

At 7:30 P.M., a training film titled, "German Labor Camps," was shown in the mess hall. The film presented the three stages of youth "molding," namely, "Yugendvlok" (Young Boys), "Hitlerjugend" (Hitler Youth), and "Reichsarbeitsdienst" (Reich Labor Service) that are important in Hitler's "molding" process. I would like to deal briefly with each category. Remember our C.C.C. camps, which no doubt did a lot of good to a lot of unemployed young men, but in which public sentiment would not approve any semblance of military training. Hitler thought our C.C.C. set up worthwhile, for German representatives were sent to the United States to observe its operation. The system was replicated, except with different purposes: to develop and train potential Army officers and men.

The "Yugendvlok," a state supported institution (as is most every institution in Germany), is designed for boys between 6 and 14 years of age, in which a normal primary education, along patriotic lines, is given. This category excludes the military aspect. The

"Hitlerjugend" is a militarized institution for young boys between 14 and 17 years of age. In these camps the boys wear the blue uniforms (swastika on left sleeve), drill in elementary tactics, study German history, sing patriotic march songs, and engage in ceremonies and athletics. They receive the best ration of the German Army and do no manual labor. The enrollment is voluntary. However, families are urged to send their "yugends" to this institution. Personnel leadership cards are accurately kept on every boy. Those showing outstanding leadership are "marked" and observed carefully as the potential Army officers. Four blocks from this camp is a Hitler youth camp. For our edification the "yugends" march and drill up and down the street, adjacent to our camp. Boy! How they enjoy it! The Reichsarbeitsdienst is a continuation of the "molding," with the added features of labor, physical conditioning, frugality and self-sufficiency - preliminary to inductions into the Army.

Every boy, upon reaching the age of seventeen enters, compulsorily, one of these camps. They work six hours daily upon such projects as land reclamation. They grow their own vegetables, raise their own livestock and poultry, and learn self-sufficiency and frugality. After each day's work, they shine and polish their shovels. With these shovels, they drill and mount guard, using the shovels as rifles.

Before each meal, they repeat in unison, "Service to the people shall be our aim." After six months of this, the youth are given the opportunity to continue in this phase, go into farm labor or continue his college education, until reaching the age of eighteen. All boys of this age, unless they are select college students, become members of the armed forces. The "Leadership" card is complete, up to this stage.

There you have what I gathered from the film. It was meticulously informative.

November 15

At 7:30 P.M., a German film with English subtitles, "Women Made to Order" was shown. It was a good picture, quite "sexy," risqué, and comical.

One thing is characteristic of the German people. They all shout very loudly at the top of their voices, even in the movies. Their movie equipment is very good but cumbersome, unlike our modern light projectors. Two German soldiers carried in the equipment for thirty minutes, to complete the movie set up. On the other hand, a simple projector and speaker constitute the movie machinery of the United States Army.

November 16

Two inches of snow fell today. The temperature is fifteen degrees below freezing.

"These Yankees are indeed queer people. They are always celebrating defeats," quoting today's front page of *Volkisher-Beobachter,* a Berlin daily paper. The paper also carried news that Lt. Gen. Mark W. Clark has received an honorary degree recently from the University of Naples.

"Kriegy Cakes" - those luscious, delicious, homemade cakes! Everybody is making them, so I made my first today. My first "Kriegy Cake" concocted like this: (1) brown bread (German spud bread) always hard but good, ground up and dried out; (2) Powdered milk, orange-jam, sugar and water; (3) raisins or prunes; and (4) a bicarbonate pill (stolen from the medicos) for "expansion." Stir and mix thoroughly. Place in a can or your steel helmet, cook for one to ten hours, depending on the present supply of coal. Try it!

While on the subject of "eats," I might say that our eating "habits" rarely change. Neither does the German ration, or the Red Cross parcel. Once a week, the "Hauptman" (Captain) issues per person the following: 1-1/2 oz. cheese, 4 oz. sugar, 6 oz. jam (pressed stock beets), 1/4 lb. margarine. Our daily issue: 2 slices of bread, 40 grams meat (which goes into our noon soup), and four potatoes. Incidentally, the U. S. Army meat ration is about 18 oz. daily per person; however, with our Red Cross parcel, we fare splendidly. Probably, those who were once prisoners of war, such as how they lost ninety pounds by eating boiled weeds and chewing shoe leather will tell many fictitious stories! The Russians, I know have eaten boiled weed soup, but not so with the American POWs in Germany. I know that there is a food shortage inside the "Goonland" - except for potatoes. Brother, the German people have millions of acres of potatoes and utilize them for every purpose.

November 17

The entire front pages of the newspapers carried news of the Japanese "victory" at Bouganville Island. The press claims that eighty-seven battleships were sunk by Japanese torpedo bombers. We wonder? No front space article mentioned the Russian front on this date. Sgt. Maj. C. J. Edwards, Ashford, Kent, England, and seven British orderlies arrived back at this camp. They were taken prisoners at the fall of Dunkirk, 1940. I will quote his story:

After capture at Dunkirk, we (all
POWs) were marched to Belgium through
Holland, where we were shipped in battle
cars to Germany. In 1941, we were sent
here. (Oflag 64 was then a British Stalag.)
In the winter of 1941, there were three
thousand POWs crammed into this coup.
We slept in tents for there were only two
buildings. Twenty men died (now buried in
Schubin Cemetery). In those days, if a
POW failed to salute a German Private, he
was punished. The Polish civilians were not
allowed to walk on the sidewalk, but had to
use the alley or street. The Poles had to
remove their hats in the presence of
Germans. They still do. No church services
or public gatherings were permitted in
Poland (which holds good to this day).
The other day, just prior to being sent
here, I heard from a German guard that all
Polish and Dutch officers were being called

into Germany, away from their conscripted employment in their own homeland. The Germans fear that those officers will become instrumental in organizing guerilla warfare, in view of the Russian successes.

I must not forget to mention today's "Schubin College of Knowledge" entertainment. Russ Ford, from Newark, New Jersey, and his twenty "Black Kriegy Minstrels" and chorus, depicted the "Old South." Each "Kriegy" show gets better. The Y.M.C.A. stage equipment has greatly improved our stage settings.

Diary Two

November 18

I mentioned at an earlier date that there was something wrong with the American Red Cross representation in the international set-up at Geneva, Switzerland. Col. Thomas D. Drake's letter should back my assertion.

Oflag 64
Altburgund, Germany
Nov. 14, 1943

To: International Red Cross
Relief Division, Commercial Dept.
Palais du Counseil-General
Geneva, Switzerland

Subject:
Clothing and Food Requisition

Gentleman:

1. In reference to your letter dated Sept. 7, 1943, Relief Div., (Commercial Dept. R.R. HWI S. I.I.22/xx), please be advised that the shipment of clothing referred to as having left your warehouses at the end of August was received here, but, due to not being completely filled, was inadequate to meet our increased number.

2. There are now 326 American prisoners of war and 26 British enlisted men, as orderlies, totaling 352 POWs in this camp.

3. The following requisition for clothing has been sent, as detailed, but only one shipment referred to, has been received.
    The numerous requisitions have been made as groups of new officers have arrived from the battle front,

and of course, there was no clothing, nor is there any for them now. There are Americans here who have not been issued clothing, though they have been prisoners for nine months.

Part of us have been fortunate in having passed through British Camps, where we were supplied from their ample stocks, but in this freezing weather, approximately 100 Americans have no overcoats or winter clothing, though I have been trying to get them some since May 7, 1943.

4. I am fully aware of the fact that I do not know all the difficulties which you encounter; but surely I could expect a letter of explanation, at least, as to why you are unable to furnish the clothing requisitioned. But outside of your acknowledgment, I have no explanation to give those officers except that I have submitted requisitions.

In regard to blankets, we are in the same situation. We received one shipment of 599 blankets, but that shall leave 52 without blankets. Of course, all officers have made donations of clothing to the absolutely destitute, but it is impossible to stretch overcoats and the like, to care for all. The luxury of pajamas, slippers, and bathrobes are something we have not seen, but we have heard that you have them.

Your request for explanation on my assertion that we have not received food parcels during the months of June and July: please be advised that the statement is correct.

The shipments you refer to, [were] made to Oflag IX AZ, which is an entirely different camp, hundreds of miles away from here. The two shipments [sent] in Feb. and March, to Oflag XXI B, were received by the former prisoners (RAF), who left here before our arrival.

The other two shipments to Oflag 64, made from Geneva during July and Aug., were received here - but not during the period, which I wrote you about, June and July, during which period we did not have any parcels from Geneva.

5. In reference to your explanation on determining "camp strength," you state not that this is inferior information - but must wait until the German Authorities officially notify you. The inference being, that in event of delay or loss of official notification, though you may have the POW representative's word, you can do nothing. That of course, explains why I got no acknowledgment of my two telegrams (which Col. Drake had to pay for) to you in June, stating that American POWs had arrived at this new camp and were without food parcels.

I do not propose to suggest a method of operation for you, and I can understand your requiring notification on figures of strength from French, Serbian, etc. POWs in giving out American supplies, but I can assure you that there is nothing more official than the word of the Senior American Officer, in reference to needs of American POWs; furthermore, American people have donated money and supplies to the Red Cross for the benefit of their prisoners of war. Any system which frustrates or delays the expressed benefit is not in accordance with their wishes. Regardless of the merits of the whole situation, the facts are that we are badly in need of clothing and blankets. We have been for some time and cannot get either the supplies or a definite word as to the reason.

6. May I assure you that I regret having to write so plainly, and do not have any doubt as to your good intentions or integrity, but I feel that there is something, somewhere, that we do not know about. Hoping that the situation may be cleared amicably, I remain,

Sincerely yours,
Thomas B. Drake
Colonel, U.S. Army
Camp Senior
(The above is a true copy of the original)

November 18

Several officers arrived today, including Lt. Col. Max Gooler (see Oct. 19 1943 date), who, after being at large about 31 days, was recaptured in Italy. Some of his former inmates were curious to know why Col. Marshall, S.B.O. at Chieti, Italy, gave the order for all officers to remain in the prison camp, after the Italian capitulation. Col. Gooler's answer to this situation was that the S.B.O. had received information from the outside or through the underground, to remain in camp, in case of Italian capitulation. With Col. Gooler were Capt. R. M. Rossbach, (820 Fifth Ave., New York City) and three other officers, all of whom had been recaptured. Capt. Rossbach had been at large 35 days and here is his experience:

An Air Corps officer and I "jumped" the train at Ancona, Italy. We made our way on foot, slowly southward across the country, avoiding towns. 99% of the Italians were nice to us, giving us food, shelter and clothing. The rural homes were full of refugees, usually young men, escaping German forced labor. The farmers and sheep-ranchers were in a precarious position. The Jerries were requisitioning the livestock. This was the season to transfer the sheep to the warm Foggia plains. To do this meant going through the German front lines, which we would not do, for then the Jerries would take the entire herds. Near Popoli, a group of Italian communists were exceptionally nice to us. They urged us to stay and organize them into guerilla bands.

On Oct. 29th, the Air Corps officer and I were making our way across the mountainous country, near Villa St. Maria, which is north of the Sangro Road. The weather was very foggy, and we had no fear of being seen or captured. Contrarily, the two of us walked right into a group of Germans. We were captured. I created a diversion, and my companion slipped away. Incidentally, I learned from an Italian Captain that the Germans had planned to delay the Allies on their main lines, namely, (1) Spezia-Bologna, Ravenna, (2) the Po River Valley, and (3) the Brenner Pass. Five Divisions, namely, the 6th, 16th, and 26th Panzer Grenadier Divisions, 1st and 2nd Parachute Divisions and the Hermann Goering Division, all under Gen. Kesselring. Their mission: to delay as long as possible in the south. In Northern Italy, Field-Marshal Rommel has 15 other Divisions in reserve to defend on the 3 main lines. We shall some day know how reliable this information is.

November 19

Lt. Col. W. H. Shaefer, from Baltimore, Maryland, and four other officers were brought into camp on this date. Col. Shaefer had been in solitary confinement at Luckenwalde, Germany, for failing to answer questions and for "raising Cain" in general. He resembles, to a marked degree, John L. Lewis. According to a companion, the German guards were afraid of him. His remarks about the Germans could not be placed in "black and white," just now. The rugged little Colonel is to be admired for his "contemptible" behavior towards the German Interrogator, Capt. Williams (previously mentioned). In camp there are now 10 Lt. Colonels, 4 Majors and, of course, Col. Drake. Fifteen field officers, whose salaries are worth $81,000.00 annually, would like very much to earn their pay some other way.

November 20

A blanket of white, 2 inches of snow, greeted our eyes this morning. For a Texan, from the sunny lower Rio Grande Valley, snow is still a novelty. Several made ice cream, by concocting a mixture of snow, sugar, powdered milk and British Red Cross syrup.

November 24

The "Goons" made a shakedown raid on Barrack 3-B, looking for indelible pencils, derogatory diaries, radio equipment, etc. The searching party consisted of German officers, 3 Gestapo and 2 SS men. Twenty-two Americans were searched. Col. Drake immediately protested on the grounds that under Article 21 Geneva Convention, the searching of the officer's person by soldiers and civilians is forbidden.

November 25 - Thanksgiving

A special menu was prepared for this oldest American holiday.

Breakfast
Red Cross Oat Meal
Hot Water

Lunch
Red Cross Stew

Supper
Scrambled eggs and bacon
Peas and carrots
Hot Spam
Mashed potatoes
"Schubin Pudding"
Tea

Every item on this menu came from American and British Red Cross parcels, except the carrots and the mashed potatoes, and the apples in the "Schubin Pudding." Lt. Col. Oakes, just prior to supper, made this announcement: "Gentleman: at 4:45 P.M., everyone will march into the mess hall and remain standing while

Chaplain Steven Kane (Des Moines, Iowa) says "Grace," then the chow will be served by courses. If this scheme works well, we may try it again this time next year, here." Someone in the back yelled, "Hang him!" (For his last remark.) The meal was the best since being a "Kriegy."

Following the splendid supper, local "Kriegies" gave us the play "Brother Orchid," directed by Frank Maxwell from Jersey City, N.J. It, too, was a tremendous success.

November 29

This week's issue of *Signal*, a German propaganda magazine printed in English, contained a lengthy article on the Allied bombing of German cities. It stated that, "Germany bombed London in 1939-40 as part of new scientific strategy, affecting only military objectives. It is true that a few civilian casualties were unavoidably produced. With the Allies, there is a different objective: to destroy civilization." I am certain that the relatives of some 30,000 dead, caused by the German Blitz in the St. Paul and Thames districts of London, would write a different story. The German press has just announced that Berlin has received three devastating night raids in five nights. Their reticence to expatiate on the bombing effects, speaks enough to reveal the true story.

December 1, 1943

Issue No. 2 of "The Oflag 64 Item" came out today with the headline "Oflag's six months anniversary to be celebrated with Erzatz Scotch, Films, Thunderous Oratory." "Gigantic celebrations this week will mark the first semi-annual anniversary of Oflag 64." Note the entertainment calendar:

Oflag Calendar

Dec.	Event
1	"Wednesday At 7:15"
2 & 3	German and Silent Films
4	Quiz Program-Messes 26 vs. 27
6	Travel Talk "Hawaii" Col. Van Vleit
8	"Wednesday At 7:15"
9, 10	Orchestra Concert
11	Quiz Program-Messes 28 vs. 29
13	"Raising Money" Lecture - Lt. Waful
15	"Wednesday at 7:15"
16, 17	Hooker - Waful Review
18	Quiz Program- Kansas 30 vs. 31
20	Travel-Talk "Mexico" - Lt. J.T.Jones
22	"Wednesday at 7:15"*
23-25	Christmas Show -Lt. Duckworth
Sundays	Catholic Services
	General Services

* "Wednesday at 7:15" is a popular oratorical program by Kriegy "orators."

December 2

Though the Berlin newspapers do not state so, we know the three recent raids, in which 7,000 tons were dropped, must have been the most devastating to date. Furthermore, the newspaper here-to-fore appearing in

English style type, today appeared in a new dress, Gothic style. No doubt, Allied bombs affected the press buildings.

"German POWs in the U.S. sing over NBC in a 'We the People' program, emanating from a POW camp in Texas! They tell what a good time they are having and how they like the U.S.," quoting an extract from a letter from a wife of one of our inmates. A friend of another American prisoner of war in Oflag 64 wrote "Nazi POWs in a camp near Jackson, Miss. live in steam-heated buildings. I hope you are as well off." Larry Allen splashed this news on our news bulletin board. My only comment is that the people in the U.S. no longer have to tune in on Berlin to hear the Nazis sing. They hear it over NBC.

December 3

Four Geneva Convention representatives paid an eight-hour visit to this camp. It was an informal inspection in the presence of Col. Drake and "Oberst" Schneider. The Colonel pulled no punches. He told them plenty while the Oberst's face grew redder and redder. This occasion also afforded Col. Drake the opportunity to "spill the beans" in reference to negligence of American Red Cross representatives in Geneva (see Nov. 18 date).

Mr. Wilcox, one of the visiting representatives, obviously, learned something. He was surprised to learn that the American Red Cross had not forwarded the Christmas packages for prisoners of war. "There are loads of them in Geneva, and I am surprised that you have not received your share," said Mr. Wilcox. Further, Mr. Wilcox stated that the Red Cross in the U.S. was now publishing a monthly paper, in which it explained how American POWs are being taken care of immediately by the American Red Cross, and that American representatives visit each camp monthly to straighten out any difficulties with the camp senior officer.

Please be informed, my friends, that Col. Drake's POWs have not been visited by a representative from the American branch in over nine months! This is a fact, not fiction. Prisoners of war have no suspicion or antagonism toward the American Red Cross, but they do against the representatives in Geneva. Our food is holding out, and stocks will not be depleted until March, provided no more prisoners arrive. Where are our winter clothing and Christmas parcels? They are available, in abundance, according to Geneva members.

Propaganda and More Propaganda!

The German "propaganda" ministry graciously handed us two pamphlets, titled *England Faces Europe* by John Amery, and *My Ally* by Winston Churchill. I quote the preface of *My Ally*. The text has been taken, almost without exception, from the original. The sources are the speeches delivered by Winston Churchill during the period 1918 to 1940, his press articles and his books. In certain instances, preference has been given to the original version of the speeches and the articles, as they appeared, in print, in English and American newspapers, rather than to the revised editions in book form. Some extracts from *My Ally:*

(1) "Of all the tyrannies in history, the Bolshevist is the worst, the most destructive and the most degrading. It is complete rubbish to say that it is not far worse than German militarism. The great misery of the Russian people under Bolshevist rule far exceeds everything they had to suffer under the Czars." [Winston Churchill's April 11, 1919 speech at a dinner at the Aldwyck Club.]

(2) "This awful catastrophe has been brought about by a comparatively small gang of professional revolutionaries, mostly Jews, who have seized on the wretched Russian nation in its weakness and in its ignorance, and have applied to it, with ferocious logic, all of those doctrines of Communism, which we have spouted so freely in this country." [Winston Churchill's 24th Sept, 1921 speech in the Chair Hall, Dundee, as reported in the Sat. Sept. 26th, 1921, *Morning Post*.]

(3) "If Soviet Russia, for instance, were to make an unprovoked attack on Germany, British sympathy would whole-heartedly be upon the German side, and Germany would be entitled to assistance, which would be given, under the Covenant of the League of Nations."[Winston Churchill's Oct. 22, 1936 statement to the press as reported in the *London Times* on Oct. 23,1936.]

(4) "Finland is behaving magnificently, yes indeed, sublimely. The service which Finland is rendering to humanity is superb." [Winston Churchill's Jan 20, 1940 speech broadcast from London and reported by the German News Agency on the same date.]

Incidentally, opposite each extract, there appeared an anti-Russian cartoon, taken from such papers as the *Washington Post*, the *Chicago Daily Times*, the *Journal American*, and the *London Times*. It's a funny world, Ach, Folk? Beats the "Dickens" out of me.

December 7

From 9:30 A.M. to 1:00 P.M., Mess Table No. 1, consisting of seven Lt. Colonels and their Majors, peeled Irish potatoes, putting in their time in this daily

Lieutenant colonels peel spuds!

"Kriegy" routine. Due to the shortage of orderlies, officers must perform certain mess jobs, such as peeling potatoes. I can just see German Lt. Col. POWs, in the states, performing such menial tasks! My guess is that the German orderlies do not even peel potatoes, because there are electric peelers to do this job. Mind you, the work doesn't hurt us - it's the principle that irks.

While in the kitchen, the carving of a hog's head (less brain and tongue) by a British orderly, captured my curiosity. The orderly informed me that this hunk of hide, hair, fat and bone, was the day's issue of "meat." The daily issue of meat (if you can call it meat) is 40 grams (less than two ounces) per person - hardly enough to flavor the soup. The orderly remarked, "The issue to their own troops is 50 grams." If this is true, the circumstances speak for the scant meat ration. "Greater Germany" just doesn't have the meat to issue.

December 9

The German Press today disclosed two of their many "secret" weapons for reprisal against the British; namely, (1) loud speakers installed in planes, which will blare noisy warnings to the people, as the Luftwaffe flies over England and (2) paratroops, especially trained, to capture the King of England (as easily as they had rescued Mussolini).

December 11

Lt. C. S. Jones, Swarthmore, PA, a prisoner of war for ten months, received news from the folks, for the first time since captivity. Forty-four letters, all bound up and thoroughly "Gepruft."

Hauptmann, (Capt. Mallmann), our German "Camp Officer," on leave to visit his family in Leipzig, was reported killed during an Allied raid on that city. Mallmann had often "gone to bat" for the American officers.

"Herr" (Warrant Officer) Hille, has just been "relieved" from this camp for acting too friendly to the Americans. He was our "welfare officer." It might be of interest to review his past. Prior to World War I, Hille emigrated from Germany to settle at Grant Pass, Oregon, where his uncle, another Hille, lived. When war broke out between Germany and the U.S., Hille was interned. After the Armistice, he became a business partner with his uncle at Grant Pass. They owned a hotel and operated an orchard and hops farm. In 1939, the Germans "ordered" him back to the Homeland (according to one Hille). He has been a German soldier ever since.

Coincidentally, Pfc. Henry Winblab, an American prisoner of war here at this Oflag, hails from Grant Pass, Oregon and had been an employee (prior to 1939) in the Hille orchards. I obtained the above facts from Pfc. Winblab.

December 15 (refer to Christmas Box, 1944)

Lt. Gravin Fitton from Harrison, Ark., received forty letters (the first from home) and a notice from the War Department of his promotion to Captaincy! He formerly commanded a rifle company.

The Red Cross is now out of our "dog-house." Today, 304 Christmas Food Parcels (34 short for our strength) and the much-needed clothing arrived from Geneva.

Contents of the "American Red Cross Christmas Package:"

1 Fruitcake, 1lb.
4 Hershey chocolate bars (D-Bars), 2 oz.
4 Fruit bars, 2 oz.
1 Damson preserves, 5-3/4 oz.
1 Cheese, 4 oz.
1 Preserved butter, 6-1/2 oz
1 Nut crunches, 1/2 lb.
1 Coffee, 4 oz.
1 Prim, 8 oz.
12 packs Cigarettes
1 Peanut butter, 6 oz.

December 16

While on parole walk today, I asked, "Why do all horse-drawn vehicles have a metal plate attached which gives the owner's name and address?" "For his owner's protection. If he is a Pole and cannot speak German, he is liable to be shot as a spy, if there is no identification plate present," was the answer. Teamsters (most of them) lift their hats upon meeting a German soldier. This is compulsory in Poland.

Lt. Col. C. W. Kouns of the 504th Parachute Infantry, a Ranger, and two other officers arrived in camp. This makes a total of eleven Lt. Colonels now in Oflag 64, Altburgund, Germany (or Szubin, Poland). The following is Koun's story:

I was dropped in the wrong place, as is Standard Operating Procedure for Air Corps, in Sicily, July 9th. Lt. Ott's planeload was dropped near me. We immediately came under fire from the Hermann Goering Division. The next day, Lt. Ott and two "Bazooka" men destroyed several tanks and fired point-blank at two personnel trucks, killing about forty Germans. We operated alone for three days, and finally had to surrender in a house surrounded by Jerries and Italians.

After considerable interrogation, I was sent to an Italian POW camp at Capua, Italy. On Aug. 27th I was sent to Chiete, where I remained until Oct. 2nd. On Oct. 3rd, while enroute to Germany, I jumped the train and remained at large for nine days, when I was recaptured at Riva. Italian civilians were nice to me during the nine days at liberty. I was transferred to Moosburg, Germany, where I was kept in solitary confinement for twenty days. While enroute to Luckenwalde, I cut my way out of a freight car and escaped near Munich. I bribed civilians for food, but could get no aid otherwise. In Munich, air-raid shelters are being prepared underneath old ruined houses and buildings.

December 20

Like seven others in camp, I was admitted to the hospital with symptoms of acute gastritis. Dr. Henry Wyneen, Youngstown, Ohio, formerly of the 1st Armored Division, attributed the trouble to malnutrition and sour rye bread.

December 23

No. 3 of the Camp paper, "The Oflag 64 Item", came out with these slogans: "Enjoy Christmas while you wait" and "Home in forty-four or bust."

December 29

Amon Carter, Jr., prisoner of war and son of Amon Carter, well-known Ft. Worth, Texas newspaper owner and cattleman, sent this message to his son:

The people of the U.S. are treating German prisoners of war like hotel guests. For breakfast, they have . . . cantaloupe, other fruits, bacon and eggs, coffee and other beverages.

How the above information ever got through the German censors is more than surprising!

December 31

The German Press has just released news of the sinking of the 26,000-ton battle-ship "Scharnhorst," December 26, off the coast of Norway. Why the delay in the announcement, Herr Goebbels?

Chapter Thirteen
January 1944

New Year's Day -1944

The New Year was ushered in by all-out aerial bombardment of the Reich. For the prisoner of war, it means liberation (we hope)! For the German, total defeat (we hope)! The German Press and radio persists, tritely, to publicize the Gen. Patton incident, in which he allegedly struck a soldier, in Sicily. Our opinion is that it is another Ben Leer (Yoo-hoo) incident, in which some newspaper reporter attempted to make a sensational news scoop.

January 3

"The mighty Russian Army crosses the old Polish border!" Through an outside liaison, we learned this momentous news. Neither the radio nor press mentioned this fact. On the other hand, Goebbels expatiated on the great U-boat victories. On the 10:30 P.M. News-in-English broadcast, Lord Haw-Haw (William Joyce) expostulated on everything from U-Boat victories and "the weeping-willow" Teheran conference to the immoral behavior of Yanks in England. He made no mention, whatsoever, of the Russians crossing the old Polish border!

January 4

Since officer prisoners of war spend the greater portion of their time reading, the library carries on an active business. Travel books, with histories a close second, surpass all others on the "reserve list."

Being in the hospital, I have more time than ever to "travel" with the authors, having just completed reading Dwight Long's *Sailing All Seas in the Idle Hour*. Did you know that about 150 years ago, a whaler by the name of Masters had to abandon his ship and take refuge with the natives on Palmerston - one of the Cook Islands? And did you know that all of those natives today speak perfect English? Masters provided himself with three native wives, raised many children, taught the natives to speak English and discarded the native tongue entirely!

Reichsfueher Adolph Hitler stated to the press today: "The German defeat at Stalingrad was due to the failure of the Italian fighting units, fighting on the Eastern front." He further charged, "The Italian betrayal in capitulating to the Allies necessitated the employment there of troops previously designated for the Russian front." "This," he continued, "is the reason for many sorrows and troubles you have had to suffer, comrades of the East front."

One year ago today, I received my promotion to the Lieutenant-Colonelcy at AFHQ, high up on the hill, Hotel St. George, Algiers.

January 8

It's Saturday Night Quiz Night! Never before has there been so much good-spirited rivalry at Saturday Night Quiz Programs - this week's in particular between "Zimmern Swei und Acht und Zwansig" (Rooms 2 and 28). The anti-climax came when each room elected its propaganda minister, to more effectively obtain support by "hurling acid charges" and defying others, prior to the "imminent engagement." Each room claimed to have a "secret weapon" for the ensuing "battle of wits."

Well, the program came off in this order: Roy Chappell, a Texan, Propagandist for Room 28, armed his men with wooden pistols and rifles. Hollis Wood, also a Texan, dressed his men like "professors of the elite school." The "Master of Ceremonies," Joe Seringer, of Cincinnati, waved a white flag and declared, "I am strictly neutral!" Room 28 won! Larry Allen of the AP, flashed this "bulletin" on our news board: "Room 28's Minister of Propaganda accused Room 2's Propaganda Chief of attempted bribery of the judges with "D" bars (Army chocolate bars)." Lt. Wood announced: "All-out Russian Aid for Zimmer Swei." One statement said, "Ivan Raccamanico, (a Russian orderly in camp whom we call 'Big Operator') the Quisling, is the only Russian pledged to Acht und Zwansig. In spite of heavy Russian support, Zimmer Zwei lost!"

January 10

Silver Taps blow in memoriam today for Richard Torrence, who dropped dead at roll call. Autopsy revealed that a blood clot on the brain was the cause of his death. Capt. Torrence, who fought with distinction in Italy, has received the Purple Heart and has been recommended for valor. Services were held in the camp chapel. He was buried in the Altburgund Cemetery. We have lost a cheerful companion, the army a courageous soldier, and his country a faithful servant. He was a member of the second battalion, 143rd Infantry. His father of 2211 Bernard Ave., Waco, Texas, survives him.

January 11

"A man is no longer safe in the states without a chaperon, especially in Washington. D.C. and Chattanooga, Tenn. (WAC HQ.). Girls now whistle when a good-looking man walks by. Why? For the old bachelor and the 4-F fellow, it's a dreamland! I'm afraid this 'Leap Year' will be 'poor picking' for the lonely females here," writes a wife of a prisoner of war in Oflag 64.

Washington D.C., Jan. 11 (via Berlin), Under-Secretary of State, Edward Stettinius, declared today that, "The Allied Invasion must be strong to beat the Germans!" My reaction: Mr. Stettinius must have lost a whole night's sleep trying to think that one up.

January 12

Lance Corporal Proctor, British "Sanitator," received a letter from a recent "Repat," back in England. After four years of POW life, he writes: "Upon arrival here, the Army granted us an eight-day furlough and immediately reassigned me to a unit! When you return home, Proctor, you can expect two days furlough for each year you were a guest of Germany! Jolly nice of our Army, don't you think, old boy?" Warrant Officer Hille was returned to camp, but is not allowed inside our wires. His welfare work for us is all to transpire outside the wire! (See Dec.11 date.)

January 13

Hitler's newspaper, *Das Reich*, carried pictures of Eisenhower, Tedder, Montgomery, Spaatz, Maitland Wilson and Alexander, with brief stories of their careers, comparing their experiences with those of German Generals.

From New York (Jan. 12, Berlin), "The United Features Syndicate announced today that Mrs. Franklin D. Roosevelt and the German biographer, Emil Ludwig, would write on War!" In Berlin, the newspaper *Volkischer-Beobachter* commenting, "Emil Ludwig Cohen and the beautiful Mrs. Roosevelt as spokesmen and experts on the Fighting Front."

January 14

If one wishes to read books, which have a chuckle on every page, then he should read *Tortilla Flat* by John Steinbeck and *Big Spring* by Shine Phillip. Comical Lt. Col. Oakes, of Oflag 64, has a philosophy on reading books: "I read books by color. After I read all the red colored ones, I start on the green ones."

In Barrack 3-A, the presence of a match creates riotous excitement. The "Goons" haven't issued matches in about three weeks. Ordinarily, they ration a box, penny size, every fortnight. When some "Kriegy" decides to expend a match, he yells, "Come and get it while it's burning." Whereupon there is a mad scramble in the hall to get that precious cigarette fired up.

The thirteen Air Corps officers in this camp have been sent to Stalag Luft No.1, Barth, Pommeria, Czechoslovakia, where American pilots are imprisoned.

January 15

Last evening at roll call an announcement was made: a wristwatch had been lost. If found, please turn into the company commander. At the morning's roll call, another announcement was made. The watch, reported missing, was found in the owner's bed last night! "Sincere apology and thanks to all who might have inconvenienced themselves in the search."

Poor Penn was late for roll call again (fourth time) this morning and again had to do his "thirty minutes" (fourth time also). For Col. Drake has a little method for dealing with these, "Aw shucks, there's plenty of time, besides it's too cold to crawl out just now, fellows." They have to walk thirty minutes out in the "early cold" before breakfast. The method works pretty well on everybody except poor Penn. "Penn," by the way, is Lt. Holmes E. Penn, Jr. from Virginia.

Penn has the darndest time; he is always losing or forgetting something. If it isn't his cap, it's his Red Cross box or his library book. Lt. Col. Jones (who is sympathetic to Penn's amnesia) says, "Poor Penn is the body from which the soul has fled." He is a likable cuss, though, and usually the neatest-dressed officer in camp, i.e., when he has a complete uniform at any one time. Penn, however, does have a few good, original ideas. A short time back, he happened upon the idea that he could add meat to his ration (having lost his Red Cross meat) by making a rabbit trap, as rabbits wander inside the "wire" at night. Sure enough, it worked. Penn caught six rabbits! This "beat-the ration" trick worked fine until everybody in camp built a rabbit trap. The rabbits had gotten wise by this time, anyway.

Now for a news flash: "Vienna, Jan.15, A special military court sentenced Aranda Vetrovsky, 28 years old, to 18 months imprisonment for 'forbidden sexual intercourse' with a prisoner of war." The POW was not named. Larry Allen discovered the above item in a German daily paper.

January 16

Going down to "breakfast," I spied three "Ruskies" (Russians) energetically engaged in retrieving a frantic crow that was dangling by a rope at the top of a tall post. It seems that the "Ruskies" for some time have been trapping crows to eat, by setting snares on post tops. Maybe Penn's idea wasn't original after all. Shortly Penn, too, may be snaring crows to eat. I suppose people back home, who have no POW relatives, wonder what items of necessity, or luxury, a POW writes home for. Usually, they are things that are not supplied by the Red Cross or the Y.M.C.A. In the first letters home, a POW writes:

Dearest, I am well so don't worry. Please send me the following things (as soon as the War Department sends the labels): A pair of pajamas, house slippers, cigarettes, my textbooks, some dehydrated cereal and fruits, vitamin pills (hoping Vitamin E is included), pepper, catsup, mustard, popcorn and flour. Oh! Yes, and some toilet paper.

January 17

Disciplining a group of American officers is not a simple task for any superior officer. Firmness, tact, diplomacy, and leadership are essential in coping with that "cockiness," that arrogant, carefree, independent attitude, which is typically American. No one here envies Col. Drake his job as "Senior American Officer" (SAO). To illustrate my remark, the Germans recently, published an order that, "Tin cans must not be thrown in trash-cans," as cans are salvaged (so are razor blades and everything else). Well, as expected, cans keep "cropping-up" in the trash, even after the Germans had threatened to cut our parcel issue. Friend, what would you do, as SAO? The SAO took disciplinary measures, as was done for roll call. I am not stating whether it was right or wrong, but I do know that it was effective. The action taken was thus: no more tins to be taken from the parcel "hatch," which, in effect, meant that all the food drawn had to be dumped into plates, cups or any conceivable container, in order to get it out of the "hatch." Of course, this is a darn nuisance, punishing everybody collectively for lowdown shiftlessness of a few individuals, but a necessary expediency.

January 20

Having been abroad for almost two years, it is hard to imagine the goings-on in the States, but it seems that every time someone there suggests something good, or introduces to Congress what seems to be a good bill, everybody else, from Westbrook Pegler to Harrison Spangler, President of the GOP, etc, immediately attacks same. Take, for example, the President's recent speech to Congress, in which he urged the enactment into law, five main points, viz.
1. Establishment of compulsory labor
2. Alterations of tax laws
3. Restrictions of war profits
4. Regulation of living costs
5. Steps to prevent inflation

Not as an expert, but as a civilian soldier, they seem to make "horse sense" to me. Brother, just ask any soldier what he thinks of Point 1.

Dr. Goebbels recently predicted that the ensuing Allied Invasion Troops would, no doubt, gain a bridgehead, but that the advance will be the same "Snail's Pace Advance" as that on the Italian Front. Time will tell, and we shall see, Dr. Goebbels.

January 19

The greatest event in "Kriegy" life comes when he receives that first letter from the wife, sweetheart or mother. From the day I wrote my first letter, to the day I received a reply, the time interval was 108 days.

January 20

The twenty Russians are being transferred from this camp. Prior to departure of ten of the "Ruskies" this morning, there occurred the usual "shake down" inspection. On one of the "Ruskies," a German officer found 500 American cigarettes and some Red Cross candy! The officer was furious. The very idea of a Russian having luxuries, which not even the German soldier enjoys! Anyway, the POWs were allowed to keep them, for American officers had contributed. This, of course, is characteristic of American generosity.

In North Africa, it was not uncommon to see Arabs plowing with teams paired up as follows: an ox and horse, an ox and jackass, or even an ox, jackass and camel. In Germany, I have seen more oxen as motivative power than horses. But to see an ox-horse team in Poland was a new surprise! That is exactly what I saw on a parade march today.

January 22

Capt. L. H. Warren, New York, and Lt. V. C. White, Texas, who were at large in Italy from Oct. 2 to Dec. 3, 1943 when they were recaptured, are now inmates of this camp. According to a story told by them, human nature is still the same the world over, even in "Greater Germany," where morals are not always to be praised. While at Moosburg, they saw three French POWs who had just been sentenced 2, 3 and 5 years of hard labor, respectively, for illicit affairs with German women. In the latter case, the Kommando (POW) worker had been sentenced five years for sleeping with the wife of a German officer, who was on the Russian Front at the time! This, of course, is hearsay and I have no proof of its validity. Any story, which makes a POW chuckle, is worth listening to.

January 23

On the 10:30 P.M. "News-in-English" broadcast, Lord Haw-Haw, the Berlin commentator, informed his English audience that Gen. Eisenhower, Invasion Commander, had created a Psychological Department. "I think," retorted Haw-Haw, "the department's first job should be that of analyzing Sir Archibald Sinclair's mind. He has just made a statement that Allied Bombing would pave the way in civilizing the Germans."

January 24

Five new officers arrived today. Two are Texans, now making 36 Texans. Among the group was Capt. Philip Foster, a former professor of economics, State College, PA.

January 26 - "Luftgangsters and Murder Incorporated!"

About two months ago, Lt. Kenneth Williams of Charlotte, N.C. was shot down in his fortress while on a mission over Germany. On the nose of his fortress and on the back of his flying jacket was inscribed, "MURDER INC." Since that date every newspaper and magazine in Germany has fervently reminded the people, by special mention, cartoons, illustrations, etc. of the American "Luftgangster's" (Air Gangster) slogan, "MURDER INC." *Das Reich*, Hitler's own paper, carried photographs of Lt. Williams and his flying jacket. "Foolishness" which cost lives of "bail out" pilots. Officers, like GIs, must have their fun!

Lt. W. E. Davis of Chicago, received a letter, which contained photographs of his wife, and on her dress there appeared a tiny object that vaguely resembled an Air Corps insignia. The pictures were passed around (an old Kriegy custom). Due to the presence of this object on Mrs. Davis's dress and due to the fact that Lt. Davis is in the Infantry, great speculations were aroused.

"Well, Davis, you have now become a member of the Brush-off Club," we said, poking fun at Davis. In great humility, poor Davis borrowed a magnifying glass. The little object was not an Air Corps insignia after all, but the heckling goes on.

"There will be no more vulgarity or derogatory remarks in camp shows," read the decree from the SAO. This "decree" came about as a result of the recent camp performance, entitled, "Your Kind Indulgence, Please." For one thing, Hitler was impersonated. Among other things, Lt. John Jones from Houston, Texas, (nephew of Jesse Jones) portrayed a World War II veteran, who had an amputated arm (Sidi Bou Sid Battle) who played the trumpet on the street, and passed the hat for his up-keep. The SAO objected to some of his actions.

January 28

In my brief military career, I have seen American Generals frighten their subordinates, but not to the degree, indeed no, that German Generals scare the "living wits" out of their own little "Unterfuhrers." For the past week, German camp officers have frantically prepared "us" and the camp for an expected call from a German Inspector General. This A.M. he came and we "Kriegies" enjoyed the comedy from a window-view. The German sentry was posted at the entrance to every building, to give the warning of "his" approach. When he entered Barrack 3-A, I snapped-to and yelled "tention!" The old camp Kommandant and his subordinates were so afraid that something would go wrong that their knees practically trembled. The General (who incidentally wore more red than a British Brigadier) asked the Kommandant five questions and I saw the Kommandant salute him five times. It's a custom, evidently, in the German army, to salute every time addressed. I must say they are the most military souls I have ever seen in uniform.

January 29 (The Sequel)

At the morning roll call, the old Kommandant made his appearance to express his gratitude for the splendid cooperation in yesterday's inspection. "I know real soldiers, when I see them," and he concluded, "And I know you are real soldiers. Oberst Drake and all of you are to be commended." It will probably keep the old boy from the Russian Front, if the German General, too, was impressed.

January 30

In order to defray minor camp expenditures, we "throw" a monthly "Gay-90's" program. An old time 1890's saloon is depicted, with all its bars, pictures, wagon wheels, cowhand costumes, and slogans such as, "Check your shootin' irons at the bar." Plenty of minus two percent beer is sold, and all sorts of gambling devices (poker wheels, Blackjack) get you Reichsmarks for the house. Plenty of music by the band and impersonations by "Daisy May." "Gurtie-from-Bizerte" provides the interlude hilarity. The total proceeds from our "brawl" last evening: 600 Reichsmarks.

Chapter Fourteen
February 1944

February 1, 1944

News developments: Heile Salassi, Emperor of Ethiopia, notified the Allies that Mussolini should return his pet lions!

Gen. Franco, Spanish Dictator, emphatically assured the Allies that, in the future, the oranges shipped to England would not contain time bombs.

"That's what you think!" wrote a German censor in the margin of a POW letter from a father in the states, who wrote, "Well, son, it looks like the war will be over pretty soon, and you will be back home."

Statistics show that 3,128 letters were received in this camp for the month of January, with 89 days average time in transit. The best time was 30 days.

February 3

Mail from England is more than twice as fast as mail from the states. I just received a letter from Gordon Fraser, a friend from Hungerford, England, in exactly 30 days.

February 4

This evening the SAO published an order that no Red Cross food items or U.S. Government equipment, in their original state, would be used in conjunction with an attempted escape, i.e., cheese, chocolate, crackers etc. must be melted. Since canteens cannot be melted, the use of canteens is to be construed out of the question. As to be expected, clamors of protest went up. 'I suppose we are to milk the old house cat to get milk to make chocolate!' cried one. "I'm gonna stamp 'Bolivian Army' on my canteen," shouted a second. "What escape?" queried still another. The SAO's reason was that the Germans might take retaliatory action, which seems a logical reason to me. Young officers, however, cannot see it that way, due to lack of judgment, foresight, etc.

February 6

All war news was shelved on back pages of today's *Volkisher-Beobachter* to make space to feature, verbatim, "The Allied School for Murder," in translating a quotation, which appeared in *Reader's Digest*. The article quoted a British Major (an acquaintance of the writer), who conducted this course in "Murder" for Allied troops. Quoting the Major in *Reader's Digest*:

This is a school of murder; murder is my business. Not the impersonal shooting of unknown people in war, but the personal and individual murder of one man. To kill a Jerry should mean more than the mere smashing of a fly. Think about it; put yourself in the same position; and offer the bloodiest slaughter; you will sleep like a baby. Only two things will interest you: commit the act, and get away from it safely.

The moment I saw those familiar expressions, I knew their author. It is Maj. Grant Alexander, who conducted this course for British Airborne and my former parachute battalion near Kairouan, Tunisia, in July 1943. His method, to murder in the use of the killer-knife, Tommy gun and pistol, was by far the most practicable and adroit known to me. This "Tom Mix" of the pistol could cut a straw in two, at close range. I saw him do it. In civilian life, the Major was a Scotland Yard detective and a graduate of both the Scotland Yard and the FBI schools. He instructed us to fire the pistol, from the center of the belly, using the navel as a checkpoint position. I should like to tell a true story of one of his military feats. (It may be verified at the British War Office.)

After the fall of France, the War Office desired the destruction of three notorious German Luftwaffe Instructors, who had been successfully directing "terror" air raids on England. Their school headquarters was located just inside the coast of France. Each night, at about eight o'clock, these three Germans rendezvoused at a certain table in a certain pub to sip French beer. That much the Intelligence Department knew. They must be destroyed! Maj. Grant Alexander was selected for the job. By submarine, the Major landed on the coast of France, near the pub. Having rehearsed the job, using a model "pub," to scale, the Major visualized the scene perfectly. Stealthily, he crept to the building, imperceptibly opened the door and with two pistols, killed his victims. He retreated to the submarine, and returned to England with a perfect record of "murder."

February 10

Agriculturists are graduated weekly, since our weekly agricultural lectures were initiated several weeks ago. The AAA could be rewritten (in so many million words) by them and many new bureaus could be created (to more thoroughly confuse the poor farmers), when the war is over and those brain trusts return to the States. Col. ("a la") Oakes has become the foremost authority on the subject. "Apres la guerre," (after the war) he plans to purchase a farm in my "neck-of-the woods" (the lower Rio Grande Valley, Texas), just to prove some of his theories. One idea, "a la" Oakes has is to provide poultry feed by electrocuting bugs, thereby reducing the feed cost. He describes his gadget thus, "The best damn phosphorus food for chickens, is bugs and grass-hoppers. Bugs, by the millions, are attracted to a yellow light at night. Then, why not set up a yellow neon light at night and cover with an electrical screen, which will electrocute millions of bugs in one night? Go out the next morning and shovel up several bushels of the best chicken chow known!"

Lt. Rauck tells a good story on Col. Oakes. Last summer, when some of the officers were working on our little quarter-acre garden, Col. Oakes gave the order, "Pull off all the leaves of the tomato vines. You can't grow good tomatoes and good leaves at the same time, so why not grow good tomatoes and to h___ with the leaves."

February 11

Gen. Dwight Eisenhower is the "Tarzan in uniform" and the "Woman's Idol," paraphrasing today's issue of the *Hamburg-Fremdenblatt* in its description of the Invasion Chief for the impending operation. The article went on: "He is a typical person whom American women idolize. They even wear panties carrying 'Eisenhower and McArthur' trademarks. This fellow, with a muscular neck, typical of a Madison Square Garden promoter, will lead the Allied troops in their attempt to invade Europe. He was selected for the job, not for his genius, but because of his national popularity."

February 16

More of the above laxative: The Feb. 16th issue of the same paper expounds on the political situation in the States. "Thomas E. Dewey, Republican aspirant, seems a promising candidate for the coming Presidential election. He is a man of breath-taking beauty, sex appeal and stylish dress - the type that will win millions of votes from the American women. He was once ambitious to become an opera star, but found the political racket a more feasible one," states the article.

Col. Thomas E. Drake, SAO, wrote another scorching letter, similar to the one written Nov. 14, 1943, to Mr. Norman Davis, President of the American Red Cross. The theme of the letter: unsatisfactory service from the International Red Cross, Geneva, Switzerland.

Wednesday is Shower Day

Typically American (as though plutocrats), the shower, after a day's use is always extremely cluttered with articles left by bathing officers. At the evening roll call, the following announcement was read:

"Left in the shower room today was a pair of gloves, two drawers, one sock, two soap dishes, a cup bearing 2nd Lt. Carter's name, but with Captain's bars on it! Also someone got the wrong pair of shoes (Lt. Cole Shaefer was guilty). To claim these articles and to exchange shoes, come by Capt. Harker's room, immediately after this formation."

Immediately after supper, our camp strength jumped to 362, because 28 officers, captured in Italy, arrived. Eighteen of these are Texans, now making a total of 44 Texans in Oflag 64. The majority of them are from the 3rd, 34th and 36th Infantry Divisions. From the new officers, we learn the following:

Only one of the original battalion commanders of the 36th Infantry Division remains in command of his unit. The rest have either been killed, captured or relieved.

The Allied soldiers have a most profound respect for the German soldier's tenacity and fighting efficiency. Treatment received from German front-line soldiers was extremely good. This bears out all previous reports that, not until inside the Reich do prisoners receive bad treatment, and then it is usually from the hands of some jackass who has formerly lived in the States or England or is a Nazi.

No, Rome is not destroyed, nor the Brenner-Pass, plugged by Allied bombs; neither is Berlin "practically in ashes." The railway system is still functioning. From the train that carried them through the Berlin terminus, damage was observed, certainly, but they expected to see the city in ashes, as the Allied Air Communiques had led them to believe.

February 17

From a German paper, we learn of the capture of Capt. Milton H. Steffen from Weimer, Texas. Due to the fact that his diary was taken, that he is of German extraction, and that there is a Weimer, Germany, considerable space was given to this article. Capt. Steffen was the last of the original company commanders of Lt. Col. Jones' battalion. Steffen is expected to join Jones very soon at Oflag 64. He was captured Jan.16, 1944.

February 18

American censorship is a peculiar animal. In North Africa, soldiers could not disclose their location; yet, *Time* magazine came out with an article on Lt. Gen. Mark W. Clark, and mentioned that his headquarters were located at Oujda, French Morocco! No American POW is allowed to receive magazines or papers from the States (occasionally, however, one gets by the U.S. censor) yet, the German Propaganda Ministry obtains all the latest issues, loads of them, through Portugal, Geneva and Sweden! The "Goons" then reprint certain paragraphs of certain "desirable" articles in their propaganda magazine for POWs called "O.K." (OVERSEAS KID).

February 21

An American: a person who is never satisfied with what he has, wants too much of something else, uses one-fourth of it, wastes the rest, then complains about not having enough of anything.

Last fall the SAO approved a requisition to the Y.M.C.A. for 400 ice-skates, 40 barbells, 24 ping-pong sets, etc.! Actually, the camp strength is 362, of whom only 18 ever skated; furthermore, there is one tiny pond available, which will accommodate 8 officers. Nobody wants the ping-pong table, for the players create too much noise. The "Y" knew better. Even they overestimated and sent 275 pairs of skates, 175 of which have never been unpacked. Now mind you, a requisition has just been forwarded for 24 footballs, 48 suits, etc. We have one cramped court that might afford a game of touch football! "Kriegies" will now curse the "Y" for not having the forethought to send this in the first place.

Diary Three

Chapter Fourteen continued
February 1944

February 21 - "Kriegy" Eccentricities

Maj. M. A. ("Ma") Meacham slices his parcel cheese so thinly that he can plainly read Larry Allen's news board through a slice of it!

Dick ("Roses Red") Rossbach is the only one in camp who can write a play, read Walt Whitman and toast "Goon" bread, all in one operation!

Most of the married men from the North believe in twin beds - or so they say! Capt. N. W. ("Tex") Lantron swears, "I'll never go to ____ for sleeping in one of 'em!"

Lt. Col. J. H. ("Medals") Van Vleit has just contrived a bulletproof jacket. "A blouse, adorned, decorated and armored with all the campaign ribbons and decorations, conceived by the War Department prior to and during the war."

Lt. Col. ("King Kong") Shaefer speaks seven languages, but swears he will never tell the Germans. Confidentially, though, he once linguistically engaged a mail orderly in his room with "gut morgen, mi amigo, comment allez vous?"

Lt. Sid ("Mouse") Waldman definitely does not like cheese and trades his issue for "D" bars.

Lt. Carl ("Professor") Hanson reads philosophy, while Warrant Officer Roger ("Slick") Cannon studies books on "sex."

Lt. L. W. ("Old Folks") Spence was endeavoring to procreate a complete squad of boys when the war came along and interrupted his "scheme of things."

Lt. L. W. ("Sitting-Bull") Lowe went out for a hundred-yard hike one evening, dropped before he got halfway and had to be carried in by his bunkmates. The "Bull" handles camp welfare.

The German security NCO, who prowls about camp looking for tunnels, has the title of "Ferret." We call his assistant "Weasel."

February 22

In Washington's Farewell Address in 1797, he said, "It is our true policy to steer clear of permanent alliances with any portion of the foreign world." In 1938, Roosevelt declared, "I hate war." In 1939, Hitler boasted, "I love war!" The next day, Mussolini states that his comrade, Adolph was not original. So the war goes on! But, "Mein Got" above, when will it stop?

February 23

Two days ago, Col. Drake received a letter from the International Red Cross, Geneva, informing him that a committee photographer would soon visit this camp to take moving pictures and photographs of camp activities. The Colonel immediately replied, and I quote extracts of his letter:

I have been informed that a moving-picture photographer of the International Red Cross is expected shortly at this camp, to take pictures of personnel engaged in different activities and of the camp, in general, for showing in the United States. This, I respectfully protest, on the grounds that I, as senior officer, and other prisoners of war, feel that the film is to be used for spreading the doctrine that all is well - which, in fact, is not true. We believe that, instead of sending a photographer, a person capable of looking into our real needs and to get information, would be more human.

After having queried the Colonel more about the subject, he told me a story that ran somewhat like this:

In 1943, a similar mission by the aforementioned organization visited the British Oflag at Chieti, Italy. Prior to the visit, however, the camp was placed in an entirely artificial state, to depict the salubrious existence of the inmates.

Outside dishes and chinaware, fancy tablecloths, flowers etc. were brought into camp. The delegate arrived. The best dinner, to date, was served. "Kriegies" in camp costumes and hobby-arts were photographed. As a token of gratitude, the British senior and his entire staff were photographed, under a Nazi flag (to their embarrassment upon seeing the photograph)!

Now, the Colonel's reprobation and remarks were not placed in black and white to bring discredit upon this charitable organization; on the contrary, to tell the truth. The truth hurts nobody or anything.

The Red Cross is helping millions, but they, like any bureau or organization, have subtle propaganda agencies.

February 23

Larry Allen's AP Board: Oflag 64, February 23, Flash! "First repercussions were felt today (as a result of the Germans issuing a week's supply of loaf bread), when a loaf of solidified bread tumbled out of a locker, smacking Lt. Curtis Jones on the nose! After having received first-aid treatment, his nose is resuming its normal composure once more."

February 24

Yesterday, the Germans sent in to our medico a great quantity of serum and we were inoculated for "typhus." Today, we learned that a German medico had made a mistake; and consequently, we were inoculated with typhoid serum instead. The "Kriegies" are now a bit skeptical about the cholera injection supposed to be administered next week.

February 26

The editor, of *Der Angriff*, recently described Mrs. Franklin D. Roosevelt as "The hyena of the White House, who approves and applauds the Allied Terror Attacks on our civilians, our churches, schools and homes!"

February 27

The only amusing occurrence this Sabbath day was the inebriation of "Oberst Lieutenant" (Lt. Col.) LeViscan and "Hauptman" Zimmermann, German commandant and security officer, respectively. Both drunk as a skunk, and happy as larks, walking down the street, arm in arm, outside the wire!

February 28

From Larry Allen's AP Board: "Dinner, then toothpicks!" "Capt. Amelio Pallaconi received, from his Michigan wife, today a parcel of food and 750 toothpicks."

February 29 (No Invasion Yet)

Yes, my weekly agricultural lectures turn out experts - weekly.

Lt. Col. Jim Alger, Regular Army, plans to grow, via remote control, coffee, tea and apples on his wife's farm in Maine, after the war.

Lt. Col. Oakes has calculated that a hen laying 200 eggs annually, eating a 20 percent protein ration will cost him 1.034 cents per "hen berry."

Chapter Fifteen
March 1944

March 1

From Larry Allen's AP Board: "They're really hurting."

Washington, D.C. (via Berlin) March 1: "'American doctors report that mental disturbances are increasing among women. Indicator: in a prominent hotel occupied by government officials in Washington recently, a woman was reported walking through the lobby, dressed with only a feather!'"

March 2

A Berlin War Correspondent writes: "It looks like the Allies are using everything except the Siamese Twins, in attacking the German troops at Cassino. Comprising the Task Force, there are six assorted divisions, namely, Algerian and Tunisian Colonials 'Sphis,' a division of Moroccans 'Goums,' two divisions flying the American flag, from the wild west to the unopened south, where wine, women and song mean everything, a division of Hawaiian Japs, and lastly, a division of New Zealand 'Maori' Head-hunters."

March 3

For the month of February, this camp received 3,005 letters. Average time in transit - 99 days. Assuming that at least one letter per day is written in the States, for each officer here, this would make a total of 12,090 letters, written monthly (camp strength, being 402). Then, what happened to the other 9,085? What happens to them every month? Never more than 25 percent of the letters, written to us in the States, are received. Paper does, no doubt, make good fuel for starting fires.

Russia reports that she has lost 15 million men killed since the beginning of the war; the United States, 143,000!

March 5

By the expedient of "Foods and Feeding," by Henry Morrison, Cornell University, Lt. Col. Oakes, Dr. Abram and I worked out the "nutritive value" of the German issued ration (using Morrison's digestive table for cows). The compilation (daily issue for one person) is as follows:

Food	Grams*	Calories*
Potatoes	400.0	261
Field peas	16.0	49
Mangels	6.8	2 (Texas cow-feed)
Barley	7.1	20
Cabbage	476.0	90
Beet jam (pulp)	25.0	11
Bread	349.0	890(?)
Sugar (beet)	25.0	98
Margarine	25.0	187(?)
Fat (cooking)	31.0	251
Meat (mixed)	15.0	45 (for soup only)
Wurst	12.0	38
Total daily	1387.9	1942

(* 1 pound = 453 grams + 1 gram pure carbohydrates = 4 calories, 1 gram pure protein = 4 calories, and 1 gram pure fat = 9 calories.)

The above figures are based on animal equivalents, for, unfortunately, figures for human equivalents were not available. Based on my knowledge of animal nutrition, I would say that these figures are nearly correct for humans, remembering that cattle's rumen contains bacteria and micro-organisms which will digest fiber, cellulose and pentosans, etc., while the human stomach will not. Let us assume that the human body is 80 per cent efficient on this ration - then the ration provides 1,554 calories daily. The Red Cross provides 2,200 calories daily, making our daily total 3,754. This is far greater than needed, which explains why most of the officers have gained weight, in spite of all the complaints. An idle man needs 2,200 and a workingman needs 3,000 calories daily. Well, what is wrong with the ration? Plenty! There is no variety, the same, day in and day out. There is a deficiency of phosphorous and calcium. Much of the cabbage and potatoes is unsuitable to cook. There is not enough bulk in the Red Cross parcel and too much of the wrong kind in the German ration. The important thing, we are not eating "boiled weeds" and "shoe-tongues," as some may say, after the war.

March 9

Yesterday, the German mail and parcel censor presented himself at the "Parcel Hatch" to "Gepruff" books. From an envelope, which "vaguely" resembled an American type, he drew out his censor stamp. One of the officers, through curiosity, picked up the envelope to discover that it belonged to (i.e., it was addressed to) Capt. H. M. Spalding, Waseca, Minn., and the letter was post dated Dec. 3, 1944. Spalding had never received the envelope or its contents. The SAO asked the Commandant for an explanation, which was politely, but cunningly given: "The letter contained so much propaganda that it was destroyed," which is an obvious "fib," and the act in violation of the articles of the Geneva Convention. Recently, Lt. P. D. Lampru, Jacksonville, Ala., having received no mail in over a month, asked the "Goon" mail orderly, "Why don't you bring my mail in now? You've had it long enough." The next morning, he brought in seven letters for Lt. Lampru, giving no reason for the peculiar action! It is a well-known fact that the officers, who "treat" the mail orderly with cigarettes and coffee, got much better service, more letters than anyone else, and, occasionally, a mail case full of eggs. Apparently, there is a "racket" in every conceivable thing under the sun. Those of us, not in on the "racket" do not fare as well, but there is a thing called pride and self-respect.

March 10

Mr. Roland Marti, Investigator of the International Red Cross and an Estonian movie photographer, called at Oflag 64 to discuss details of the SAO's letters, which were more or less reproaching. Mr. Marti asserted that the delay in clothing shipments was due to the fact that no reserve stocks were maintained in Geneva, and that the shipment came directly from the States, as a result of requisitions. All requisitions from American camp officers were referred directly to Mr. James, American Red Cross representative in Geneva, and upon receipt of such requisitions, Mr. James used his own judgment in determining their priority. Food and clothing, for the French, Serbs, etc. were marked for them in the States and not in Geneva, and therefore none of it has priority over American POW shipments. He stated that poor mail service was caused by the U.S. Government and not the Red Cross at all, because the government refused to allow POW mail to go on Red Cross boats, and instead it was sent on any boat from Portugal via England (which I don't believe). The SAO refused to allow the Estonian, who wore long fuzzy hair over his ears, and pantomimed his expressions (as "art-i-s-ts terr-i-fi-que"), to take movies.

According to German sources, President Roosevelt has appealed to Congress to permit soldiers to vote in the coming Presidential elections by airmail postcard. Being true or false, the Oflag 64 poll showed that ninety-five per cent of the officers were against such an absurd thing. The ten million soldiers will have their say after, and not during the war, which is yet to be won, to quote my simple-minded thought.

March 12

Atta Boy! Good old American "esprit de corps!" Today, a list was placed on the bulletin board, which informed all those needing a pair of eyeglasses to sign below. The Y.M.C.A. will make an attempt to get them. Exactly 178 signed up (almost half of the camp strength) and the only reason the rest did not sign up was there was no more space to sign on!!!

What a "Kriegy" says when he drops his bread or cheese, on the floor, "Darn, I'm glad 'that' piece of paper was on the floor," and he goes ahead and eats the morsel.

March 13

I have just seen the unusual. A 2nd Lieutenant closed the barrack door as he went out!

In "Kriegy" vernacular, a "Who-Done-It" book is a mystery book; a "Shoot 'Em Up" is a westerner.

The recent historical novel, *Moment In Peking* by Dr. Lin Yu Tang, is the most superb of its kind ever written, I think.

Capt. Sid C. Brockman, Louisville, Kentucky, formerly with the 168th Infantry and captured in Tunisia, reported January 1943 into this camp this evening. Briefly, his story is as follows:

After capture by the Italians, I was sent to Sfax, to Tunis, where I was turned over to the Germans, and later, sent to Capua, Italy. From there to Stalag 3-B on the Oder near Berlin, where I remained an American Medical Officer. Here, there were French, Serbs, Slavs, Russians and about 1,800 Americans. The housing and facilities were fair. The 168th band, almost complete, entertained. Recently, the Germans made a raid with 200 soldiers and 40 Gestapo agents. Some personal items were confiscated; and later, they issued an order prohibiting the accumulation of more than one day's food supply for the individual. When I first went to the Stalag, young guards were on duty, to be relieved shortly, by older ones. Now, there is an old-timer on guard, who was turned down, during the last war, for old age!

March 14

Timesaving devices are all-important, obviously, to the "Kriegy." He rushes to the mess, gulps down the food in five minutes, grabs another cup of water, rushes to his room, slumps in another spoonful of "Nescafe" and reaches for the "Who-Done-It" book and pushes his way to the community stove to settle down to the daily routine. Even daylight saving time is observed!

March 15

Lt. Cary L. Demott from Bessemer, Ala., our newest arrival, was captured in February at the Nettuno Beachhead, Italy. At that time, he was a part of the 45th Infantry Division. In a comical Alabama accent, he related the following:

I was wounded at the time of capture, and carried to an old barn, which was used as a German aid-station. One day an Italian civilian came in and asked "Are you an American?" and I said "Yes," whereupon, he kicked me in belly, just for the h___ of it, I suppose. Then, the German medical orderly swaffed the "Ite" on the head with the butt of a rifle, and took on another patient. At Rome, I met a German Sergeant, who had been a "Fuller-brush man" in New York. He married an American girl and would like to go back, after the war. (They all would!!!) Rangers and Paratroopers ain't half as hot on the battlefront as they are at a Red Cross club. The Yanks fight well, but so do the Jerries.

March 16

Lt. John Hannon from Bedminister, N.J., gave us his best performance, as Sheridan Whiteside in the play, "The Man Who Came to Dinner" at our little theater this evening. Prior to the war, John, had just started a career as a professional actor. My prediction is that John J. Hannon will someday be a nationally known star!

March 17

They "done" it! The Germans finally broke down and allowed us to attend movies in the Altburgund Theater, outside the wires. At 2 P.M., the "Kriegies" marched to town to see "Women are Better Diplomats," a good German color film. The language was "Deutsche" but that did not matter; to get the same privilege as German POWs in the U.S. is what matters.

Observations from a critical viewpoint:

Music and songs: beautiful.

Settings: elaborate.

Irony: Germans have a sense of humor.

Male characteristic: big "tummies."

A fact: There are more corn-fed "gals" in Germany than Carter had oats.

The film was very sexy.

March 20

Returning from Gniesen, where the SAO went for an ulcer X-ray, he reported as follows: "There was more clothing and fresh meats on display than I have ever seen in Germany. The Nazi salute is still a common sight."

March 23

It seems that mail service from Germany to the States is about twice as fast as from the States to Germany, just now.

Lt. Teddy Roggen, Houston, Texas, received a letter with plenty of "black-out," which is obviously ridiculous censorship. An example: "The Longhorns played (blackout) Bowl."

March 24

Lt. ("Lightening") Lou Lowe from Gilbert, Arizona, is the man dripping with vitamins! He received 24 "vitaminized" candy drops from home yesterday. Smacking his lips and beating his gums, Lou ate all 24 in about 10 minutes, discovering later that the instructions read, "Eat one each day, by dissolving slowly in the mouth."

March 25

Capt. Lou ("Lou-ege") Salerno, M. C., arrived back at this camp, after four months absence with American "Commandos." His observations are as follows:
The Allied bombings of Berlin, Nurnburg, and Frankfort, have damaged considerably the civilian districts, and in the case of Nurnburg, the railway system. Very little damage has been done to the war factories. They are practically all under ground.

Two members of the "Swiss Delegation" visited this camp to talk over confidential matters with Col. Thomas D. Drake, SAO. The mail irregularities being the main complaint, the SAO handed them a letter, addressed to the Adjutant General, Washington, D. C., which pointed out some of the facts the War Department should know. Some extracts of the letter are quoted below:
1. Lt. Col. Max Gooler, a prisoner of war for twenty months, has received only twenty-four letters and two private parcels. The last letter was written July 1, 1943.
2. 2nd Lt. Sid Waldman's wife (1200 Chesterfield Ave., Cleveland, Ohio) has informed him that government censors requested that she write only three or four letters per month.
3. 2nd Lt. Paul LaChance's wife, 2302 5th Ave. Phoenix City, Alabama, informed him that the censors, without explanation, had returned 32 of her letters.
4. Capt. Francis D. Burdick, Medical Corps, was informed by his wife, 104 Cresent St., Shenandoah, Iowa that 50 of her letters had been returned September 1943, without explanation.

5. 2nd Lt. H. L. Tallman's folks had received word from a charitable organization, stating that they could write only four letters per month. (This is not true, for the Germans place no restrictions on number of incoming letters.)

6. 1st Lt. Roy Chappell, Jr. received word from Miss Helen Ruth Moore, Kemp, Texas, stating that U.S. Censors had returned all of her September, October and November letters.

7. Both the censors and the Red Cross have informed wives of American prisoners of war that they cannot send letters by "Atlantic Clipper" (30 cent air mail), yet this camp receives them each week!

8. U.S. Censors often blackout football scores, yet the German published paper, "O.K.," publishes all scores.

Prior to departure, one member of the Delegation summarized the Reich, thusly:

1. About 90 percent of the people (German civilians) are "fed up" with the war, but realizing that they have all to lose, they continue the effort.

2. If it were not for nineteen Nazi leaders, the government would sue for peace immediately, first with Russia and then with all remaining Allies.

3. One sees on the streets of Berlin: fire wardens, police and foreigners.

4. 60 percent of Berlin has been damaged, mainly, however, the residential districts. Many of the war plants are under the ground (as in England). (This concurs with Capt. Salerno's information.)

March 27

For the second time, the "Kriegies" were permitted to attend the German movie in Altburgund. It was an excellent two hours of entertainment. During one of the soul-stirring scenes, a Baron von Bomberg, as the "wolf," was about to seduce an innocent blond, when a "Kriegy," who reached an emotional-pitch, completely obsessed, "barked" like an excited dog, then, practically had a spasm. The newsreels showed close-ups of a "Fortress" attack over Berlin, fighting on the Nettuno and Russian Fronts, right among the clouds and ground troops, respectively. They, no doubt, were "doctored-up" but, at that, the most realistic movie projecting this "Kriegy" has yet seen, even in the States.

Lt. Col. Charles Jones, whose barrack failed to hear the roll call bell and almost missed the formation, is now called "Col. W. Lee O'Jones" and his Early Birds.

From the German Press: "Allied Headquarters had the absurdity to report that they had recaptured two houses at Cassino. How stupid! There are no houses left at Cassino! Only piles of rock, occupied and defended by Germans."

Lt. Col. Jones reports that he now knows "more about sex than ever before," for that is all his barrack of new officers talks about, in the most vulgar manner, sixteen hours a day. "That is their one and only thought, all day long," says Jones.

Obviously, the "Goons" are tightening up to prevent an escape, ordering three "appells" (roll calls) a day and requiring can for can to be turned in at the Parcel Hatch.

March 28

"Doc" Harry Abraham, one of our five Jewish doctors who was ordered from here three weeks ago to Stalag III B, Ferstinberg, Germany, where he was to have been the American camp doctor, returned today with the following story:

When I reached the Stalag, I was

placed in confinement in the compound, where I remained, without letterforms, books or explanation. Finally, the German "Kommandant" brought me a post-card and ordered my return to Oflag 64, still without explanation. Here I am.

March 30

Lt. Teddy Roggen received a letter from his mother, Houston, Texas, stating, "Many of your letters have been returned by the U.S. Censors with instructions for me to write only three letters per week, and to write only one page, and that only next-of-kin may write prisoners of war. I'm sorry if my letters have not reached you. Love Mother."

Not only several, but dozens of officers in this Oflag, have failed to get mail for the very same reason. Why should prisoners of war not enjoy the same privileges as other members of the armed forces? Because we fought for our country and are now unable to serve any longer, under these circumstances, are we to be kicked in the pants by some confounded censor, who says, "By complying with these instructions, you will greatly alleviate the mail situation?" What he actually means to say is "So that I will be able to knock-off at five o'clock!" I am certain that this will be corrected as soon as Col. Drake's letter reaches the War Department.

"HOT ZIGGITY"

Arriving from International Y.M.C.A., 36 footballs, 84 basketballs, 4 hockey sets, 200 more ice-skates, rowing equipment (should have been amphibious), 432 soft balls (with the life of a baseball being 1 week and there being four months playing season per year, there should be sufficient number to last us twenty years!). I hope this is not a "Thirty Years War." It would not be surprising to see, any day now, deep-sea diving suits in Oflag 64.

The Hooker-Waful production, "What Next?" a fantasy with marionettes, a modern operetta, mixed with song, music and "Kriegieitis," came off very well this evening. Feminine roles, such as the "WACs", which was the case tonight, always draw hilarious response. One "WAC" said to another "WAC," "Oh, this awful life in the States without my Freddie." Some "Kriegy" in the audience, while all was quiet, sighed deeply and injected, "Ah, yes - - yes, yes!" I learned that it was Lt. Ed Spicher, Pleasant Gap, PA.

Chapter Sixteen
April 1944

April 2

The "Goons," the "Wehrmacht," the "Storm Troopers," and the "Gestapo" moved in today, just after breakfast, to give us what they thought to be a surprise search. It was not, for we had been expecting it for a month and had been alerted to it. When the bell sounded, everybody walked out with a book to read. They were perplexed by the books and wondered how we knew about the search. Each room commander was ordered to his room to witness the procedure. Lt. Col. Gooler, my roommate, said, "A 'Storm Trooper', a soldier and a 'Gestapo' agent came in. I gave them each a cigarette and a cup of coffee. They casually looked into the wall locker and walked out. They carried out the Berlin orders, but not in spirit."

Thinking into the future, however, they confiscated identity cards, civic membership, Masonic and all club cards, driver's licenses, etc, which will be reproduced for spies, in laying the ground for World War III, no doubt. All in all, it was a stupid search. One year ago, even six months ago, the story would have been different. The "Storm Troopers" are Hitler's great hope and they are softening to a certain degree. (This is my opinion, of course.)

April 3

It's German "Movie" Day. This time two blondes were seduced instead of one. Marching, to and from the theatre, is always interesting. On the way down, a poor, old crippled "Pole," in the act of removing his hat and bowing to the "Master Race," stumbled and almost fell. All the girls, children and mammas always came out to see the American "Kriegies." The children follow to pick up the cigarettes. A squad of old "Poles," both men and women, sixty and seventy years old, are always on the job, sweeping the streets, for the "Master Race." "Alles ist besseren Deutschland!" (Everything is better in Germany!)

During the German search, April 2, a war log of a certain Captain was taken; upon request by the SAO, the diary was returned. In the diary, personal thoughts were written down, some of them revealing light military information and bitter sentiment against the Escape Committee for their non-aggressiveness. One of the extracts read as follows:

The Escape Committee is composed of three West Pointers and one National Guard officer (naming each). One of the West Pointers tried to make it all West Point. Five tunnel plans have been submitted and all five have been rejected on the grounds that it would result in collective punishment. My God, what a hell of a thing to have officers like these to represent us.

Tonight, these extracts and others were read to every POW, revealing the name of the owner of the war log. Subsequently, an order read to the effect that all POW diaries would be censored tomorrow.

Now, let's analyze the above. Two violations of War Department regulations have been committed, namely, by the owner of the diary, by revealing light military information, and by the field officer, a member of the committee, who publicly belittled, by name, the writer. It is strictly against War Department regulations to publicly defame a member of the services as a disciplinary measure. It should have been handled in this manner. "Now, due to the fact that a certain officer (not naming him) has written these things in his diary, all diaries will, commencing tomorrow, be censured by appointed American Field officers." As it was handled, bitter feeling has been created. One POW yelled, "Hell! Give Captain _____ a medal!" So there is how it stands.

The weekly German movies aid greatly in breaking the monotony, this week's in particular. The main feature is "The Horrors of a Bathtub," a very amusing

153

picture of the introduction of the bathtub during the Middle Ages in Germany. A traveling merchant visits a mayor in a remote village. He falls in love with the young, beautiful wife, who is fascinated by the merchant's bathtub and bath perfumes and his smooth flattery. The mayor is annoyed with the merchant, his wife, and particularly the bathtub, which will likely create a scandal. The mayor agrees to allow his beautiful wife to keep the tub providing she takes her baths in the stables.

The merchant, delighted with his success, takes leave for another village, but promises to see the young Maria upon his return. Maria, thrilled and happy with her new "way of life," instructs Nina, the maid, to prepare the bath in the stables. In the meantime, a village clown, who learns of the coming event, passes the word to all the husbands, who gather outside the stables and fight for the key holes and cracks in the walls. Maria disrobes and takes her first bath. Ah, how wonderful it is! The mayor discovers the men around his barn. Maria is indignant as well. The mayor throws the tub in the creek. To get even, Maria has the clown recover the tub and contrives to have the maid take a bath. Nina, immodest and agreeable, prepares the bath. Maria notifies all the wives. She also paints smut around the keyholes and cracks. The mayor learns from the clown that the maid, who, too, is voluptuous and pretty, is taking a bath. Nina disrobes and takes the bath, while all the wives assemble in the parlor. At the opportune moment, they all sneak up to the stable and catch their husbands, red-handed. The smut is convicting evidence, and they give the husbands an old time flogging. Later, the mayor comes up with smut around his eye! Maria is avenged and things are "ironed out."

A week later Maria, who learns that the merchant is on his way back, prepares to give herself a perfumed bath for the handsome merchant. In the meantime, however, the clown has installed wheels on the bathtub. As the merchant approaches the village, Maria steps into the tub. Immediately, it starts rolling, out of the barn, down the street and comes to a stop at a gathering in the street! The mayor is scandalized; Maria, in the tub, all but naked, is horrified by her ignominious fate. She screams and weeps; the mayor places his cloak around her and carries his now hysterical wife home. The merchant is driven from the village and the clown is thrown into the river with the tub. Maria and the mayor are happy once more.

The newsreel: It appears that we have seen a Flying Fortress shot down three times in three weeks. The left engine explodes; the left wing falls off the plane, falling over to the left. (Perhaps the German people haven't noticed it.)

In Barrack 3-A the "Kriegies," learning that Wendell Wilkie has dropped out of the presidential race, decided to nominate their own: "W. Lee O'Daniel for president and Bob Hope for vice-president."

Capt. "Roses Red" Rossbach wonders what his New York wife will do when he says to her in the Texas vernacular, "Honey, get the cornbread hell up and fix my breakfast!" or will she know what "Kiss my cotton-pickin' foot," means?

Easter Sunday, 1944

There are serious moments in camp. On this Easter Sunday, in old Poland, Lt. Paul N. Carnes, Ellettsville, Ind. delivered a very fine and fitting sermon, in the theater, with a pulpit beautifully painted and adorned with flowers from our little greenhouse, to a mixed Catholic-Protestant audience. The service ended with hymns by the choir and communion for those wishing to partake.

April 10

The SAO is in receipt of a very nice letter from Mr. Maurice Pate, Director of POW Relief, Washington, D.C., in an effort to eliminate some misunderstanding, mainly in regard to mail, food and clothing shipments and their priority. Mr. Maurice Pate advised the SAO to contact Mr. Francis B. James, Hotel des Burgues, Geneva, directly in any matter pertinent to American POWs.

"Two or three International Red Cross boats leave Philadelphia for Marseille each month. Prisoner of war mail goes on these boats (contradictory to Mr. Roland Marti's statement - see March 10). Arrangements exist for Airmail Service," states Mr. Maurice. At the present time, the Red Cross has met all our demands, and then some.

Why the Poles "Love" the Germans

This evening at 5:45 P.M., the writer and some thirty-five Americans (including Lt. Colonels John Waters and Jim Alger), sitting in the evening sunshine and watching the holiday walkers strolling up and down the street, witnessed a German atrocity against a Pole.

A young Pole with his wife or sweetheart, walking down the sidewalk failed to remove his hat when met by two Brown Shirts of the Schutzpolizeir, (Protective Police) of Schubin. The "mobsters," who were riding in a buggy, stopped the horses and assaulted the defenseless Pole in the presence of the woman. One struck him in the face while the other knocked him down. Nose and face bleeding, he struggled to his feet and walked on to catch up with the lady. So help me God, this is a true story.

April 12

The first air-raid alarm sounded here in Schubin at 4:00 P.M. The Germans ran for their gas masks and hit the ditch until the "all-clear" sounded. The German radio programs are now interrupted to announce the location of "Terror Bombers" within the Greater Reich. Thus, when the speakers are connected up, we follow the bombing pattern with interest.

April 13

This week's film, "Star of Rio," was amateurish indeed. One of those "two-steps-to-the-right-and-then-emotion" films! The newsreel gave close-ups of the Cassino Front and, to compare German Fighting with that of the Allies, injected a supposedly "captured action film" of the British in action on the same front. Actually, the British were dressed in slimmer uniforms. Furthermore, many of us recognized it as part of a British training film on street fighting tactics, having seen it in England.

Spring is here, and work on the garden is under way. Those muscle-bound boys (the ones having supple athletic physiques) work in only shorts. Those skinny, slender ones (like myself) work with their pants and shirts on! Admiring young Schubin lassies stroll languorously by these enterprising young "Kriegies." They are, of course, on the other side of the fence.

April 17

A German newspaper says that, according to an American commentator, the crooner, Frank Sinatra is causing the nation to lose thousands of work hours, for when Sinatra goes on the air, "swoon-sick" women rush to the nearest radio.

In Oflag 64, a "Jerk" is just anyone referred to casually.

Very few parcels have been received lately. The railway at Posen "ist aus gesperrt" (is all blocked up) by Allied bombing.

Bob Rankin and his fifteen-piece band gave us an hour of swing last evening. Jack Marlowe, our "Sinatra" (without a female audience) gave a grand rendition of "A Cowboy Ridin'." The number arrived recently from the states via the Y.M.C.A.

The generous-hearted "Goons" issued a roll of toilet paper per officer for the first time since October! Sears-Roebuck catalogues would bring a premium in Oflag 64. The Y.M.C.A. at Geneva sent us (eleven Lt. Colonels, six Majors, and four-hundred other officers) little game books titled "100 games for you," for our simple-minded amusement. Last evening, a "Goon" guard spent an hour inside the wire picking up cigarette butts! Today, a second order, by the SAO, was published to the effect that all "Kriegies" destroy all cigarette butts. Americans would "snipe" too, if they did not have any cigarettes! I suppose someday we may be out of cigarettes.

April 18

According to the German High Command, the Kertch Peninsula was evacuated "in accordance with the planned retreat, after the destruction of all important war sites. The city of Tarnopol had to be evacuated because of a shortage of water."

The press carried an article, purporting to be the exact quotation from a British magazine (not named) that "Every conceivable thing has been planned to provide the soldiers (of the impending west front invasion) with delicacies, refreshments, radios, and magazines. 'Club-mobile' units, with three army nurses as hostesses, will follow the front-line troops to keep their morale high!"

The SAO has just confined (and rightly so) an American captain "to the stockade for one week, for direct disobedience to orders." In the Army, one does not disobey; he executes the orders, regardless of personal sentiment. That is what makes the Army click.

"Oberst" Schneider, the German Kommandant, met with us at evening Appell, to deliver another famous speech, covering several points, viz, our cooperation in inspections, our failure to salute the Nazi civilian doctor and our furniture (we are to get new wall lockers). The Nazi doctor gets very mad upon our failure to salute him. Col. Drake has maintained that we should not salute him. The "Oberst" says we will. This means one thing. The Nazi has enough power, even though a civilian, to over-ride a decision of a German Colonel. The "Oberst" is too smart to oppose him.

April 19

While rehearsing a coming play, Lt. Wilbur Sharp, the high-school "girl," the flirt, all dressed up with skirt, brassiere and wig, ran out of the theater, pursued by a "Kriegy." The "Goon" guard, outside, got all excited and called the Sergeant of the Guard. He thought a Polish female had been smuggled into camp! Our stage make-up man had done a good job.

April 20

One hundred and eight officers arrived from the Italian front today. In the group were two young Majors. One of them, "Maj. Whirlaway," cornered W. O. Cannon, an old "Kriegy," with these inquiries: "Do you sleep on sheets?" "No." "What kind of beds do you have?" "Double-deckers, board bottom and straw mattress." "You mean you don't have sheets and spring beds?" "No." "Do you escape on 'parole' walks?" "No." "What are you, a soldier?" "No, a warrant officer." "Well, where are your insignia? "I don't have any and can't get any." The Major, more nonplussed than ever, walked away. He asked Lt. Col. Waters if field officers had private rooms with bath!

New "Kriegies" arrive. Lt. Joseph Shimatsu, Japanese American, was among the group. Five officers from my old outfit afforded me the latest information. Lt. John Martin of Eagle Pass, Texas, had this to say:
All officers and soldiers "look forward"
to being killed, wounded or captured.
There's practically no rotation for the old-
timers. They are in the trench, month after
month! Last winter, we didn't receive
overcoats until practically half of the men
were evacuated to hospitals with colds, flu
and pneumonia. Half of the rest were killed
in action.
C'est la guerre.

Waste! Waste! Waste!

Yesterday, I personally picked up a whole loaf of bread from the trash box. Today, I got seven pieces, enough to feed an officer for one week. Yet they constantly curse the "Goons," for the short issue of bread. There are other officers, especially the new ones, who would be glad to have the bread. Everybody seems to "cuss" the Jews because they always have more than anybody else. What we Gentiles need, are a few lessons in frugality from them. There's a lot of truth in the saying, "Take the waste from the American Army and feed the British Army. Then, take what they have left and feed the Chinese Army!"

April 25

From the new officers, we learned that Camp Pine, N.Y., one of the most beautiful army posts and the most elaborately landscaped in the United States, has been converted into a POW camp and that a beautiful resort hotel has been provided for German submarine and naval POWs. One of my Battalion officers recently from Anzio stated that, of the original Battalion, only 120 officers and men were left. The others have been wounded, captured, reclassified or killed!

"Alles 'Nix' besser fur der 'Kriegies.'" (All "Nix" better for the Kriegies.)

Samples of the German issue of barley, which was varicolored with rat feces and dehydrated cabbage that looked like sun-baked ragweeds, were displayed in the mess hall today. "Oberst" Schneider, learning of the exhibition, replaced our barley with a new sack, void of rat dung.

Hot Rumor! Rudy Valle is now a POW at Luckenwalde. He was in charge of the Nettuno landing at the time of capture!!!

Here's the low-down on the "Goons." The "Ferret" (Security Sergeant) has returned from the Russian Front. He, along with several others, got "sick" and was returned to this Oflag. Incidentally, the "Ferret," it is learned, threatened several German guards for smoking American cigarettes. One tells the story that the "Ferret" was seen smoking them while at the Front!

Another "Goon" says it is worse behind the lines than in the lines, because of the intense guerilla activity.

They are now replacing our old lockers for better ones. One German says that the warehouses at Posen had to be cleared out. Another says they are being nice to us, for only Sergeants in the German army rate these lockers. Our own guess is that they intend to move us out and set this camp up as an evacuation hospital.

We have nick-named the Lagermeister, "Glutteral Fluteral"; the Essenmeister, "Porky," the Postemann, "Gepruft"; Brandice, a mail censor, "Ed Winn," the Corporal of the guard, "Onion-head."

A wife of a "Kriegy" writes: "The Postmaster of New York City has informed correspondents of prisoners of war to write only one letter a week!!!" What authority does he have to put out such instructions, we ask.

Doc Abraham is avenged - accidentally (refer to March 28)! Today the "Goons," while searching the building for contrabands of war, gave the hospital a very good once-over. Vainly ransacking, they descended upon the surgical room. Coming upon a little object, sort of round and neatly wrapped in a little can on a locker, a searcher with an "Ach! I've found it" look, yelled, "Komme Sie Hier!" The object, sort of unpleasant smelling, too, was pulled out, handled, and unwrapped. A discovery was made: it was a bowel evacuation of an ulcer patient! Doc "Abe" had taken it and prepared it two days ago to be sent to Walstein for chemical analysis! The Doc is now a hero to the "Kriegies."

April 29 - A Typical Spring Day in Oflag 64

Roll Call is at 7:45 A.M. For breakfast, hot water plus Red Cross items at 8:00 A.M. Gardening, in mess plots. Each mess of ten officers has a ten-by-twenty foot plot. Softball, volleyball and basketball are played all day long. Reading is in off moments. Orchestra and play rehearsal is in the evening. "Lights out" at 10:30 P.M.

The weather in Poland is like that of central Texas. You never know whether to wear your shorts or your overcoat. This morning it was sunshiny; this evening it is snowing.

"Maj. Whirlaway" is "red hot!" (Refer to April 20). He has a theory that the "Regular Army" will eliminate the 'rabble' soon after the war is over, and that each Regular will do the work of twenty, if necessary. He volunteered his services to Captain Foster, educational director, as a French instructor. "I have had one year and would be glad to organize a new class." There are already two classes. He promised a Lieutenant a promotion if he would help him escape!! This morning, having joined the choir, he shamed Tom Holt, a semi-professional artist, for hitting high "D" too soon. Russ Ford, who had directed the choir for nine months, said, "Sir, if you don't mind, I will do the directing."

Syndicates and rackets flourish because "suckers" always bite. There is now a Red Cross Parcel Syndicate at Oflag 64. A parcel worth 27 "D" Bars (1,350 points on the Mart) goes for 40 "D" Bars (a profit of 650 points). If the Red Cross knew this, they would probably have a stroke.

Waste! Waste! Waste!

As barrack Commander, I have tried to instill a little comradeship by sharing with others what would otherwise be wasted. Yet, this morning, I picked up almost two gallons of spoiled potatoes from the trash basket. The new officers would eagerly have eaten them the day after issue.

Chapter Seventeen
May 1944

May 1

There is very little betting now on the Invasion date. Larry Allen has already lost six hundred dollars. Others have lost their pants.

Many of the old "Kriegies" have received in private parcels, as many as twenty cartons of cigarettes, yet the new officers got by on three packs a week. The old-timers have forgotten how it is to be short of cigarettes.

Lt. Ken Goddard rigged up a wooden "candid camera," that folds like an accordion, and excited the "Goons" by "snapping pictures" out by the wire fence!

The right size but the wrong hat!!

Lt. E. O. Ward, Clewiston, Florida, received in a private parcel from his wife, a cap, which he had previously requested, with laundry mark and name of a "Lt. Miller." Ward does not know him, but is sure his wife does!!

Col. Thomas D. Drake, Lt. N. J. Meadows, and five others have just passed the "Repat" board at Posen. My guess is that neither Drake nor the others get back before we do.

Last night while the "Goons" were making the usual bed check, the "Obergefreiders" (Corporals) jabbed Lt. Meadows in the ribs to see whether the form in the bed was what it should be - a man instead of a dummy. Meadows let out a yell and the "Goon" was convinced. Meadows' bunkmate below, also aroused, asked, "What's the matter, Meadows? Are they trying to steal your pass to the States?"

May 5

Keeping in good standing, the Y.M.C.A. sent sixteen musical instruments! With all the others, the camp will now be able to organize another New York Philharmonic orchestra.

May 7

Currently showing for three nights is "Three Men on a Horse," an old timer starring Larry Phelan, Charles Eberle, Carl Burrows, Sid Thal, Richard Van Sycle, James Bancker, Willard Duckworth, Donald May and others.

Upon return from the Repatriation Board, Col. Drake wrote this letter:

The Swiss Legation,
Schweizeriche Gasandtschaft,
Ableitlung Schutmarchtengelegenheiten
Pariser Platz 2
Berlin W8

Gentlemen:

This is to inform you of the shocking ill treatment and lack of care displayed on the part of certain German officials toward sick American prisoners of war.

On May 1, 1944, I and nine other officers went to Posen to appear before a mixed Repatriation Board. Seven of the ten passed.

Upon arrival at the railway station, a Sergeant was there to march us to the headquarters. He instructed us that we, as prisoners, would have to walk in the street and not on the sidewalk! I informed him we would only at the point of a bayonet. We were broken up into small parties and allowed on the sidewalk.

We were taken to an old barrack to wait for further instructions. The barrack was rickety, dirty and unsightly, and had formerly been occupied by tuberculosis patients! I informed the Hauptmann (Captain) that we refused to stay here and to send for the Kommandant. He stated: "This being May 1st, is a holiday," and that "this is war." The board beds were filthy and upon turning over a mattress, a bed bug scampered to concealment. One of the blankets had vomit on it. Eight of us were to be placed in one room!

After standing outside for three hours, a Major came and apologized. New blankets were issued. (While outside three hours, one officer got so ill that he was forced to lie on the cold ground).

It is requested that your office inform the High Command of this, and remind them of their country's agreement in the handling of prisoners of war.

Thomas D. Drake,
Colonel, U.S. Army.
Senior American Officer.

May 8 (Full Moon)

The new musical instruments are marked "Property of the U.S. Quartermaster," as is all the clothing we have recently received.

Larry Allen, AP Correspondent, who has been with us since October, has just left for a German "Hilag" where he, along with other civilians are to remain until an exchange can be made between the U.S. and Germany. Supposedly the exchange is to take place in June.

The exchange of the seven POWs has been postponed indefinitely. The exchange was to take place at Barcelona, Spain, June 10, 1944.

The Germans are now issuing vinegar and we are to get bed sheets today.

"Come Up To See Me Sometime, Big Boy!"

There is a girl's Hitler Youth camp near this Oflag. On a "parole walk" last week, some twenty officers halted for a rest at the edge of a wood near the youth camp. About one hundred yards from the resting "Kriegies" sat six voluptuous blonds (about 17 years old). To tantalize the boys, they fondled, kissed and 'pecked' each other (among other things)! Even kisses were gestured by the hands. One "Kriegy" asked "Feldwebel" (Sgt.) Holland, the English-speaking guard, "How about it, Sergeant? Can't we step over to see 'em?" "If I allowed that, it would mean five years in the 'jug' for me," he answered with a laugh. (Note: Sgt. Holland formerly lived in the U.S., having worked in a hotel at Lima, Ohio, and also on a Mohananburg newspaper!)

This week on the "parole walk," the number of participants has increased from twenty to 150! Wonder why?

"Beaucoup" Patriotism, Less Pay and Allowances!"

Lt. R. M. Mason has just received word from his wife that she has joined up with the WACs. Prior to this, she was secretary to one of the larger oil firms in Tulsa, making $180.00 per month, plus $60.00 rental allowance from the War Department, totaling $240.00. Now, she gets $50.00 per month and Mason gets his salary, less ration and rental allowance for the wifey!

In a parcel from my mother, there was a cotton handkerchief with a tag marked Perry's K-3, 15¢. Prior to the war, one could go to any chain store and get them a penny apiece! The material was the poorest quality I have ever seen. Lt. Medlen, textile expert, says one 22¢ pound of cotton will make at least 25 of these handkerchiefs! Who makes the 2000 percent profit?

May 11 - "Plenty of Instruments for Everybody!"

I "am" Bob Rankin, the Schubin Orchestra leader. I have gone through the barracks and saw all the new instruments (some $5,400.00 worth) upon tables and chairs, uncovered, dusty and damp with Schubin dew. I call my boys together and make a speech: "Boys, we've gotta lotta new instruments from the "Y," and we'll probably get a lot more, probably three per man. The cases are just a damn nuisance. No good, anyway. I wouldn't bother much about the instruments, either. They take care of themselves. Let your buddies play 'em, too - if they want to - just to get along with 'em. You know how roommates are. Besides, Uncle Sam has plenty of dough; he'll give the "Y" more when we call for them. O.K.? O.K.!"

The group pictures that were taken in December have just been handed over. They're late and thoroughly "Gepruft."

A wife of a "Kriegy" writes, "A very sad thing has just occurred. My friend has just died from taking too many sleeping tablets. Last evening she was visiting me and we were listening to a radio program. Now today she is dead." The "serious Kriegy's" comment, "I'll bet it was Frank Sinatra!"

Amon Carter received a letter for "you sons of Texas:"

Albany, Texas
January 12, 1944

2nd Lt. Amon G. Carter, Jr.

I have been wanting to write to you
"Sons of Texas" ever since I learned of your
whereabouts, and I have just received from
your dad an addressed envelope. How are
you tonight? I hope you are warm and do
not have the "Flu." I know of one "Cow
Town" that will be happy when you got
back home. I will thank you if you pass the
following little messages on to your
comrades. (Officers were listed and some
interesting little anecdotes told about their
hometowns.)

Lt. Snyder, I lived in Colorado City for
thirty years, not far from your hometown.
There isn't a thing as grand as youth.

167

Well, boys, we are happy that you can study and read. The people in the land where you are can't understand how you Yanks can laugh, sing and joke so much, even in the hardest and toughest times. They don't know the swell "red-blooded," high minded, noble character and Christian youth of America.

When you come home, come to Albany and we'll fix a steak and fried chicken, pecan pie (Hush!) and the hottest biscuits and say, 'Boys, let's go fishing.' Mr. H went fishing Christmas Day and caught a 5 lb. black bass and a 3 1/2 lb. one, too. Please write sometime, each of you, for I would be thrilled to hear from any of you and I wish for you the best.

Your friend always,
Mrs. J. L. H.

(Even though the letter is typically amusing, we know that this humble, old lady meant every word of it.)

May 15 - "Big City Boy Learns Gardening"

"Leftenant" V. D. Danylik, N.Y., N.Y., went up to hoe the weeds out of his carrots and the only mistake made was that he mistook the carrot for the weed. Now, he has a perfect stand of weeds!

May 16

Capt. Don May, Washington, D.C., received a letter from his mother stating, "I am only writing you one letter a week and telling all my friends to be sparing in their writing also, so that the U.S. Censors won't 'bog down.'"

Every time a civilian comes into our camp, we say, "Ach! The Gestapo is after our driver's permit or Rotary Club card again." This morning, a civilian came into camp and we said, "Ach!" But he was an old one-eyed piano tuner!

The searchers are a nuisance, to put it mildly. What we have they know, anyway. So, why this harassing?

Two weeks ago, Russ Ford got a letter from his missus, stating that she had just bought a "swell Buick convertible." "Leftenant" George L. Durgin bragged, "I'm certainly glad my wife is conservative. I wrote her last week complimenting her." Lo, and behold! Today Durgin learned, through another "Kriegy's" wife, that HIS wife had bought herself a "swell" new car!!

From "Insomnia" to "Lumbago"

Lt. Mossberger, who fought in the Tunisian Sidi Bou Sid area and who was sent back to the States because he couldn't sleep, is now in the States. He writes Ed Spicher:

> Dear Spicher. I am now working for a ship construction company in Frisco and the work is pretty tough. I make $50.00 weekly, have lost twenty pounds and am having trouble with my back. (!) By the way, when in New York, I spent a swell night taking in Jack Dempseys and the Stork Club. Right now, I am drinking a bottle of real old time beer. Wish you were here. Can I send you some beer?

May 18

Convoys and bicycle brigades have been streaming by, going north, all afternoon. From ten to twelve bicycle men were observed being towed behind each vehicle! It means one of several things: (1) maneuvers, (2) reinforcing East Front troops, or (3) Baltic reinforcements for the expected 2nd front there.

May 19

Last evening, torrential rains beat down for about one hour, carrying away topsoil, garden slips and plants and causing the ripping in two of the volleyball and badminton nets. Mother Nature caused this - but Mother didn't leave the net out overnight to be ripped apart. ("O.K., the 'Y' will send us more, so what!")

During the last two days the German mail censors have deliberately neglected to bring our mail into camp. (Another German said so.) Col. Drake accosted "Hauptmann" Menner, German welfare officer, about it and demanded an explanation. "Sir, I was not aware of this," replied Menner (who seems to be rather nice) - whereupon, the mail was delivered in camp!

May 24 - "Things That Make Kriegies Bitter"

The U.S. Censors, or Customs Bureau, continue to remove such items as cake mix, biscuit flour, sweets, and garden seed from our parcels. Typical examples of censorship (taken from letters of POWs) are "_____ is now a Corporal." "The price of shoes is now _____." "Mary is now working in _____, and John is in ATTU." "Your blouse came back and I have sent it to the_____ tailors."

It is regrettable that the U. S. Government employs "Nit-Wits" to cause bitterness towards one of its Departments. And it is gratifying to realize that all departments do not employ "Nit-Wits." The U.S. Government could do well by censoring and controlling the distribution of all the newspapers and magazines, instead of heckling military personnel with stupid, trivial censorship. Germany obtains current copies of *Life, Time, Fortune, Collier's*, etc. Some of them even give blueprints of so-called military weapons! There are examples of "The Flying Fortress," the M-I Rifle and the L.S.T.s and L.S.I.s.

"Things That Amaze Kriegies"

We are amazed that there are "Military Experts" in the states and in England who criticize Gen. "Ike" Eisenhower for not getting on with the second front. (Gen. "Ike" is nobody' s fool; he knows better than "they" do from his experience in Africa, Sicily and Italy and what it will take and how much of "it" it will take to whip "Jerry."

The Yardley Diaries span Col. Yardley's three years as a soldier overseas in Europe and as a German POW in Poland.

Doyle R. Yardley as a private in the Texas National Guard.

Soldiers of the 509th Parachute Infantry Battalion,
Doyle Yardley's unit, were dropped over Avellino, Italy.

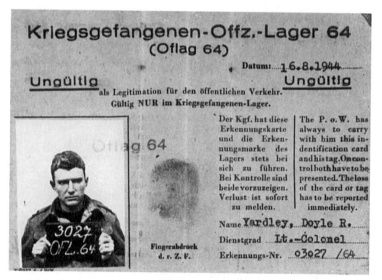

Lt. Col. Yardley's Prisoner of War identification
document.

POW James Bickers drew this rendition of Oflag 64, Szubin, Poland for the camp paper, "The Oflag 64 Item."

Texas POWs from Oflag 64, Szubin, Poland. SAO
Yardley front row, left.

POWs at Oflag 64 pay tribute to a fellow soldier during
a graveside service at the camp.

Bar of soap made from Polish prisoners given to Lt. Col. Yardley after his escape form Oflag 64-Z POW camp.

Photos like this of the "Glee Club" were often included in the camp paper, "The Oflag 64 Item."

Comic strips in the "Item" confirm Col. Yardley's introductory statement that as "typical Americans," the POWs "always found something funny to do."

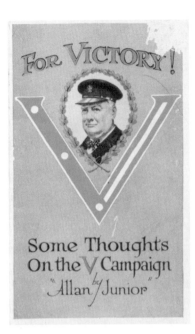

Booklet found in
Col. Yardley's
footlocker.

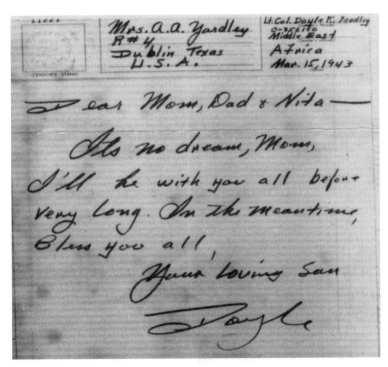

Lt. Col. Yardley writes his parents as he travels home
through Africa.

Official U. S. Army photo following Col. Yardley's return to the States.

Col. Doyle R. Yardley is photographed in combat gear to promote his South American lecture tour.

In July 1945, on an extensive lecture tour throughout
South America, Col. Yardley is photographed with three
South American military officers.

Juanita (Nita) and
Electra (Peggy)
Yardley,
Doyle Yardley's
sisters.

Col. Yardley (center) at home with mother and father, Emma and Al Yardley.

Charlie Turnbo as a young boy at his uncle's gravesite in East End Cemetary, Lingleville, Texas.

Diary Four

Chapter Eighteen
June 1944

June 1 - "Very Cheap Sensationalism for Americans!"

It is no wonder the German people think all Americans are either lovers, divorcers, robbers, jukebox operators or murderers. (The majority of the people of any country believe almost all they read.) Not only do our leading newspapers, magazines and movies give people "sensationalitis," but also now, even the Red Cross has this affliction. I give you facsimiles of proof by quoting extracts of a Red Cross News pamphlet recently sent to POWs in Germany, "poop" that might well read like a J. Edgar Hoover crime report. Judge for yourself the number of crimes, felonies, frivolities, etc., mentioned bluntly, subtly, or by inference:

A.	Crimes and Felonies	55
	1. Homicides	
	a. Murders	13
	b. Suicides	4
	c. Other degrees of homicide	10
	2. Robbery	4
	3. Burglary	3
	4. Theft	10
	5. Forgery	1
	6. Draft evasion	1
	7. Prison break	1
	8. Conspiracy (Jukebox)	2
	9. Manufacturing illegal liquor	3
	10. Counterfeiting	1
	11. Embezzlement	1
	12. Blackmail	1
B.	Crimes and Misdemeanors	8
	1. Drunkenness	2
	2. Traffic Violations	3
	3. Gambling	2
	4. Juvenile Delinquency	1

C. Civil Law Suits   28
    1. Divorce   24
    2. Breach of Promise   1
    3. Workman's Compensation   1
    4. Suit for possession of property   1
    5. Impeachment   1

D. Miscellaneous "Crap"   122
    1. Manpower shortage   20
    2. Deaths   51
    3. Fire outbreaks   10
    4. Auto/train/plane crashes   6
    5. Dog fights   5
    6. Practical Jokes   2
    7. Births   5
    8. Crop damage, shortage   5
    9. Disease outbreak   3
    10. Marriage   7
    11. Engagements   2
    12. Marital squabble   1
    13. Rattlesnake bite   1
    14. Shortages
        a. Ice   1
        b. Transportation   2
        c. Metal   1

(Published by the American Red Cross. Printed in the U.S.A. and distributed to U.S.A. prisoners of war by the International Red Cross Committee, Nov.1, 1943, Vol.1, No. 3.)

Noted in *The News,* "It is not possible to supply each prisoner with a copy of *The News.* You are therefore urged to handle your reading copy with 'Particular Care' so that its value to the next man will not be impaired!" (If the Red Cross thinks POWs read this bunk with "Particular Care so that its value . . . will not be impaired," they are either crazy - or ignorant - with the "heat." Read this junk and ask yourself if it is representative of what Americans like to read.)

June 6, 1944 - THE INVASION IS ON

By strange coincidence, indeed, the "Invasion of Europe" has begun on the Northern coast of France, on the same date as the anniversary celebration of "One Year Behind the Wire" at Oflag 64, Schubin. Following the announcement of the fall of Rome yesterday, June 5th, the German Radio broke the news to its people at 2:00 P.M. with a laconic communiqué. "The long awaited invasion has begun with the landing of Allied troops in great strength in the Normandy area, North France."

Now the celebration is really in full swing with music, laughter and plenty of "bashing" of Red Cross food at Oflag 64 (a Y.M.C.A. representative who arrived yesterday, presented Sports Badges to several "Kriegies" before learning the news). To climax today's glad and long awaited event, 650 new No. 10 Red Cross Food Parcels arrived. These No. 10s are the best yet! They have peanut butter, relished by everyone. It's a great day, this.

June 7

About 200 Y.M.C.A. cooking kits arrived this morning with excellent Akta Kockum Emali (brand name) utensils. Each kit contains one spoon, one knife, one fork, one plate, one saucepan, and one frying pan. All of which aids "bashing" proper.

From 9:30 P.M. "News in English" Broadcast

"The enemy has effected a landing at great cost. Practically all Airborne Troops have been destroyed. An American paratrooper states 'We were told it would be 'hell,' but I never knew it would be like this.'" Only four of his unit came out alive. Being a paratrooper, I feel for the boys.

June 7 - From *Der Angriff* (News Board)

"At Moscow's order, the Invasion begins;" "Invasion troops on the Cherbourg peninsula were thrown back to the beach-head;" "Thirteen hundred giant gliders were either captured or destroyed. The gliders contained 120 men plus equipment." (Actually these gliders will carry one Jeep or seventeen men!)

June 8 - From 930 P.M. "News in English" Broadcast (William Joyce)

"Jew Guggenheim, New York financier and philanthropist, offers $500.00 to the first Allied soldier to set foot on France. A British Naval officer was the first, but he was killed, so the award will be made posthumously, no doubt!"

"No Letters, No Photos"

The following is a true copy of a letter:

June 7, 1943
Subject: Second Visit of Dr. Roland Marti, Special Representative, International Red Cross, Berlin, 8:15 P.M. this date, accompanied by "Hauptmann" Menner, German Camp Officer

Dr. Marti described his last visit and presented a letter signed by Brig. Gen. B. R. Legge, Military Attaché, Berne, Switzerland, addressed to a Mr. James, American Red Cross, Geneva, stating that "Inasmuch as I now understand that Col. Drake has no objection to taking pictures, I do not either."
He also had a letter from Mr. James attached. I explained my previous statement and my letter to the War Department to Dr. Marti. The letter clearly pointed out that I would not object, provided the War Department directed the pictures to be taken. Dr. Marti stated that the letter from the Red Cross was sufficient. I carefully explained that the Red Cross could not "direct" it, but they

should have the War Department send the order to me that I did not object to the taking of films, but in the absence of an answer from the War Department, requesting their decision, I could not give my sanction.

Dr. Marti became angry, saying, "I am a fool. I'll not do anything more for prisoners of war; I'll dismiss my men and the American Red Cross will have to pay the expenses incurred."

Whereupon, I said, "Yes, of course, they will pay for it. They have the money."

He said "Yes, that's all I hear, 'they have money, lots of money, money to throw out the window.'"

Dr. Marti appeared very angry. I believe this attitude is corroborative evidence of the nature of the desired film taking. The attitude of the I.R.C. is 100% diametrically opposed to the Y.M.C.A.

Thomas D. Drake,
Colonel. U.S. Army
Camp Senior.

C'est la Guerre

Two English paratroopers were captured soon after D-Day, according to the press, and here is the "interrogation" between a Jerry and the two captives, Mortimer and Goddard:

"Sie sind Inglisch?" (Are you English?)

"Ya" (Yes)

"Was wollen sie heir im Frankreich?" (What do you want here in France?)

"Zu befreien Frankreich!" (To liberate France!)

C'est La Guerre, Again

2nd Lt. Lawrence Thibideau received a letter from the Office of War Information to inform him that he is definitely a Lt. Colonel. (The War Department had sent letters to his father addressed as "Lt. Colonel," whereupon his father made inquiries. To jump from 2nd Lt. to Lt. Col. just doesn't happen in the Army!) "Now, if I can convince the finance department, everything will be O.K.," says Thibideau.

It's a funny thing, these 'I-went-to-war stories` by reporters like Mr. Reynolds:

They are also tossing high explosives at us from rifles . . . perhaps two hundred thousand men (20 divisions!) are huddling behind whatever covering is available. [I'll bet Gen. Mark Clark and Gen. Alexander will be surprised to learn this, when they actually had about six divisions!] To date we have had very little success with our parachute troops. [It's true that the troop carrier pilots scattered paratroops all over Africa, Sicily, and Italy, but the panic created by their scattered presence is a well-known fact. In the African "show," when the Germans dropped a planeload of them behind the lines, troops were alerted from Tunisia to French Morocco!] The 36th (Infantry) Division was hurt badly at Salerno, because it dug in instead of forcing itself into close quarters. [He doesn't even know how to designate an Infantry Division properly; furthermore, the 36th Infantry Division had definite orders to dig in, once about twelve miles inland!]

Lt. Col. Barron and Lt. Col. Jones, of the 36th Infantry Division, state that Mr. Reynolds never got beyond any Regimental Headquarters at any time, when he wrote this "tossing high explosives at us" story! Where was Mr. Reynolds when he wrote this eyewitness "us" story of Dieppe? The British say he was several miles out in the English Channel on a battleship! It's like Ernie Pyle's writing when he wrote up "Lt." Bergman's Rapido River crossing. Bergman, Mr. Pyle, was a Captain, not a Lieutenant! Bergman says Mr. Pyle was miles from the river at the time of the crossing! (Bergman is now a POW at this camp.)

June 22 "Concerning Food and Recreation Equipment"

Because of connections, two officers in camp have received eight each, either No. 8 or No. 10 Red Cross parcels! This is over and above the one per week issue. The Red Cross has informed this Oflag that parcels will not be sent to individuals, but to the camp as a whole. Yet, this evil exists because of "connections" and because some Red Cross employees in Geneva violate their own orders. Why don't you "clean house," Red Cross?

During the past week several thousand new No. 10 parcels have been received - also athletic shorts and tops, and footlockers from the "Y" for practically every officer.

June 26, 1944 - Carter's Crow

Oflag 64 now has a mascot, Amon Carter's baby

crow, which prematurely got ambitious and fell out of its nest. "Ronnie Dougald" is its name, after a British Major who was always "yapping." "Ronnie" now yaps, rides on "Kriegies'" fingers, eats Red Cross food, hunts bugs, "picks off" mosquitoes that molest Carter, and yaps in anger if things don't go his way! Carter spends most of his time now digging for worms. Ronnie is always along on these hunts. Ronnie stubbornly refuses to use the latrine or to learn how to talk (he only yaps).

June 21

Germany now has an equivalent to our "bazooka." Several months ago the "Goons" belittled the "bazooka;" now they have a weapon just like it.

June 23

"1940 Waffenruhe mit Frankreich" - Guns all quiet in France (from the calendar). This day also marks the end of "Jugend Sportsfest," a Sports Festival for local Hitler Youth. Hundreds of young, smart, neat, healthy boys and girls, 6 to 14 years of age, from the adjacent youth camps, have carried out three days of gala sports, marching, singing, drilling - in perfect cadence, unison, etc. - in a salubrious fashion. If you don't believe that the youth believe in Hitler and everything he stands for, then you are as crazy as a "loon." Little, big, old and young are so well disciplined that they even think and react "by the numbers." Little boys, hardly big enough to walk, march in the "brown shirt" uniforms. Little girls, cute little blondes, all with their hair braided, dressed in white skirts and brown vests, march with light packs, also in perfect cadence. Little Hitlers in the making!

Chapter Nineteen
July 1944

July 16 - West Front Boys Arrive!

With a great deal of excitement and surprise, Oflag 64 became the new home of about fifty American POWs (mostly Airborne) from the Western Front! They include Col. George W. Millet, my C.O. in 1941, from Saratoga, Florida; Lt. Col. Nath R. Hosket, Carmel, California; Lt. Col. "Bob" Palmer, 82nd A/B Division; Maj. H. R. Cole, West Medway, Mass.; and the first Airborne officers from the West Front. Chaplain Robert M. Hannon from St. Louis, Mo., who bears the nickname "Jumpin' Jesus" is the first ordained Protestant minister at Oflag 64. This camp now has two full Colonels, thirteen Lieutenant Colonels and fourteen Majors.

"Grossen" Tales of Optimism

There is a little warning sign in Lt. Col. Barron's barrack that reads like this "Boys, we've all been in combat, so, watch your 'Bull____'!" New officers have heap big stories, but as "Kriegy" life grows, they realize 'bait' has been prepared." All West Front officers are optimistic, believing that Germany will capitulate in about three months!

July 20

Plot to murder "Der Fuhrer" fails. The papers all carried front-page news and photos of the attempted assassination of Hitler. War news was shelved on back pages. Following this incident, Hitler reshuffled his government, giving four Nazis over-all power.

July 28

The Germans featured a captured American "Handbook of Modern Irregular Warfare" pamphlet in all the newspapers. This type of propaganda was very effective on the German civilians. Such pamphlets make it hard on POWs and should never have been printed in such straight language.

Chapter Twenty
August 1944

August 2 - "I Feel No Pains"

Lt. Seamour Bolton received a letter from "Kriegy" Larry Allen, written while on the S. S. Gripsholm. To quote Larry, "I told everybody everything about everything . . . I feel no pains . . . life is wonderful." Nothing has changed.

$1,000,000 Reichmarks Worth!!!

Der Fuhrer has offered one million Reichsmark for information leading to the arrest of Dr. Karl Gordeler, "Oberburgermeister," who was involved in the plot to assassinate "Der Fuhrer" and other leading Nazi leaders! (He is still at large as of 8-2-44!) (Sept. 10, he was captured and executed!)

August 5 - Skulls for U.S. Citizens!

Tokyo pronounced the Yank soldiers as criminals and cannibals, who disregard all ethics of modern warfare, who murder prisoners of war, who send skulls and letter openers, made from arm bones of Japanese dead to Roosevelt and to movie stars. The Berlin papers carried a caption of "American Beauty" with a skull as a souvenir from a soldier in the Pacific.

"Ites" in a Bad Way

The "V-B" (*Volkisher-Beobachter*) carried a front-page article, supposedly taken from *Reader's Digest*, titled, "We can't solve the problem," painting a dark picture of Italy under AMGOT (Allied Military Government of Occupied Territory).

Thousands upon thousands of Italians are starving . . . The Lire is down to one cent per . . . The black-market is widespread, and somehow, one-third of our Allied food earmarked for the civilian markets goes to the black-market . . . Girls, thirteen to nineteen years of age, are offering themselves as prostitutes in exchange for calories . . . Children are crying for bread. An

AMGOT official at Naples, commenting on the situation, said, "If we had to round up all black-market operators, we would have to string a barbed-wire fence around the entire city. If we follow the same course in other occupied countries in Europe, the peace will be lost before the war is won..."

August 11 - Berlin

Reuter's reports that U. S. Admiral Con Pardee, who commanded the U.S. Naval Forces during the Normandy invasion, committed suicide last Sunday, Aug. 6, 1944.

August 12 - From the German Press

According to *Der Angriff*, while the Polish emigrant chief, Mikolajczyk, was in Moscow waiting to see Stalin, the Bolshevist in London formed the "Polish Progressive Club." They immediately declared themselves to be on the side of the 'Polish Soviet Committee of Liberation,' thus stabbing Mikolajczyk in the back. To quote *Der Angriff*:

"Mikolajczyk is down on his knees before Stalin, begging his case, but so far he is just the object of daily surprises. After a fairly friendly reception, he was surprised to hear over the Moscow radio that the Soviet government had appointed an 'agent' for this political job!"

Roosevelt, concerned about the U.S. Polish and Catholic vote, and hoping to appease both sides, got the State Department and Foreign Office to work on a plan that would be acceptable to both!

"Stalin subsequently formed the 'Polish Liberation Committee.' The result of the above is that, actually 'Liberated Poland,' in the end, will become a Soviet Union state!"

The "Schweinhund" (Pig-Dog) Hoppner!

Following the abortive attempt on Herr Hitler's life, the "People's Court" tried and convicted the following "Convicted Schweinhunds": Erich Hoppner, Witzleben, Stieff, von Hagen, von Hase, Bernardis, Klausing, and von Wartenburg.

The press gave a word-for-word summary of the "Plotters' Trial." "*V-B*" headlined it:

Dr. Gordeler to have been Chancellor of New German Government and Witzleben, Commander-in-Chief. There were plans for a complete new government, which would immediately negotiate with U.S. and Britain for peace. Terms for the peace, if 'Der Fuhrer' had been killed, would probably have been unconditional surrender. All Nazi leaders were to be arrested and tried. All prisoners were to be released and their guards arrested. Chancellor of the new government was to be Dr. Karl Gordeler, former Mayor of Leipzig (still at large on this date). Field Marshal von Witzleben was to be new Commander-in-Chief of all armed forces, with Col. Gen. Beck as Military Reichschancellor. Secretary of State was to be Count von Wartenburg, cousin of Count von Stauffenberg, planter of the bomb. Col. Gen. Erich Hoppner was to be commander of Home Forces. The Plotters arranged to hold back tank forces, which Col. Gen. Guderian was to have taken to the East Front.

At the 'Peoples' Court,' Dr. Freisler, president of the court, called Hoppner a 'Schweinhund' as he appeared on the stand. On the stand, Col. Gen. Hoppner said he had allowed himself to be arrested because he didn't feel like a 'Schweinhund.'

'What animal do you resemble?' asked Dr. Friesler.

'A jackass,' replied Hoppner.

'Nien, nien, Mein Herr, you are and will remain a Schweinhund. Nothing further; the court rests.'

From the *AAA Observer* (Barrack 3-A news sheet taken from German papers; translated by Fred Johnson, Winter Park, Florida, and edited by Teddy Roggen, formerly with the *Houston Post*, Houston, Texas). This is their translation:

According to the "*V-B*," a Samuel Mosche Levy of Palestine wrote the classical letter to Stalin, taken from Pravda radio-press:

Stalin the Savior,

As your warriors place foot on despised enemy soil, please accept from one of thousands of tortured Jewish hearts, the old testamentary blessings, which Jacob invoked on Joseph. "Joseph will grow; he will grow like a tree at the spring, a tree that raises its branches over the wall (Genesis 49)."

Hurrah! You most brave soldier, who has covered himself with fame and glory, you, with Roosevelt and Churchill, have surpassed all men in war history! In the eyes of the world, this is a symbol that you three have elected to sweep the enemies of Jewry from the face of the earth, and to set up an authority in the world, which will give back to the Israelite his beloved homeland!

Your admirer,
Signed: Samuel Mosche Levy.

"Unruhestiffen, Streithahne, Aggressoren!" (Unrest, Strikes, Aggression!)

Many of the German papers during the past weeks have gone all out for anti-American propaganda, covering American political history with a series of derogatory articles on some of our past presidents. These are authentic interpretations from Johnson-Roggen, *AAA Observer*:

> Dr. William Koppen, German historian, says, 'Monroe established in 1823 the famous doctrine, which had the complete ascendancy of the U.S.A. over both American continents. Lincoln, despite English and French intrigue, led the U.S. to unity by the Civil War (mild!). Cleveland was the last Lord of the White House to reject dollar imperialism. In 1905, Teddy Roosevelt utilized a peace between Russia and Japan for the advantage of the U.S. and to the disadvantage of Japan. Wilson meddled with the Mexican chaos and flung the U.S. into World War I against the will of all the American people. Franklin Roosevelt, under whom dollar imperialism has entered into open discussion of world domination under the current Jewish and Free-masonry symbols, has spread his colossus effect to every part of the earth.'

August 16th - South France Invaded

Exactly twenty-four hours afterwards, the "Goons" disclosed to us the news of the new landing in Southern France "intended to take Britain's mind off of 'V-1'" (to quote the press!).

August 17th

Lt. Col. Robert M. Cheal, San Francisco, 133rd Infantry, and 38 other West Front officers arrived. The majority was Airborne, who had, as expected, been dropped in the wrong place.

Where is Tunisia?

A new 34th Division officer asked an old 34th Division officer (one captured 18 months previously), "Where were you captured, in France or in Italy?"

"Neither! In North Africa!" answered the old-timer.

"Why, I know some of you were captured in Tunisia, but I didn't know any of you were in North Africa!"

"Wow! Man, the 'V-1' must have made you 'coo-coo!' Tunisia is in North Africa, for your information," was the retort.

"Kriegies" of Oflag 64 are now seeing, "The Front Page" - A Comedy-Drama in 3 acts, directed by Lt. John Glendinning, from 138 E. 60th St., New York City.

August 17

The Story of Lt. Col. Cheal, as told to me:

I was captured July 20, 1944, S.E. of Carentan, France. I was originally with the 329th Infantry on the landing on "Utah Beach," and the next day got the Third Battalion. On the landing, the casualties were very high, particularly among the field officer grade. The 38th Division was again ordered to attack S.E. toward the Taute River. My battalion reached its objective with 8 officers and 126 men! This was in the course of 4 days, in which 5 attacks were launched. The remainder of the regiment with the rest of the division reached this area 2 days later! The battalion then went into division reserve, where it received complete reorganization and replacement. Shortly afterwards, the battalion received orders to attack across the Taute River, to secure high ground, where the Germans were using observation posts, watching our supply roads. The attack came off at night; the objective was reached, but the "Das Reich" SS Panzer Division overran our position. It was here that I was captured. The Germans placed us in a boxcar, which was strafed three times by P-38s and P-40s near Chateau-Thierry (famous in World War I). Five men were killed and 23 wounded west of Paris. There was a scene of burned-out vehicles every few yards, particularly on the Alencon-Paris railroad.

From here to Chalons, where we remained in solitary confinement, we were given propaganda talks. Rather than questioning, the "Goons" talked politics and appeared to cry on our shoulders, wondering, 'Why would the Americans allow the Bolshevists to conquer and massacre the Germans; why were the Americans bombing their cities; and why were the Americans fighting with the Bolshevists?'

To go back to where I was, when we relieved the Airborne Division on July 27th. It had been effectively reduced to nothing. Prior to my capture and while in Normandy, our division had the mission of clearing out the Cherbourg Peninsula. The Germans fought fanatically. The front line troops treated us as nicely as could be expected. Rear troops did not.

The S.A.O., Col. George Millett, was suddenly dispatched, supposedly for interrogation, to Frankfurt-on-Main, Germany. No American interpreter was allowed to accompany him. Speculations are afloat as to his mission. Was he sent to an interrogation? Where could he be going? Was he sent to look over accommodations for a new camp to which we might be moved? Time will tell! We shall know . . . or will we?

August 18

A number of officers, including myself, received our new Rolex Oyster Perpetual watches from Rolex, Geneva today (an international agreement). Now the proud owners roll their sleeves up instead of down.

The common question, "What time is it?"

"8:31 and 2 seconds!" (Isn't it just like human beings?)

August 20

Lt. Col. Charles (Witta Wabbit) Jones, Jr. is now a big mail operator, as is Amon Carter, Jr., having today received a letter dated August 6. While in Ireland, Carter's "Pop" flew over to pay him a visit. Since nylon hosiery stood high with the Irish lassies, "Pop" gave him twelve pair; however, so the story goes, the next day, Amon, Sr. asked Amon, Jr. for six pair back.

My hobby is that of collecting "war stories" from persons having had interesting experiences. One of the most interesting is that of Lt. Col. Max Gooler, Military Attaché with the British 8th Army, Egypt and Libya, 1941:

In January 1941, I was called from Fort Benning to Washington, D.C., where, to my surprise, I was handed credentials directing me to take a Clipper and fly to Cairo, where I was to report to the British Middle East Command as Military Attaché. I caught the Clipper in San Francisco and flew to Hawaii; to Guam (a beautiful island Naval base); to Midway, Wake and then to Manila, Philippines, where I stayed at the Bayview Hotel (I recommend this hotel as it is clean and reasonably cheap); southwest to Mindanao; Singapore, where everything was very much Europeanized. Here, I changed over to the British Overseas Airways, and flew across Burma to Rangoon, which was surrounded by dense vegetation and cluttered with dirt, and then from here across India to Karachi. Here, we waited several hours for Duff Cooper, his wife and page of servants. (Incidentally, they appeared snooty, cold and indifferent.) We had no trouble, however, as I attended to my business and they to theirs! Two American Shell Oil officials joined us, and we were off across the Indian Ocean; up the Persian Gulf to Bassena; from here across Syria to the Sea of Galilee, where we had fine British tea and a brief rest. (By the way, I recommend Galilee. It's pretty, cool and clean.) Then we went south over the Dead Sea (a God-forsaken place), across the Sinai Dessert, Suez Canal (a big ugly ditch), and on to Cairo in exactly 14 days after departure from San Francisco!

After presenting my credentials to the American Consul, I took up my quarters in the Metropolitan Hotel (one I recommend highly, unless you wish to stay with the chosen ones at Sheppherd's). I was received with courtesy by the staff, Middle East Command, where there was always plenty of 'reserve' tea and 'skotch.' Imagine, 'skotch' in American Army Headquarters with work to do, and where I was never allowed to pay a cent for anything. It was always difficult to obtain the information on operation and equipment - to comply with my orders. It seems that some news correspondent had spoken his mind; and, consequently, their G-2 was airtight; however, I did eventually get the inside on operations. I was attached to various units, throughout the many skirmishes in the Libyan Desert, from January to June 1941.

The first break-through at Tobruk - by Foxy Rommel, which ended at the very approaches to Alexandria - came as a great shock to the Middle East Command.

Rommel had superiority in planes and armor and his choice of command, no doubt, at the time, was better coordinated than the British.

During all this time I was busy on the Front collecting German Ordinance material and secret documents and forwarding them to the War Department. To digress a bit, I would like to mention an amusing incident

About this time, the Maxwell Commission arrived in Cairo, where it immediately took over the consulate set-up, its numerous villas, etc. Then representatives from the Chicago Military Exposition came to collect a Mark III tank and other German accoutrement, with the approval of the State Department, for their museum! (I had already sent a Mark III to our own War Department, and the British couldn't see why another should be sent; however, they got their Mark III.)

On June 17th, once more I joined the fighting forces, the 2nd South African Division, which consisted of the 4th and 6th and another Indian Brigade. I reported to the 4th Indian Brigade, with whom I had worked previously, where I dropped off a case of coveted 'skotch.' The war clouds hung low over the desert around Tobruk. The 2nd South African Division, which had just occupied Tobruk, had orders to hold a 30-mile perimeter around the city, with the 4th on the right, the 6th on the center and the other Indian Brigade on the left. At this stage there seemed to be no continuity of command; furthermore, the RAF, which had suffered heavy losses, and the Royal Navy batted brains against a decisive stand to hold Tobruk.

So, at early dawn, Saturday, June 23, 1941, Rommel launched his powerful thrust through the famous 'Gap.' In order of events, the Stukas attacked for one hour, long range artillery pounded the Indians, the sappers moved through the 'Gap' - to find no mines! Colored smoke screen laid down, two Panzer divisions moved in on Tobruk, and actually sank two ships - by rank cannonade! At 10:00 A.M. Sunday, Maj. Gen. Klopper's division, which had sustained only 300 casualties and which had not committed either the 4th or 6th Brigade, facing the Italians, surrendered. Although Gen. Klopper had in his headquarters a copy of Rommel's "Battle Order" of a year ago which had used the same general tactics, the 'Gap' wasn't even mined!

In this action I escaped to a cave along the coast north of the harbor. Some "Ite" gave me away, and a German officer poured fire with his carbine into the cave. Between bursts of fire he'd scream and laugh at me. Finally, he said "Kommen Sie," and I did.

Some interesting sidelights and hints to those who might be interested. At the time of arrival at Cairo, there were only six American officials and prices were reasonable. In fact, the British controlled the prices in Egypt. When more and more Americans arrived, prices jumped and jumped some more, to the horror of the British! (I told Lt. Col. Gooler that I found the same thing to be true in French North Africa, 1942 and 1943, and upon my five-day visit to Cairo, July 1943!)

In 1940, young King Farouk had overproduced cotton and left the mess for the British to clean up. Under this and

201

accusations of intrigues with the Nazis, the Egyptian King fled in a yacht, to be apprehended in the Red Sea. Allowing the crown to remain on his head, provided he remained a good 'boy,' appeased him! (I told Lt. Col. Gooler that I learned, while in Cairo, July 1943, that Farouk is a 'big operator,' owning two night-clubs and the controlling interest of the Hunt Club on Gizeh Island.)

I recommend visiting Jerusalem, where you should stay at the Y.M.C.A. and visit places under their advice. Other places will 'verneuk' you! Port Said is interesting. In Damascus, you should stay at the Y.M.C.A. (where food is cheap and where you can visit the Church-of-All-Nations without being pestered by guides). I actually saw Jews doing an excellent job of farming in ancient ruins between Beirut and Damascus, Palestine. In Biblical days in Matruh, Cleopatra bathed in perfumes, and, in recent times, the Duke of Windsor and 'Wallie' frequently met. The 'City of the Dead,' just outside of Cairo, is where Egyptians bury their dead and remain there one week to mourn and feast. The Barracks-of-the-Camel Corps and Mt. Sinai are also interesting. (I told Lt. Col. Gooler that I recommend seeing the Bazaars, Minarets, Mosques, Pyramids, without a native guide!)

If the Egyptians get disgruntled with the British, they engineer a student demonstration and hope that it impresses the British! There are four famous prices in

Egypt; 1) a price for the Egyptians, 2) a price for all Europeans, 3) one for the British, and, 4) one for the Americans!

To our surprise, six French officers from an Ack-Ack unit, captured near Florence, arrived here today. Two of them speak English - Capt. Henri Lemaria, 6 Boulevard du 4 Zouaves, Casablanca (or 37 Rue de Petien, Paris) and Lt. Yves Poussier, 76 Fants-St. Honore, Paris 8.

Col. Millett's campaign to prevent officers from throwing cigarette butts on the ground was effective. You see, American officers, when they are flush with cigarettes, throw the butts on the ground. The "Goons" come along with flashlights at night and pick them up! They, too, like American cigarettes. Col. Millett saw no reason why Americans should furnish the "Goons" with tobacco, so he got Jim Bickers, camp artist, to paint subtle cartoons on this "butts" business. It was effective!

August 25

If you remember, Col. Millett was sent away a few days ago. After he returned, I got a story of his experiences:

When I left Oflag 64, the German guard, Fexler, who lived many years in the Philippines, carried me to Oberusel, near Hammelburg. A disinterested "Goon" interrogated me. On the whole, they were nice to me, giving me freedom to walk around. After signing a 'parole,' I was allowed complete freedom of the hospital and its surroundings, without guards. There were sixty American pilots here, many of whom were in pathetic condition. The hospital was also being used for mental cases for German civilians and army patients. In one room was a cousin of Count von Stauffenburg, the man who planted the bomb intended for Hitler. The cousin was a former Private in the 'Wehrmacht.'

Among the American officers who have been through this place was Brig. Gen. Vanaman, former Military Attaché at Berlin. He was flying a bomber on a sightseeing flight over Germany when he was shot down! A Maj. Helm, an interrogator from Berlin, questioned me for four successive days. I believe that I was called here because of a previous statement I had made when being questioned at Chalon, France. I had stated, 'If you would get rid of Hitler, the war wouldn't last much longer!' (This was before the attempt on Hitler's life.) On the return trip, the trains were crammed with German civilians from France. I annoyed them by smoking 'Prima' cigarettes and eating food from my Red Cross box! One lady, who spoke English, enjoyed one of these 'unbelievable' cigarettes, while chatting with me. An old man, who sat across from me, ate from my Red Cross box and asked me what I was doing with American food. When I told him I was an American officer, he looked rather chagrined! After all, what else could he suppose? 'Postum' Fexler was sound asleep. Forced laborers are digging great tank traps just east of Szubin (Oflag 64).

August 25

The Ostdeutscher-Beobachter in Posen scooped the *Volkisher-Beobachter* mouthpiece in Berlin on the "Treacherous surrender of Romania to the Bolshevists."

August 26 - Beaucoup Mail, But . . .

International Red Cross headquarters has just handed the German Press facts of its "gross" operations - that:

In 1939, I.R.C. had one small building and a very small staff to handle charity affairs, but by 1943, through four years of war, has expanded to twenty-seven buildings, and handled one million letters for 58,085 prisoners of war each month! (Or about 25 letters per "Kriegy" per month!)

All overseas mail comes via Lisbon, or Genoa to Geneva, where it is reclassified and distributed to various camps by a mailing staff, four-fifths of whom are volunteers, and seventy-five percent of whom are Swiss!

"Kriegies" are asking "Where are our twenty-five letters which we are supposed to be receiving each month?" I, for example, have received exactly two letters this month. To date, and after almost twelve months behind the wire, I have received 23 letters. Now, where are the other one hundred and fifty-seven? Across the wire, I think!

August 30 "My Heart Stands Still" (!)

William Joyce (Lord Haw-Haw) is famous for his pet expressions, for example "My heart stands still" (when he is always seeing those secret weapons, such as a V-1, which are to let the Allies in for a big surprise!), and "the German Nation," which he says has mobilized all its manpower to destroy the "Calluses," which are spreading over Europe!

"American Gangsters Won't Stop to Fight" (!)

The German Press now says, "The American Gangsters won't stop to fight our brave soldiers" and, "The fighting in France has taken on a highly mobile characteristic."

Beaucoup Babies

Since 1933, the National Socialist Party has encouraged marriages and big families by grants or exemption of taxes on new homes or baby bonuses to couples of limited income. During 1938, of the 925,000 couples to marry, 825,000 babies were born! (Facts were taken from "Hitler Germany" by Cesare Santoro, Italian writer.) Each town or city has its own marrying agency, to bring couples together. Nearby Posen has one, and many widows, widowers, etc. are matched by this agency. For example, here are some ads from *The Ostdeutscher-Beobachter*, Posen, Freitag, den 18, August 1944:

Heirat (Marriage)

1. Mechanic, 35 years old, looking for a young girl
2. Fraulein (unmarried woman), 47, wanting to marry
3. Dipl. Ing. (City official) with pension and plenty of goods, etc., wants to marry
4. Witwe (Widow) pretty and has money
5. Junges Madel (young maid) wants to correspond with man 20 to 50 years of age.

Germany "Bleeding," Germany "Bleeding"

Nightly at 9:30 P.M., Germany "bleeds" for fifteen minutes to the English-speaking world. The newscast opens with "Germany calling, Germany calling" (Americans substitute the word "bleeding" for "calling.") The narrator, with an Oxford accent, opens with "American and British POWs, do you know that you are fighting for the Bolshevists and International Jewry?"

Under Hitler's new total war effort, Dr. Goebbels has decreed that cabarets, nightclubs, movies, newspapers, periodicals, etc., will be limited, cut out or greatly curtailed. Furthermore, "Strength through Joy" (Kruft durch Freude) is no longer possible!

"Achtung, Achtung!" (Attention, Attention!)

"Gentlemans, I'll tell you," says Billy ('Gentlemans') Bingham, "the only 'line' Jerry has left is the one under his eye! And, I predict that Hitler's next command will be 'Fall out! Fall in at Berlin!'"

"Home-by-Xmas" Clubs

Last year before Christmas, "Home-by-Xmas" Clubs were formed. Recently, membership has reached an all-high record! There is also a "Home-by-Thanksgiving" Club! Vell, vot are ve vaiting for?

Chapter Twenty One
September 1944

September 1, 1944

Lt. Bill Schultz, former Oflag 64 inmate, who went out on a "Kommando" work party February 1 disguised as a British orderly (in place of Gunner, Hethcoat, British) unbeknown to the "Goons," was returned to camp today, after spending weeks at the hands of the Gestapo. Here's his story:

> I left here to get experience and to learn things outside of the wire. From Oflag 64, I was sent to Stalag (camp for enlisted men) where I worked in a veterinary hospital. I groomed Russian ponies until I could see horsetails in my sleep. Later, I was sent to a German O.C.S. camp where an Australian Corporal and I escaped. I was soon recaptured, but the Corporal got away. As punishment, I was given 21 days in confinement.
>
> On July 14, I was again assigned to a work party. I obtained civilian clothing and again escaped. I traveled from Posen to Prague, Czechoslovakia, without being detected. Posing as a French civilian, I bought a ticket to Austria. On the train, I was asked to produce identity papers, which unfortunately, I did not have. The Gestapo searched me and found my 'American' dog tags. Instead of turning me over to the Army, they placed me in an SS prison. This SS prison in Prague was the 'true story' that one reads about in magazines, books and newspapers. From my cell, I saw a blind man being double-timed; each time he fell, the Gestapo

guards clubbed him with a rubber hose until he fell to the ground again, exhausted and bleeding.

I was shipped in a prison train with German prisoners, to Dresden, to Breslau. En route, the car was so crowded that we had to stand up. In Breslau, I was slammed into a dungeon. Once a day, I was allowed to see daylight. I was not allowed to wash! In this hellhole, there were people of every description: Jews, convicts, deserters, etc., who had committed 'acts against the Reich.' It was here that I saw Jewish women, ragged and famished, being beaten and treated like dogs!

After 21 days of this, I was transferred to a prison in Posen, where I again saw women, Polish, I think, being beaten, knocked down and beaten again for getting up! From here I was sent to a civilian internee camp at Bromburg, then to a Stalag at Thorn, where there were 6,000 British prisoners.

In retrospect, I might say that in all my contact with thousands of forced French laborers, all I had to say was 'American' and they did everything in their power to help me. They idolize Americans. I saw many German deserters who seemed to be happy to be prisoners! I sincerely believe my American dog tags saved me from the cruelty and beatings the others received and I believe that if Col. Drake's and later, Col. Millett's letters, had not been written to the "Swiss Legation," I would not be back yet! If I had possessed a faked passport, I would have made a complete get-away! I don't regret having done what I did; I saw the 'true story' of the atrocious Gestapo. I'm happy to be back, though, you can bet on that!

"Kriegy Lament" - Tune of "Dark Eyes"

Oh, Rokossovsky
Bring your Ruskies
Come and Get Me
I'm 'Kaputskie'

General Bradley
You Have Normandy
You Have Burgundy
Why Not Germany?

Marshal Stalin
Hear Me Calling
Keep 'em Rollin'
Right Thru Polen!

Kriegs-gefangenen
With too much time to spend
All Go 'Round the Bend'
Sweatin' out the End!

Our Outlook is Down
Our 'Goon' Bread is Sour
Use Your Strikin' Power
General Eisenhower!

Zhukov, Konev, Melanovski
Patsch and Patton
Novogrowski - Ruskies
Come and Get Me!

Maj. Jerry Sage, who was captured in Tunisia, February 1943, composed the above lyric, "Kriegy Lament."

Sept. 6

Die Woche writes about Texas (incidentally, this was the last issue of *Die Woche* to be printed, because of the "Total War Effort"):

"Kriegsgewinnler - Texas" (War Profiteer –Texas)

The following things do not at all correspond to our ideas of Texas as a cowboy paradise:

That this territory, largest of the states, should have had such an extraordinary development in such a short time, that in the opinion of many who know, it is well on the way to throwing out of the saddle, not only the old industrial quarters of the northwest coastal region, but the somewhat younger industrial center, California.

The picture that one has of the southwest corner of the United States that borders on Mexico, comes from the period when mammoth herds of cattle were being led to the slaughter houses in the northwest under the protection of the dashing riders in shaggy trousers and artistic hats, or derived from a still older period when the Indians were in control.

That this land, which consists first (going from the Gulf of Mexico inland) of a broad fruitful lowland called the 'Black Prairie;' second, of a mountain and table land that has little water; and finally, in the north, of the high plain that closely resembles a desert, should have many valuable raw materials, seems to contradict somewhat, the romantic Wild West film. (What a description!)

At the most, one knew that in the southern section of the states, cotton controlled a wide area of rich black land (Texas supplies about thirty per cent of

U.S. cotton) and that a considerable amount of oil lay underneath. Recently, this oil has come into greater and greater prominence. For example, at the moment, a 2,000-mile long pipeline is built to the west to make use, industrially, of all the oil there. The cost of production is, for technical reasons, substantially lower in Texas.

Now people are finding a very great interest also in the wooded country of eastern Texas, which is very well adapted for the production of cellulose, and which, in recent years, has been attracting many suitable production plants. Whereupon other factories will then be built, for producing artificial silk, cellulose wool, artificial resin and other cellulose derivatives. In the coastal area there are countless supplies of the heavy chemicals, such as sulfur, salt, and lime, all of which have likewise become the basis of large industrial enterprises. The chemical industry, therefore, has taken on in Texas a position that reaches out in very different directions, that, opposed to the competitive positions of other states, has the advantage of producing the most modern equipment, and which, for that reason, presents the abnormally conceited Texas people with a course for daring future plans.

Like everything else in the U.S., economic improvement is naturally being thoroughly exploited among those interested. Texas, having a decided democratic majority, hopes for great things for their countrymen! Jesse Jones (nephew, John Jones, Oflag 64), who, up to the time of his dismissal as head of the Reconstruction Finance Corporation, looked after the interests of his home state with all the weight of his very original and massive personality. It is hoped that he will have something decisive to say, when once the matter is to be considered, of what now should be 'lasting' of war productions that have been conjured up! If, of course, the Republicans should take over in Washington, D.C., then it is feared that Texas' great days will not, at the expense of the opposition, flow quite so self-centeredly, into a lengthy prosperity. (This 'jerk' has either met a Texan or has been to Texas, or both! Capt. James W. Barker, Harrisburg, PA. translated the above article.)

Sept. 10

The Berlin "News in English" Germany "Bleeding" broadcast devotes very little time to the war front these days; on the other hand, much time is spent to propagandizing. (One of these days, Germany is going to bleed to death!)

Sept. 13

Ninety-two more "Kriegies" arrived from the west front. Six field officers, including Maj. Gordon K. Smith of Fond du Lac, Wisconsin, Col. Millett's supply officer, Lt. H. M. Pike, Weslaco (the lower Rio Grande Valley, Texas), and an AMG official, Capt. H. D. Eldridge, Denver, Colorado, also arrived here.

Moments (One Year) in a "Kriegy" Camp

One year ago today, the 16th Panzer Division in southern Italy captured me.

The Last Straw

Das Oberkommando der Wehrmacht (OKW or the German High Command) ordered today that Red Cross Parcel stock would be removed from camp and that a one-day's supply would be allowed inside the wire. All private reserves of food would be reduced at the end of

213

two weeks. Red Cross parcels would be kept in a nearby warehouse, under German, not American, control. The Camp "Kommandant," Oberst Schneider, has ordered that two parcels will be issued, thus, further cutting down our supply, and the German ration would be reduced accordingly! Col. Millett, S.A.O., informed the Kommandant "You will get the parcels out only by force!" Nevertheless, 2,000 parcels were removed from camp!

The OKW motive behind this is obvious (1) To save their own ration; (2) To gain control of parcel issue (violation of articles of the Geneva Convention); (3) To prevent the POWs from giving food to the Poles and Russians, and to their own women and children upon capitulation; and (4) To cut down food stocks in case of an Allied rescue mission (which is very unlikely). The old "Kriegies" in camp remember very well what happened to the parcels in Italy, September 1943; the Germans took them over and ate them in their presence!

The Germans have made a grave mistake in their manner of dealing with Allied prisoners. Instead of paving the way for good feelings for them, the Germans have done everything in their power to instill hatred in the POWs. (No POW would ever sympathize with defeated "Goons.")

Sept. 18

The "Goons" continue to post propaganda pamphlets. Today they came into camp and tacked up a propaganda poster (escaping ceases to be a sport, etc.) in all the barracks, against the vigorous protest of the S.A.O.

Today at the noon meal, they issued bread that looked and felt like soaked sawdust! This bread was baked in July - two months ago! (The date was stamped on the bread)

Sept. 19

A current play makes a big hit at Oflag 64. Feminine characters played by "Kriegies" always amuse us to no end. Lt. Lynn Vaden, from Dallas, says, "You know it just embarrasses the very dickens out of me, the things us 'gals' have to go through."

"When Peace Reigns"

From an October issue of Berlin's *Signal*, printed in English, the following ad was taken. Peace! Ah, how wonderful it would be!!!

"Frankfurt Alright"

Capt. H. D. Eldridge, AMG officer, now a POW, and veteran "occupation" soldier of World War I states:

In the Cherbourgh area and along the
Normandy coast of France, the attitude of
the civilians was one of reserve,
indifference, aloofness, and suspicion of the
invading forces, due perhaps to the
uncertainty of the success of the invasion.
The German propaganda had its effects.
On the other hand, the civilians of the
interior met us with 'vivas,' 'vin rouge,' 'vin
blanche,' flowers and gestures of welcome.

DeGaulle was constantly on the lookout
for bad management of AMG, so that it
would give him grounds for an early
assumption of civil authority over the
French population. My task, once Germany
capitulated, was to be the AMG
administrator for the Frankfurt area. It
was here that I served with 'occupation
troops' in World War I. It was at Stalag XII
near Frankfurt where, during World War
II, that I spent several days as a POW!

Sept. 21 - "Ya, Benny Sent Me"

"Feldwabel" Hartl, local "Goon," left for the west front yesterday carrying with him a note of surrender. "I surrender. Ya, Benny sent me." Signed an American.

Sept. 29

Sixty-eight new "Kriegies," from Italy and both fronts of France arrived early this morning. Three field officers in this group now bring the total to thirty-five, or about $580.00 worth daily! Sketchy tidbits of information from them:

The 7th Army, in the rapid advance to
the north, did not slow down until it ran
out of gasoline, near Grenoble, France.
Reception by French civilians was very
good. By bribing the German guards with

American cigarettes, the Kriegies received
good treatment en route here. Of course,
everybody rode in boxcars. Col. Millett's
Regiment sustained 69 per cent casualties!
Brazilian "venereal" casualties in Italy
were extremely high!

Chapter Twenty Two
October 1944

October 1, 1944 - Holland to Schubin in Four Days!

Lt. William L. Geddens from the 101st A/B Division, attached to the British 1st A/B Division, holds record time in "Flight of a Kriegy" to Oflag 64. He was captured near Arnheim, Holland, September 27, and arrived here October! "The Germans claim 6,635 airborne troops were captured near Arnheim." Geddens says. "It's not so. They didn't have that many in the drop. Furthermore, I know that at least 3,500 got back to the Reine, where they were holding the bridgehead at the river crossings, when I was captured."

No-Man's-Land Hospital

"It might be of interest," continues Geddens, "to say that there was a No-Man's-Land Hospital used by both 'sides.' Wounded were taken here, and if recovery seemed likely, they were sent back to their side with a Red Cross band as passport. Some came back several times, wounded again!"

Goons Dance with Yank Gals!

Word came into camp to verify a previous rumor that a group of gals at Camp Atebury, Indiana, last Christmas, gave a dance to German officer POWs! Walter Winchell, on a Sunday broadcast, had exposed the incident! A chaplain (I won't name him), now in Oflag 64, says, "It's so, for I helped in putting it over. I didn't know there was anything wrong with it."

October 4

Since the Allies have occupied France and cleared the obstacle to Geneva, some letters have arrived from the States in fourteen days! Also, about 300 private parcels have recently arrived, the first ones since D-Day, June 6.

We feel, too, that Larry Allen has exposed the inefficiency of the U.S. Postal authorities. For example, last week Lt. Col. Oakes received a letter from his wife in Texas, a letter which was post-marked in San Antonio, November 1943, post-marked again at New York in August 1944, postmarked in Oflag 64 again in September 1944! "Was ist loss?" (What's wrong?)

October 5

Lt. Col. Nath Hosket, returning from the Wallstein Hospital, where he has undergone treatment for stomach ulcers, assembled a nice bit of gossip, along with a cross-section of political views. For at Wallstein, there were Pole doctors, Norwegians, Serbs, and British.

A Norwegian Naval Commander, Capt. Cameron, British Medico, learned these viewpoints, hearsay, of course, from eight Polish doctors, the latter having served, separately, with the Russians, the Germans, the Austrians and the Poles during World War I.

The Polish doctors believe the Russians deliberately left Gen. Bor and his insurgents to the fate of Warsaw, because Bor was a "Polish Liberation" selection from London. Gen. Rola, Russian selectee of the Lublin government is "rightly" the man to lead the Polish armed forces. They say there were forty to sixty Russian divisions across from Warsaw that could easily have rescued Gen. Bor from his predicament in Warsaw (Bor vs. Rola). Bor is an upstanding high-spirited cavalryman who won the Aquatic Event at the Olympics in Berlin in 1936. He is a favorite of Britain and America. Rola, on the other hand, is a leader of Polish "Lublinites." He was discharged from the Polish Army about 1936 for irregularity in the manufacture of gas masks.) A Bor officer, captured two weeks ago in Warsaw, was "disgusted."

An American Air Corps Sergeant, shot down about three weeks ago while attempting to re-supply the insurgents, stated that the supplies were dropped at 18,000 feet! When the Sergeant bailed out, he was over

Warsaw. He drifted eighteen miles west of here before hitting the ground! The Sergeant believes if half a dozen bundles landed in Gen. Bor's area, it was a miracle!

The Norwegian, who spoke perfect English, was brought in after the recent Oslo uprising. He says the Wehrmacht is "O.K.," but the SS troops, "Nix." After Norway fell, he says the Gestapo forced the Norwegians to do calisthenics, in shorts, in the snow until they keeled over. The Jews, when exhausted, were held up by Gestapo men while women were forced to march up and kick them in the groins! The Poles stated that they had seen their day, when their own women had stabbed bound Germans. Later, the Germans had done the same thing to them.

They say that the Lublin government is headed by Polish Jews, who have always been communistic, or so inclined. (It's beyond me to analyze or to draw any conclusions from this muddle. I wonder if there is a solution to this mess. Aloofness on the part of Americans is the best for America, I say!)

October 8 - "Feldwebel Holland for President"

There is nothing like a little American music to send us to bed. Feldwebel (Sgt.) Holland, an old German who lived in the States for more than a decade, switched on an American 9:15 P.M. broadcast of a short wave program. Some babe was warbling, "I love to hear the coo-coo in my clock," then silence - (the announcement, no doubt) - and, "I'm in love with someone who's not in love with me." This is the first time we have heard an American broadcast in Oflag 64! Someone recently wrote, "I know you must enjoy the popular numbers in overseas broadcasts!" (My dear, we don't in Germany!)

October 10

The "Goons" daily become more harassing. They take control of the Red Cross parcels, and now, they refuse to turn over 2,280 private parcels, which arrived this week from our families back home. No doubt some of these parcels have been inside Germany for several months. Two orderlies, who helped unload them, say that they are stored in a German warehouse some fourteen miles away. "You have too much food already," say they!

Col. Millett has written two strong protests to the Swiss but we all fully realize that the Swiss Delegation and the Geneva Convention mean nothing to them. Just after the confiscation of the parcels, an I.R.C. representative dropped in. German authorities promised that the parcels would be released when we "wanted" them! No sooner had the representative departed, than the "Goons" broke their promise. That, too, was expected.

October 14 - "Boots and Saddles"

This evening, an English broadcast from Berlin entertained "Kriegies." The scene reenacted:

A gal, who must have been Sally, the famous "Bitch of Berlin," who, incidentally, used to entertain us via the air in North Africa, Sicily and Italy, spoke a few "sweet words." Some "jerk" sang "Boots and Saddles." He must have had "tracheitis" of the windpipe. Several Bing Crosby records were played.

Their propaganda "stunk," but, in spite of this, Berlin had an eager audience by the loud speaker in the north end of Barrack 3-A, Oflag 64.

October 18

Late this evening, one hundred officers and twenty orderlies arrived. This puts the camp strength to approximately one thousand Americans and nine Frenchmen.

Col. Paul R. Goode, famously known as "Pop" Goode and two other full Colonels were among the new arrivals. Col. Goode, a graduate of West Point, class 1914 and highly esteemed by all those serving under him, now becomes the new S.A.O. The Colonel reputedly fought for the rights of American POWs from Chalon, France to here.

Back in France, when twenty Americans escaped, the Germans lined up Col. Goode and four other Americans for a reprisal execution, whereupon he made this statement "You may execute us, but I warn you that our Army will know about it and will execute every German present after the war." From then on, no further attempt or threat was made. No execution took place.

Col. Edgar Gans has become, in a few short weeks, quite a globetrotter. He left the States on August 26 and was captured September 15!

"Believe It or Not"

Three weeks ago, Capt. Lou Wilcox received a letter from Maj. Kermit Hansen, former aid to Mike O'Daniels, stating, "It won't be long now before we can have a get-together and talk things over." How true! Maj. Hansen is now a "Kriegy" in Oflag 64! A curious world, this!

Lt. John C. Simick, Waco, Texas, says, "I had rather battle the SS troops any day than the Wehrmacht. A unit of original Africa Corps captured me. They were tough boys to crack. Treatment, after capture, was good by front-line SS troops; however, the treatment inside Germany was poor. (This has been the case in previous reports brought in.)

New arrivals report that numerous German officers had asked if it were true that Negro troops would occupy Germany after the war. (The German press says so!)

October 23

Recently Gen. Reinford, the man who wiped out Gen. Bor's Warsaw insurgents, visited Oflag 64. This week's paper announced that SS Gruppen Fuhrer Reinford is in command of the newly created "Volkstrum" of the "Wartaland" (this district along the Warta River).

Of the some 3,000 private parcels that arrived "outside the wire," the Germans have condescended to hand over to "Kriegies" in dribbles, 50 to 75 daily. Red Cross food parcels have been exhausted in this camp. Five telegrams have been sent to Geneva to rush more here. The Swiss delegation lays blame for not being able to obtain food parcels on French terrorists, who supposedly raided Red Cross trains in France, confiscating many food parcels intended for POWs! The International Red Cross has made no commitments to date, nor has it answered the five telegrams. There are three million parcels in Sweden.

Command Performance (Verbotten)

At 7:30 P.M. Szubin time, the loud speaker bleated "Command Performance" . . . music . . . "Hello there, you boys." 'Click,' off went the radio. A mistake, no doubt! The voice sounded mighty like Don Wilson's. Eager "Kriegies" enjoyed the two-minute American program; that is to say, they almost enjoyed it.

October 31

When food stocks become exhausted and the German ration furnishes only 1,300 to 1,500 calories daily, then naturally, the uppermost topic of "Kriegy" conversation is food. POWs can't understand why the I.R.C. didn't send part of those three million parcels in July and August when rail facilities would have been available; furthermore, why hasn't the I.R.C. answered the five telegrams? Due to the fact that the old officers have divided their cigarettes and food from private parcels to new "Kriegies," everyone in camp is reasonably well taken care of, for the present at least.

The Germans only furnish two blankets per officer. Old officers gave up one of their blankets. Now, everyone here has two blankets, but four are needed in this damp, freezing Poland weather.

Voluntarily, old prisoners donated food to the new prisoners. Now, the "new" fellows seem to think that they should have a larger share! Surprised, the old timers retort, "Well, I'll be d___d!" Imagine! Some of these birds were eating steaks or B Ration, long after we were captured.

Chapter Twenty Three
November 1944

November 1, 1944 - "France Crumbles"

Lt. H. de Vilmorin, from Vence, France, is one of the nine French officers here. His present wife (an American), lives at 215 East 62nd St. in N.Y. City. His first wife was a granddaughter of P. Diaz, the former Mexican president, and he was one of Gen. DeGaulle's original "Free French" officers. Lt. de Vilmorin relates in detail the "Fall of France":

In 1936, the 'Popular Front' came to power. At that time, there were very few ineffective Communists and Fascists; however, there existed a strong and growing Socialistic group. No party offered a social program suitable to the masses, and everybody was against everybody else. Two factions arose from petty jealousy and political avarice, viz, the Anti-Fascists and the Anti-Communists.

The 'Popular Front' was the laborer's government. The laborers definitely benefited, whereas the white-collar workers (the civil servants, teachers, etc.) suffered greatly. Politics brewed and old politicians stewed. The government changed horses overnight, similar to Mexico of old.

In 1938, there existed one-half million unemployed. A 38-hour-week work bill was passed, with the results to the effect that no additional workers were employed, and industrial output, particularly munitions, declined to a dangerous low.

In retrospect, we must recall that the Spanish 'Popular Front' came into power, and one week later, the Spanish Revolution broke out. Then came Munich, which our propaganda played up as the great political victory of the age. M. Deladier received a hearty ovation upon his return from the conferences. The people were thankful that Hitler had been bluffed!

After the fall of Czechoslovakia, even the French still felt secure behind the Maginot Line. After all, France had the best army in Europe. France made no effort to 'Panzerize' its Army, as did Germany. Five years previously, Gen DeGaulle published his book on Panzer Armour and Tactics, for which later, Generaloberst Guderian, Germany's ace Panzer tactician, paid high tribute. But the old French Generals couldn't agree! There was the Maginot Line! M. Deladier stated that France would not understand a declaration of war when there was England, with the greatest navy in the world, as an ally.

Soon after M. Deladier's return, there evolved two plans; viz, to attack at once and push to the Rhine, or (from the pacifists) wait until spring. In the meantime, the French forces had moved twenty-five miles beyond the French border. They were ordered to withdraw. In spite of this threat, no preparations were made. France had at that time only 18 heavy bombers!

Then came the invasion of Holland and Belgium. Since the Siegfried Line stops off in Luxemburg, France had loaned Belgium several million francs to fortify its defense. The only thing wrong was that Belgium built the fortifications between the two countries and faced them the wrong way!

During the meantime, life went on in the Maginot Line as usual card games, shows, politics, always politics, and wives and sweethearts came and went without any checking whatsoever as to identity. Then in June 1940, came the invasion of France. Army units fought valiantly, but were cut to pieces by German Panzers and the Luftwaffe. The panic and commotion of the civilians, which clogged the roads, did more to hasten the defeat than anything else.

So, in seventeen days France surrendered, with France's oldest soldier, Marshal Petain, signing the armistice. It is interesting to note that Italy would not accept the armistice terms until M. Laval, Italy's favorite, was made a cabinet member of the provisional government!

Gen. Henri Giraud was taken prisoner. Gen. DeGaulle secretly initiated the resistance movement, which resulted in the formation of the Fighting Free French Force. All resistance forces went either to North Africa or to England. I happened to be one of DeGaulle's original twenty officers who formed a headquarters of the Free French Forces in London.

Subsequent events included the British Navy firing on the French Navy off the shores of Algiers, and the Free French Navy attempting to destroy the rest of the French Navy and take Dakar. This 'abortion' paid dividends for the Nazi propaganda machine in France. French morale was never lower. Petain tried to hold the civilians in order to prevent revolution, which he knew could never mean anything but tragedy for the people. In the meanwhile, dirty politicians did the dirty work under the cloak and shadow of the old man.

Winter came on with its ever-present propaganda. Great promises were made, without success, to induce civilian workers to go to Germany (Germany already had 1,800,000 prisoners of war). Finally, each town and village was given a quota of workers who would be taken to Germany. Roads out of town were blocked to prevent escape. Reprisals, in the form of shooting hostages, occurred to get results. The towns had to comply. Laval assisted the German cause. Thus began the disintegration of the French home. 1,500,000 workers were dispatched to the Reich. This meant that over three million men would not see their wives or fiancées for several years. Consequently, France would suffer a baby shortage hitherto unknown in history. This was the greatest cruelty Germany inflicted on France. We must remember that France lost 1,200,000 in World War I and 80,000 soldiers at Dunkirk, to save the British in this second Great War.

The French still looked to America for early help, which didn't come, but their patience never gave out. America entered the war. German propaganda hit a new high to play up terrorism in American bombing. But many an American pilot has been taken care of by French men, and later aided across the Spanish border. Resistance movements increased. This invisible army was most dangerous to the Germans, who haven't stopped fearing it.

November 7

"Was ist los?" (What's wrong?) The camp has been out of Red Cross parcels now for three weeks and we have to subsist on a 1,400 caloric ration per day. The German order states that no individual shall have in his possession more than twenty-four hours ration. Well, the "Kriegies" switched to the expediency of "hides" to store a few extra cans. Yesterday the Germans tore the place down and found the "hides," taking all contents outside the wire. In all, some 450 tins of food were found and confiscated.

One Joe Friedman was slugged the worst; he lost some thirty cans of food plus some of his private parcel food. The private parcel food could have been stored in the tin store, but Joe didn't see fit; if Germans are honorable, they will turn in the confiscated food to the camp mass for the benefit of all. One "Kriegy" got a bright idea. From his "hide" he took the food, and in its place went a little note that read "Was ist los?" (What's wrong?) The Germans found the note.

November 9

From the dear old Y.M.C.A. come a lawn mower, an ice-cream freezer and rolling pins! The only thing wrong is that there is no grass to mow, no cream to freeze, no biscuits to roll out!

German propaganda says, and quite prominently plays up, that Gen. Joe Stillwell was relieved of his China post because of friction between Stillwell and China's Generalissimo Chiang Kai-shek. Stillwell failed to persuade Gen. Chiang Kai-shek to use "Red" partisans aid against the Japanese. Just prior to his recall, Stillwell refused to accept Chiang's highest military decoration. Furthermore, America had fallen down in sending supplies to China. Chiang, declared, so say the Germans, that the supplies sent to China would supply one American division for one week. Then the Americans accuse both Chiang and Stillwell of a slow and poorly coordinated war effort.

German press quotes American papers in picturing gross inefficiency of the UNRRA (United Nations Relief and Rehabilitation Administration). "It is noted for its high salaried Jewish officials who have plenty of advice to give."

November 11

All quiet in Szubin.

November 16

Cocktail mixers and rolling pins, more gifts from the Y.M.C.A. arrived today! Now we shall really have amusement, shaking up 1,400 German calories and then rolling them out! These 1,400 calories are contained in the daily issue of 625 grams (1.38 pounds) of German issued food. "Kriegies" haven't stooped to boiling weeds yet; nevertheless, everybody is hungry.

November 16

The Gestapo searched the camp today for contraband. They confiscated pencils, nails, cigars, pipe tobacco, cigarettes and razor blades! This makes the fourth raid in the last three weeks. Such is the life of a "Kriegy," but we can take it.

November 19 - Pine Pie from the "Y"

Early today the Germans sent word into camp that a boxcar full of Red Cross food parcels was at the Schubin railway station. POW morale jumped sky high. Upon investigation, however, it was discovered that the car contained lumber from the "Y" in Geneva, for our Little Theater! Lou Otterbein, stage master, says, "Well, we'll saw it up and have Pine Pie!"

The German commandant ordered Col. Paul Goode to turn over 90 complete uniforms "for prisoners of war at other camps." The S.A.O. flatly refused, believing that the clothing would be used for fifth column work. Anyway, the "Goons" got them by calling everybody out for formation and then stealing them from the barracks. Some of the clothing had been sent from folks at home. Uniforms insignia were confiscated also. Now, what next?

"France Comes to Light" (A Continuation of Lt. H. de Vilmorin's Story)

At the time of the invasion of North Africa on November 8, 1942 (which was fifteen days early), the population, some million French and nine million Arabs, was anxious, confused, but happy. Gen. Henri Giraud had been 'kidnapped' from the Germans and landed on the coast of North Africa in fourteen hours. Prior to the landing, the feeling between the French and British was slightly cold, both sides remembering (1) Dunkirk; (2) the abortion of Madagascar; (3) Dakar; and (4) Syria and the estranged relations. The political and military set-up was as follows:

Admiral Darlan, under Marshal Petain, was commander-in-chief of the French forces; Gen. Nogues, Resident General; Adm. Michelier, C.O. of the French fleet at Casablanca, French Morocco; M. Peyrouton, Governor of Algeria; Adm. Esteva, Resident General of Tunisia; and Adm. Derrica, C.O. of the French fleet there, and who immediately surrendered to the Germans. With only fifteen days supply of ammunition and after perhaps three days fighting, Adm. Darlan capitulated, bringing both French Morocco and Algeria under Allied military control.

Upon asking Gen. Giraud to assume command of all French forces, he, feeling incompetent, recommended Darlan as the only Frenchmen capable of giving the order and having this order carried out! Certain British officers opposed Darlan. On the contrary, the Americans approved of the set-up, which now stood as on D-Day, except that the greater part of Tunisia went over to German control, and Gen. Giraud assumed command of all ground forces. Two French battleships had been seriously damaged at Casablanca. There wasn't much left of the French fleet. On D-Day, Petain had ordered, upon German occupation of the rest of France, that the fleet at Toulon surrender to the Germans, whereupon, the French Admiral in charge ordered the fleet to be scuttled. All were, including the battleships 'Strassburg' and

'Dunkirk.' There remained the 'Jean Bart'
at Casablanca, damaged, and the
'Richelieu' in the U.S., under repair.

In November and December, Giraud
was occupied reorganizing the remnants of
two ill-equipped and badly scattered
divisions (Gen. Giraud, with Gen. Welvert,
visited my battalion at Gafsa, Tunisia,
Nov. 27, 1942). Partial mobilization was
ordered subsequent to Giraud's return to
A.F.H.Q., Algiers.

On Christmas, a mad French boy, who
apparently thought he would become a
national hero for this act, assassinated
Darlan. Gen. Mark Clark, greatly alarmed,
asked Giraud to take command, which he
did. This time, oddly enough, Giraud
issued orders and to his surprise, they were
carried out. (Remember that Gen. Charles
De Gaulle had not yet arrived on the scene,
as the Allies deemed it best for him to
remain in London until the people in North
Africa could be united in a common cause.)
Things began to work more smoothly,
however, there was still a lack of liaison
between the Americans, British and
French. Later, however, the situation
improved when Gen. Mast became 'Chief of
Liaison' between the French, British and
American Army commanders. After
Tunisia, the French mobilized French
North Africa, and new divisions were
activated.

In June, Giraud left for the U.S. to
obtain armament for his army. When he
returned to North Africa, DeGaulle was in
power. At this time, a 'Joint Liberation
Committee' was formed as the official
government, with DeGaulle and Giraud
equally in power and equally responsible!

Such a set-up could not hope to exist very long. Eventually, DeGaulle, because of his poise, ingenuity and personality, would gain control of the political reins.

In July 1943, out of dire necessity, the 'Assembly Consultative' was formed in Algiers. This committee was composed of Giraud, DeGaulle and old 1936 members of Parliament who had been signers of Marshal Petain's armistice terms. This Assembly also included the twenty-one members (Communists) who had been arrested in Paris and sent to North Africa as prisoners. These twenty-one members constituted a small part of the Assembly. This new set-up chose DeGaulle to lead the government and Giraud to command the French armed forces. Immediately, DeGaulle ousted Gen. Nogues as 'Resident General' of French Morocco. War criminals, including Adm. Dennier, who had surrendered the French Fleet to the Germans at Bizertte, were tried, convicted, and shot.

German propaganda scandalized DeGaulle and his government in the German controlled press in France, and some Frenchmen behaved amazingly! The F.F.I. (Forces Françaises de l'Intérieur) intensified their activities in France.

It was not until the Invasion of Corsica that the French Army and Navy, under American air cover, carried out a successful combined operation. This caused certain changes in the high command and Gen. Giraud lost his post as commander-in-chief.

This brings us up to the time of the landing in Southern France in August 1944. Several French divisions, fully equipped with American material, and with excellent morale, participated with the American 7th Army. The F.F.I. using mostly captured weapons, aided materially in the northward advance. The civilians showered us with flowers, wine and kisses! Oh, there were many kisses for the Americans. I know, for I was liaison with an American regiment. Incidentally, I had the pleasure of seeing my own chateau liberated. It was located in Domaine de Molbosquet, in the Alps Mountains, near Vence, France, where I stayed three days. The Germans, fortunately, had not removed any of my property. For this, I was extremely happy.

There were some terrorists operating in France, but they were of bad character, operating against anyone primarily for their material gain. They were an avaricious and undesirable lot of cutthroats.

In concluding, I would like to add that France does not fear Communism. France's political desire is to, firstly, restore order once more under Gen. DeGaulle's leadership, and secondly, to build a new Fourth French Republic. France must have aid in rebuilding its industry, for the Germans have stolen most of the rolling stock, war materials and everything else, practically, except one - that desire of every true Frenchmen to be a part of the great and 'New' Fourth French Republic!

November 26

Now Oflag 64 has a War Correspondent from the *Atlanta Journal*, Wright Bryan, who resided at 2513 Peachtree Road in Atlanta, Georgia. We haven't had one of these birds in camp since Larry Allen left in the

Spring. Larry, we hear, is "telling the truth" back in the good old States, but, do the people believe him? It's doubtful.

Overseas Veteran

Oflag 64 is host to Capt. Eugene M. Witt, 2037 Idlewild, Richland, Michigan, where his baby twins, whom he has never seen, and his wife reside. Capt. Witt has been overseas since June 1941 at which time he landed in Iceland. Witt's resume of Iceland:

He liked Iceland and its people. The people of Iceland are great family people, who live in small houses, who believe in trial marriages and place a great deal on chastity. However, it is not uncommon for the fiancé of a girl to visit and sleep with her, in the same room with the whole family, for several months prior to marriage! Mutton is the staple meat, for the sheep are the only domestic animal that can live and thrive on the moss, which provides the only year round green forage. Entertainment is noticeably lacking. Since the coming of the Yanks, however, American movie films are becoming more and more popular, particularly with the young people.

December 1, 1944

To give a slant on "Kriegy" thought, on food mostly, here follows Number 14 of "The Item,"

Last Annual Winter Issue

The Oflag 64 Item

Circulation: 1130, Still Growing

"One ITEM 's Worth 10,000 Pictures"

No. 14   Altburgund, Germany — December 1, 1944   Price: 50 Pfg

Annual Minstrel, Swingland, Glee Club Program, Yule Festivities Celebrate Kriegy Christmas Season Here

OFLAG NEWS ● IN BRIEF ●

● In the midst of a global war, when kriegies were boiling their old shoes for soup, an outside civilian agency peered into the future last month and sent the Oflag — of all things — one each lawnmower and ice cream freezer!

● A firm believer in keeping warm at all costs, "Cheerful Charlie" Cheatham, of the White House, says appels are all the same to him now. He has to get up and dress for all of them.

● Lt. "Honest John" Rodgers, only American newsboy in Germany, has just been decorated. He has, since May 17, 1944, when he took over the job, distributed 300 German newspapers a day, or a total of 585,000 newspapers, to news-hungry kriegies.

● This really happened: The door to Altburgund Academy banged open. Principal Gruenberg rubbed his hands in anticipation as he faced the new arrival:

"Ah! and which classroom are you looking for?"

"Classroom hell, buddy — where's the Mart? I want food!"

Girl of The Month

Gay Paree is no idle rumor, according to a newly-arrived Kriegie who was there and carried this away as evidence... We're convinced.

Oflag's Catholics Prepare Spiritual Scroll for Pope

An elaborate 40-inch hand-lettered spiritual scroll from the Catholic faith in the Oflag, has recently been completed for presentation to his Holiness, Pope Pius XII.

The Scroll, containing an official See SCROLL, Page Two

Revamped Minstrel Opens Monday

The second annual Robert E. Lee Minstrel, complete w/1 ea. steamboat captained by Russ Ford, will dock at the Little Theater for six nights starting December 4th, with a full cargo of dusky comedy and Stephen Foster melodies.

Howard Holder will again act as interlocutor, while last year's end men, Syd Thal and Bill Fabian, will be augmented by Don Waful and Jack Cook, with the addition of four chocolate—colored beauties—Kermit Hansen, Keith Willis, Wilbur Sharpe and Leo Farber—the "Queenie" of last year's show.

Following the Minstrels, Bob Rankin will take over on the 16th with a four — night Swingland.

Christmas will be celebrated will carol singing by the Glee Club at the evening meal on Christmas Eve, and a musical program in the theater directed by Russ Ford and Bob Rankin to be presented continuously Christmas afternoon and evening for six performances.

The New Year will be ushered in on the 31st by the opening of John Hannan's production of the Broadway smash comedy hit "Room Service."

War's Coldest Rumor Brings Winter Olympics to Oflag's Sports

By: David Englander

According to the war's coldest rumor, plans are afoot — or underfoot — to bring the Winter Sports Festival to Altburgund.

Our winter games experts are already drafting plans to prepare Oflag 64 as the scene of the great sports fete.

The athletic field will be converted into a skating rink. Supper coffee will be used to make the ice and special guards will be mounted on the skates to keep the ice from eating into the steel.

The walk around camp will be prepared as a toboggan slide. This will be the damndest toboggan slide in the world, since it will follow the design of a four-wall handball court with several built-in roller coaster features.

Construction of a ski jump is under discussion, but will probably not be carried through because you know why.

Crackerjack, popcorn and peanut concessions will probably be assigned but transport problems may make supply questionable. Bring your own refreshments — black bread will do.

In case of inclement weather, the program will be adjourned indoors where seminars will be held around the stoves on popular novels like "Cold Journey" and "Life among the Eskimos."

December 5, 1944 - Morale Shoots Up!

After being out of Red Cross food parcels for seven weeks, a shipment of 2,350 has just arrived and every officer (some 1,145) has been issued a parcel. "It's wonderful to feel full once more," is the general murmur. "Hurray for the Red Cross," is the common feeling.

Dear Diary, Scales Don't Lie!

Three weeks ago, Col. Paul Goode, S.A.O., had everyone weighed. Each was weighed again today and it was found that the average loss of weight per officer was 7.3 pounds! Only four officers had gained. One was the new mess officer in charge! He, good naturedly, took a lot of joshing. Things could be a lot worse, though.

Lt. Col. Jimmy Lockett

To arrive recently was Lt. Col. Lockett, San Antonio, Texas, who was my company commander in 1937-38, while I was serving one year in the regular army at Ft. Sam Houston, Texas. Lockett, by being such a good staff officer, is still a Lt. Colonel. (He has forgotten more military science than I ever knew.) "C'est la guerre." He tells many amusing anecdotes, which are briefly related:

In my experience around Gellenkirchen, I found the going pretty tough, particularly against the pillboxes and Bunkers. The Hun (slang term for Germans during the War) in the pillbox is finicky when tanks approach. They readily come out waving white flags. One morning we came across two tanks in a big trench. The occupants refused to come out or surrender, so the bulldozer came along and buried the tanks and occupants under Mother Earth!

After the capture of small towns around Aachen, we found the civilians very humble, submissive and cooperative. We only took soldiers as POWs. One old man who acted suspiciously when asked why he was not in the German army, stated that he had heart trouble. I called for a medico to check his heart, whereupon he confessed, 'I'm a soldier but not a spy.' 'Well, what are you doing here?' was the question. 'I have been staying with a widow here. The bombs killed her husband. I think my wife was, too, so I just thought I'd cheer her for a while.'

Later, after I was captured southeast of Aachen on the Ruhr River, a Hun who claimed he had lived in New Jersey for several years, and who appeared to be an interrogator stated, 'By the way, I'm engaged to a girl in Jersey. Do you think she'll marry me after the war?'

'I believe she will,' I said. He slapped me on the back and led me to his house. I was treated with cigars, wine and a good dinner! The treatment at Limburg was not so bad; however, I was placed in confinement in the castle, where I was given only soup and a broth stew, in a large pan.

Some of my observations

The older Germans seem fed-up with the war, at least some of them. The younger men arrogantly say that they will win the war in 1945. Germany's motor transportation is in poor condition. On the other hand, I found their railway transportation in fairly good working order, in spite of the Allied Air claims.

December 10

From the camp News Board (Lt. Diggs, Editor):
The German Press claims protection by an extensive trench fortification, against the immanent Russian drive along the Vistula in Poland. 28,000 trenches and 100,000 "bunkers" have been constructed.

December 13 - Christmas Parcels Arrival

The Inventory
1 Game set
1 Deck of cards
1 Pipe
1 Pipe tobacco
1 Hand towel
1 Picture, Devil's Tower, Wyoming
4 Packages of chewing gum
2 Fruit bars, 2 oz. each
1 Box Tetley tea
1 Can Chef Paulin's turkey, 12 oz.
1 Can Kemp's nuts, 7 oz.
1 Can Richardson's plum pudding
1 Can Potted ham, 3 oz.
1 Can Vienna sausage, 6 oz.
1 Can Kraft cheese, 4 oz.
1 Can Kraft butter, 3-1/2 oz.
1 Can Royal Ann cherries. 8 oz.
1 Can Branch candy, 12 oz.
1 Can Pure Clover honey, 8 oz.
1 Can Chimmel pineapple jam, 6 oz.

Compare this Christmas Parcel with last year's under date December 15, 1943!

Col. Paul Goode requested of the local authorities that (1) they cut the bread ration 20 grams per officer for three days, and in lieu issue the equivalent flour for baking purposes; (2) they make available the Schubin bakery for Christmas baking; and (3) they issue spices and pickles for seasoning, etc. This will make a real Christmas "bash." "Kriegies" are making their own ovens out of Red Cross tins, using the Red Cross containers as fuel! In other words, we are celebrating Christmas, even though we are behind the barbed wire.

Devil's Tower brings to mind a parachute stunt, performed by the professional parachutist, Hopkins. He dropped on the tower and got a lot of publicity getting down! This same Hopkins was a Private in the parachute company, which I commanded in 1941. As rumor gave it, he was discharged from the Officer's Candidate's School in 1941, for being a bigamist.

December 24 (Christmas Eve in Schubin)

With the thermometer sinking to 7.5° F, but with "Kriegies" cooking, basting, boiling, baking, and bashing the Red Cross parcel, it is a Merry Christmas – even under these circumstances. Even though some of us haven't seen or eaten whole eggs and milk for over sixteen months, it could be a lot worse. We are alive, and that is a lot to be thankful for. Perhaps us Americans are the most spoiled people under God's sun - America, the land of plenty! God's Country! Ask any POW!

Hobbies in foods! For "Kriegies," after the war, food preparation will be a popular hobby!

December 25 - Christmas in Altburgund

Some 1,200 officers celebrate either their first, second or third Christmas behind the renowned barbed wire.

December 29

Two American Officers are sentenced to die for nothing! Lt. Col. William Schaefer and Lt. Carl Schmid were today sentenced by a German Military Court Martial to die for "Acts against the Reich." Several months previous to this, Lt. Col. Schaefer, upon learning that the local Germans were going to post propaganda bulletins in camp, ordered Lt. Schmid to stand at the door and protest the action. He did, but with no violence or force, and now, both of them are to pay the price with their lives. The trial, with Col. Paul R. Goode, S.A.O, and two other Americans attending, took place at Posen. In the words of Col. Goode:

> The trial was a cut and dried affair
> with closed doors to begin with. The
> German lawyer, hired by the Swiss
> Delegation, had no influence whatever over

the court. Now the case must rest for three months before the execution date. The sentence requires the Fuhrer's approval. There is a small hope for their lives, particularly Col. Schaefer's.

Every officer in camp heard the verdict with complete awe and apathy, but without any violence or demonstration whatsoever. Discipline in Oflag 64 under three senior officers, has always been and will always be, exemplary. This is American Army tradition.

Chapter Twenty Five
January 1945

January 1, 1945 - New Year in Schubin

I shall always remember this New Year, for it was then when the temperature hit 1° F. The "Goons" refused to give new arrivals (160 officers) any blankets, and we had to cut our quota to two instead of four, which was the number we had last year (everybody used towels, clothes, and paper and made bed sacks to keep warm, plus sleeping with everything on.). Three boxcars of Red Cross food parcels arrived and we went back on the one-per-week issue. (Funny, we Americans, the appreciation of the Red Cross rises and falls like a barometer, depending on the parcel supply!) Some of the new officers just arriving from Lemburg, report that Allied bombs fell on a barrack there two weeks ago, killing about eighty officers and enlisted men.

On New Year's Day everybody in Oflag 64 joined the "Home-in-45" Club.

January 4 - The Scales

Weighing of officers was carried out again this week. The average loss of weight was two and a half pounds. Now that we are back on Red Cross parcels, body weight should increase.

Flowers for the American Red Cross

The time-old saying that food is the greatest morale factor in human life could never be more definitely true than was demonstrated during the first week of parcel issue, following the seven weeks of being without them. Now that we have them, morale was never higher in Oflag 64.

January 5 - "Repats" Leave

Lt. Col. Nath Hoskett, who arrived here in July 1944, with six other officers, having passed the Repatriation Board, took leave for their homeward journey.

Save-Me-the-Bones, Pal

Capt. Clarence Fergenson, Texas, set a snare and caught a rabbit, but another "Kriegy" got it, cooked it, and ate it. Capt. Ferguson tracked him down, but it was too late! So-o-o, he informed the rabbit snatcher to save him the bones next time!

From the Press

Hans-Ulrich Rudel, Germany's greatest air ace, was decorated and promoted to Colonel at the age of twenty-six. He is accredited with 2,400 Allied planes and 463 Panzers. A squadron or group leader gets credit for all squadron or group victories. He receives his decorations and promotions, not by the length of service on the job, but by his meritorious actions. Thereby, this system gives the individual the full incentive to excel.

January 6, 1945

According to the press, the Allied Headquarters has undergone a shake-up. In my conclusion, drawn from opinions of various new arrivals, the success of the German Major offensive caught the Allied Armies by surprise. The obvious weaknesses of the Allied Command are lack of relegated operational power to Army Group Commanders, lack of Reserves, and poor air and ground reconnaissance. How right or how wrong am I?

January 7 - Boy Reaches Manhood in the "Bag"

Young 2nd "Luey" Jack Carpenter became 21 today, after almost two years in the "bag."

"I'm old enough to shave and do, I'm old enough to vote, but don't," confirms Jack.

"Men, Defend to the Last Man!"

A conversation between three "Kriegies," Lt. Col. Jimmy Lockett, Lt. Col. "Klem" Oakes and a new Captain went like this:

The Captain, "My Company was defending a mile on the Aachen Front, with every man on the line at the time of my capture."

Lt. Col. Lockett, "Didn't you hold out a company reserve?"

The Captain, "No, I didn't have enough men to hold the front line."

Lt. Col. Lockett, "You didn't hold it anyway, so why violate the regulations of Field Manual 7-5?"

Lt. Col. Oakes, "Why, in Tunisia, my battalion had 45 miles to defend. I guided a group of 'braves' to Kasserine Pass and explained, 'Now, men, the enemy is all around, and you will cover the front for 5 miles and defend this pass to the last man - all six of you!"

Diary Five

Chapter Twenty Five continued
January 1945

January 14 - Schokken, Germany - Oflag 64-Z

An auxiliary camp has been set up here at Schokken, Germany, for American prisoners of war. A staff from Oflag 64 has been sent here, including Capt. Amelio B. Palluconi, who speaks Italian fluently, Lt. Craig Campbell, who will be my adjutant, from Houston, Texas, Lt. George Muhlbauer, who speaks German fluently, Lt. Pete Lampru, from Jacksonville, Florida, eleven orderlies and myself.

This camp is to be Oflag 64-Z. This was an orphanage in peacetime, and there are now 200 Italian generals and admirals interned in this camp. Col. Gen. Geloso is the Senior Italian: Gen. Blasio, the Executive; Gen. Ationi, Supply Officer; Col. Dulchi, Adjutant, etc. They have been interned here since the Italian armistice, September 1943.

The Americans are to live in one of four big buildings. Our building, Block No. 1, is a fairly nice building, warmer than any of the barracks at Oflag 64, Szubin, Poland. The big question is, "Will we get Red Cross food parcels as does Oflag 64?"

January 15 - First "Kriegies" Arrive

Col. Hurley E. Fuller, San Antonio, Texas, and 87 other Americans arrived this evening at Oflag 64-Z. Col. Fuller relates the following story:

Just before the big German offensive started, for several days I warned the Division Commander of the 28th Infantry Division, of the imminent German offensive in the Bastogne sector. The general and his chief of staff laughed at me! The attack did come. Just prior to my capture, I allowed the chief of staff to hear over the telephone the rattle of machine gun bullets against the walls of the building, which served as my command post. My regiment was all but eliminated when I was captured. The Germans marched 1,800 Americans from the 106th and 28th Infantry Divisions inland 120 miles. They gave us no food or water for three days. No halts were called. The treatment could not have been much worse. All of the officers with me are famished from lack of food and weak from exposure. The people back home would never believe the stories I could tell about the treatment at the German hands.

January 19

The OKW (Oberkommando Wermacht - German Supreme Command) has announced the fall of Litzmannstadt, Tschenstockau, and the evacuation of Warsaw. Cracow was evacuated January 19. Litzmannstadt is about 70 miles from Oflag 64-Z in Schokken, Germany (Skoki, Poland).

This is indeed a precarious situation for prisoners of war. Will we be abandoned or will we be marched out of here on foot, in case of a Russian break-through? Will we still be recognized as prisoners of war and receive protection under the Geneva Convention? What will our status be?

January 20 - "The Kommandant Has a Grave Announcement for You"

At 6:00 P.M. this date, the German interpreter, "unteroffizier" Hegel came to my room and excitedly stated, "The Kommandant, Hauptmann Martz, has a grave announcement for you and Col. Fuller. He would like to see you immediately!" In the Commandant's office five minutes later:

"Gentlemen, due to the grave situation for the Germans, the camp is being evacuated at 4:00 A.M. tomorrow. We have no available transportation, consequently, the Americans and the Italians will be ready to march at 4:00 A.M. Any questions?" asked the camp Kommandant.

"Where do we march?" was my question.

"Westward toward the Reich. Arrangements for quartering and rations will be made along the route," was the reply. (ARRANGEMENTS!!!)

Col. Fuller explained to the Kommandant that many of the officers had no socks or underwear. "The stores will be turned over to you," was the reply. And for the first time to my knowledge, the Germans gave the American prisoners of war all the socks, coats and underwear that were needed! (The obvious reason: The Russians.)

This "bird" Hegel, who had lived in America for several years, working for Bayer Aspirin Co., came to my room to cry on my shoulder with this story:

Colonel, I'm married; I don't know
what to do. My wife and two-week old
baby are in Posen (30 miles to the
southward). What will become of them if
the Russians come? My first
naturalization papers are also there! If I
had those, perhaps I could pose as an
American, in case the Russians capture
us. Do you think I could just borrow an
American uniform - in case - Colonel?

Same old story: "I got caught in Germany and Hitler would not let me return to America."

January 21

At 4:00 A.M., 94 Americans, about 200 Italian Generals, and the German guard company under Hauptman Martz, moved out. The temperature: 15 degrees below zero, according to Hegel.

To describe the Italians in their comical, almost pathetic appearance would require an experienced chronicler, but briefly, they ranged in age from 45 to 71. Now imagine or picture these old fellows; soft, physically unfit from eighteen months of internment, and like babies - trying to carry all their personal belongings, including boots, pictures, clothing, canteens, plates, etc. etc. - in one, two or three suitcases, marching a hundred miles or so!

Before marching a mile, the Americans, following about 200 yards behind, began to stumble over suitcases, boxes, etc. After another mile, we passed one old fellow who had dropped by the roadside from physical exhaustion and old age. A German guard urged him onward, but the cry was, "Imposiblo, imposiblo." What happened to the general I could not say. Likely he froze to death. By 8:00 A.M., several of the Generals had collapsed by the roadside.

The column finally halted after 27 miles hiking at a big farm estate, where we got hot milk from the Poles, and some pork stew. We slept in a horse barn with the horses. Actually, the straw (and the manure) helped to keep the barn warm enough to keep us from freezing.

January 22 - "Schneller, Schneller" (Faster, Faster)

Rumors from local Poles have it that the Russians have encircled Posen, 30 miles to the southwest. "Schneller, Schneller" (Faster, faster) is the German frantic cry. Fortunately, the Italian Generals and Admirals couldn't march faster, faster. The roads were jammed with German civilians, who left everything behind except what they could throw into a wagon. We marched through Rogozno then marched five hours more. We halted at a "Kommando Camp" (a POW work camp). It was 11:50 P.M. at this point. I informed Col. Hurley Fuller of my intention to escape at the very next opportunity.

"Yardley, I'm not telling you not to, but I think you're doing a foolish thing. The Russians will come now any time." (The artillery and tank fire could be heard to our northeast).

"You may be right, Colonel, but being a POW for 16 months is enough for me. I'm taking off if I get the break," was my reply.

January 23 - "Freedom"

At 12:05 midnight, Underofficier Hegel asked for four men to go with him to get some coal. I threw on my roll (hoping), and got the men. I followed this detail out of the barrack, passed the two guards, and when the detail turned right into a building, I turned left and kept going. FREEDOM. It was a wonderful sensation. After walking well out of danger, I stopped in a grove of pine trees, and paused to smoke the best "smoke" in 18 months. I slept in a haystack until 5:00 A.M. and took a compass reading - eastward.

Soon after daylight, I came to a creek crossing, where I almost stumbled into a lone German, who was guarding a small bridge. In a pine forest four miles southwest of Rogozno, and one-half mile from the Rogozno-Oborniki road, I came upon a small cabin, which I reconnoitered until I saw a woman go from the barn into the house. Taking a chance, I knocked on the door for 25 minutes before a man, who seemed very frightened at my presence until he learned my identity, gave me a hearty welcome and food, including eggs, whole milk, pork and bread. It had been 471 days since I had seen such luxuries.

"A Woman and Two Men in a Bed"

Fortunately, this little family turned out to be H. Surowieka, his wife, Helena, and Marina, an old maid cousin. The couple was about 35 years old and had formerly resided at 11/9 Grudlowa St., Lodz (or Litzmannstadt, the German name). This couple had drifted into this house when the German family fled, leaving behind all their worldly possessions, including six hogs, one horse, two milk cows, a few hens and three geese. In 1939, this was a Polish home.

When Hitler crushed Poland, a German family by the name of Lenz had moved in and kicked the Poles out (as was true in all Poland), leaving the Poles without a home. They weren't even allowed to keep their personal possessions. It was all for the "Master Race" - nothing for the defeated. Not even such things as family pictures and marriage licenses. In my new refuge, I found myself, by necessity, sleeping with the man and his wife, the husband in the middle. There was only one bed! For three days the battle raged for the possession of the Rogozno-Oberniki road. Time and again, the Germans counter-attacked from the Posen area, but without success. Many shells tore the road and the villages beyond recognition in this area. Many Polish civilians were caught in the duel.

January 27

The battle having moved in the direction of Posen, I pulled stake and headed toward Rogozno, where I planned to join up with the Russians.

"Sprecken Sie Deutsch"

Traveling through a snowstorm with a compass in mid-winter in Poland is no comfortable feeling; so, I decided to find shelter at some farmhouse for the night and try to reach Rogozno the following day. I approached a little village just before dark and reported to the first civilian, whom I took to be a Pole. When I explained that I was an American, this young man carried me into a house where I was heartily welcomed, fed sweet bread and hot milk. To my surprise, the whole family began to jabber in German! ("Was ist los?") Then I began to look for a way to get out. Whereupon, they explained that they were "Volkdeutche" (German people) and had lived here for twenty-three years; and furthermore, they told this to the German authorities, which had advised them to get out. (Most of the families in the village had left.) This turned out to be the home of Mrs. Emil Zellmer. The whole family seemed happy to have me. Before supper, this Mrs. Zellmer surprised me with a POW card from America. It revealed that "Auntie" had a nephew who is a POW in the States: Gef. Heinz Steinke, I.S.N. 4 WG No. 13268, Co.No.10, Camp Clinton c/o G.P.O. Box 20, N.Y., N.Y.! She requested me to write to him upon my return to America. This family is indeed lucky to be alive. Perhaps they stood well with the local Poles. Her last words to me were, "Der Krieg ist nicht gut" (The war is no good). I wonder if she felt that way in 1939-40, when every German shouted, "Heil Hitler!"

"With the Ruskies"

At early dawn, this date, I came onto the highway just outside Rogozno. The first vehicles to pass me were ten Studebaker 2-1/2 ton trucks and one Russian truck! Next came some General Sherman tanks! On the edge of town by a railway repair shop, I observed some Russian soldiers repairing a GMC left rear spring. I walked up, rather hesitantly, and said "Amerikanski." My welcome was: claps on the back, a bottle of "Vodke," and a feast of bread and fat meat. Not being able to speak a word of Russian, I felt helpless. The best I could deduce was that they wanted me to go with them to whip Hitler. Go along I did.

So, in an American truck with ten Russian soldiers from an artillery regiment which must have been miles ahead by this time, we set off to the Front. The comrades had no suspicions of me, obviously, for I was never searched or stripped. For miles and miles on our westward trek, the road was a continuous stream of foot infantry - thousands of them, marching an average of 46 Kilometers a day, trying to catch up with the Armored units. At Wielan, (Filehne), we stopped for the night, at a German General's house. The whole family had fled, leaving everything behind. There were fresh eggs in the house and feed still in the troughs for the cows!

Next, I rode in a horse-drawn coach with a front-line Infantry reconnaissance battalion until we reached Kreuz, Germany, on the Netze River, where the Russians had run into stubborn German Panzer units the day before.

Marshal Zhukov, 20th Century Genghis Kahn - Escape to Freedom

Lucky, free American ex- "gefangeners" (prisoners), after one to twenty-eight months of imprisonment, by luck, fate or by God, found themselves in an unprecedented situation: for it was on Jan. 21, 22, 23 that Marshal Zhukov's mighty Russian Armies ploughed through the area of Poland, Szubin (Altburgund), "Skoki" (Schokken), Posen, where American, British, French, Italian, and Yugo-Slav prisoner of war camps were located.

Many tales and yarns will be told about this "liberation" business. Here is what actually happened: POWs either escaped or joined the first Russian unit, Armored or Infantry, or similar units liberated them. In any event, the moment they were identified, by word or by other means, as "Amerikanski," the welcome was extremely friendly, hearty and cordial. The reception or welcome consisted of too much "spiritas" (a potent 192 proof Russian drink) raw fat meat, whole grain bread and anything else the "Rusky" soldier might have. In many cases, the "Rusky" gave his fur-lined mittens, his fur-lined coat or his wool cap to a needy American comrade! Out of the bigness of his heart, anything he had was yours.

On the other hand, there were instances of "roughing about," taking of personal watches, etc., but this very rarely happened. For example, I know of only two positive cases. A drunken Russian soldier slapped Lt. L. W. (Old Folks) Spence, from Emory, Texas (formerly in my barracks, Oflag 64, Szubin, Poland) in the face. The Russian also took his G.I. watch. Lt. S. E. Solmer lost three rings (why wear three rings, anyway?) and a watch. These cases were exceptional and occurred where drunken "Ruskies" were encountered or where there was a doubt of identity. The thing uppermost in every ex-"Kriegy's" mind, quite naturally, was immediate evacuation, first to the rear and then to America. And here is where the difficulty and disappointment occurred. The "Rusky" soldier, with a shot of "spiritas" under his belt, wanted his comrades, the "Amerikanskies" who, by this time were spirited up, to go along and "kill more Germans." So, many found themselves, quite unavoidably, moving along with front-line Armoured and Infantry Units. (Oh! For one of those fine Studebaker trucks and a ride back to Moscow!) Americans all over Poland and Eastern Germany were wandering around, going forward, going to collecting points or trying to hitchhike to Moscow. The situation for everyone except the Russians was one of confusion, discontent and anxiety. But for our allies, the Russians, there was no confusion or doubt as to their task; "Onward to Berlin!"

Marshal Zhukov - His Ruskies (Russia's Number Two Man) - An Observation

To better understand and to visualize the operations of Marshal Zhukov and his mighty hordes, read Charles Lamb's *Genghis Khan* and *The Earth is the Lord's* by Taylor Caldwell. Combine this picture with one of a 20th century army that is successfully driving the Wehrmacht and Hitler's troops westward through Germany, and methodically cutting the guts out of "Deutschland."

Zhukov, defender and hero of Stalingrad, is the number two man in Russia. He and Marshal Stalin hold the highest order of decoration in Russia, "The Order of Victory." Zhukov is the favorite of the Russian G.I.. According to Maj. Gen. Pawel Firsov, Commander of the Russian 5th Army, Marshal Zhukov was given the central Poland sector (Litzmannstadt, Posen, Landsberg, etc.) because it was considered to have been the hardest nut to crack. Zhukov's armies crossed the Vistula at dawn on January 12, 1945 (as did Marshal Konev's armies).

400 Kilometers in Sixteen Days

In an almost unprecedented lightning drive, Zhukov's advanced Panzers rolled the German line back 400 kilometers in 16 days, from the Vistula to bridgeheads across the Odor. According to the "Rusky" soldier, no prisoners were to be taken during the first three days of the great offensive! (Incidentally, the order is still in effect, as far as the "Rusky" GI is concerned.) I traveled with a Russian artillery section from Rogozno to Wielan (Filehne), then from Wielan to Drieson, on the Netze River with an infantry battalion. During this trip, I saw only six living Germans! They were the only prisoners of war whom I saw until I returned to Filehne, one week later. Here, there were fifty! Many of the German civilians who could not get out met a similar fate. I saw many dead civilians along the roads in Eastern Germany. The towns were not destroyed, however, unless Jerry defended it. In this case, artillery and tank fire quite naturally did a thorough job. One Russian lieutenant, who spoke English, explained, "There's nothing too severe for the Germans. When they invaded Russia, they destroyed our towns and many of our factories, burned our cultural buildings and homes. In many instances, they entered our towns, locked the people in cellars under the homes, and upon departure, the houses were set on fire and the people slowly baked to death. You wait until you have traveled a few miles inside Russia, and you will see." (More eyewitness stories shall be related later on.)

The Russian Officer

The Russian officer is university educated, or self-educated, smart in appearance, very friendly and quite democratic with his follow soldiers. From what I can ascertain, the requirements for a commission in the Red Army are higher than in our army. Captains frequently command battalions; Majors, regiments; and Colonels, divisions. In the Russian Army, discipline is an understood thing. Officers are quite friendly and close to the soldiers. The front line officers and men, by necessity, work, eat, drink and sleep together - but that doesn't lower the standard of discipline one bit. When an order is given, the soldier quite often argues his point. The officer does not get offended or "rattled"; but he,

after a great deal of patient listening, directs the
execution of the original order, with or without changes
or recommendations.

The Russian Soldier

To be quite frank, I never met a bigger hearted
individual than the "Rusky" GI. Carefree, cool, collected,
generous, fatalistic, lovable are words, which weakly
describe the "Rusky." I say he is a fatalist because I'm
almost certain of it. Lt. John Siska, from Warren, Ohio,
who speaks Russian, and I were with an infantry
battalion on the road just outside of Krenz, Germany,
which is on the Netze River near Driesen, when
attacked by four ME 109s. The planes made four sweeps
up and down the columns, strafing and dumping out
"butterfly" grenades. But, did this incident excite the
"Rusky?" Not in the least! In fact, the column never
stopped, but doggedly marched on "come what may!"
Were there wounded and killed, you may ask?
Certainly! And horses were killed, too. We placed the
killed and wounded beside the road and removed the
harnesses from the wounded horses. The stragglers
rejoined their unit in Krenz.

The "Ruskies" laughed at Lt. Siska and me for
hitting the ground each time the planes came over. Lt.
Siska asked a captain why such fatalism, "Oh, well." he
answered, "If we die, we die for our people and comrade
Stalin. We are here to kill as many Germans as fast as
we can, so that we may go home." The hate for the
Germans, the will to kill them, plus the effect of Vodka
or "spiritas" produces the toughest soldier in the world:
the "Rusky." This hatred for the Germans, plus the will
to kill them, forms a common tie among all Russians.
What is that but discipline? That is discipline.

The age range of the soldier is from twelve to sixty-
five. Often father, son and daughter are in the same
unit. The "Rusky" can, and often does, march sixty-five
kilometers in twenty-four hours. (So do the "Rusky"

girls, who, with the Infantry, are usually nurses or ordinary soldiers.) At halts, which might be every two or four hours, he plops in the snow and sleeps.

The "Rusky" soldier lives off the land as much as possible. He is an excellent forager and ransacker. All German houses were thoroughly ransacked but not burned - as was the case in vice versa. The emergency ration, which is usually American canned goods, is never touched as long as the land will furnish the necessary requirements.

The "Rusky" travels very lightly, carrying only his weapon, ammunition and a bottle of "spiritas." The "spiritas" not only supplements the fat meat in calories, but also fires up his fighting spirit!

The discipline while marching, too, is a funny thing. If a "Rusky" sees a bird, he drops out of the column to try his skill. If it is successful, the rest of his comrades, including the officers, have a big laugh. He also practices on dead "Goons" (Germans) along the roads! The dead often remained unburied for weeks. "The cold weather freezes the bodies, so there is no hurry," explained one officer.

When the Russian GI is on guard duty and becomes tired after three or four hours, he usually fires off his weapon either into the air or at the top of the building where his relief is sleeping, until he is relieved. A funny thing, this! It became a saying among the Americans, when the "Rusky" fired his weapon, "Well, it's time to change guard!"

There is another saying that "War is fought for rings, pocket-knives and watches." The "Rusky" got his share of them in Poland and Germany. Unfortunately, but not as a rule, a lot of Poles lost their rings and watches. I saw one "Rusky" with a pocket full of rings and watches! He tried to give me a handful. No harm was really meant. I have seen Americans fight this war of rings and watches in Africa and Sicily.

The soldier never complains about his food or treatment. Give him "spiritas," a newspaper for cigarette paper, some Russian tobacco, and fat meat, and he is happy - if he can move on and kill more Germans. One may ask, "How can the soldier fight if he is spirited up or drunk?" I personally saw very few drunken soldiers. If he got drunk and unruly, his commanding officer beats the stuffin' out of him with his fist or the butt of his pistol. Lt. John Siska, Capt. James Maher, Jr. from Huntington, Indiana, and I saw a Russian major knock a drunken soldier down three times with his fists, and stomp on him until he was sober or lifeless - I don't know which! That's the Russian way of disciplining a drunken "Rusky."

The "Rusky," to my great surprise, is pretty well informed on international politics and American generals. Many of them knew that Generals Eisenhower and Clark had been decorated by Marshal Stalin.

On January 31 at Wielan, the soldiers informed us of the Roosevelt-Stalin-Churchill conference in the Crimea. An *Izvesta* newspaper, sort of a Russian *Stars and Stripes*, carried news of Marshal Stalin's congratulations to President Roosevelt upon his inauguration into office for his fourth term. Lt. John Siska interpreted the article, which read:

> The U.S.S.R. hopes that the same
> friendly relations between Russia and
> America shall continue for many, many
> years . . . after Nazi-ism is completely
> destroyed . . . so that the world can once
> again live in peace. Americans can never
> know the Nazi as we know him. He came
> to our land, killed our civilians, and
> destroyed our homes, towns and factories.
> It is hoped now that the President will visit
> Russia to see for himself this wanton
> destruction inflicted upon us by the Nazi
> armies. All Russians sincerely hope that
> some day all Americans will know the
> truth.

This same little paper also carried the news of the fall of Frankfort on the Odor River. For this magnificent achievement, Moscow gave Marshal Zhukov and his armies a twenty-salvo (a firearm discharge) salute. (The "Ruskies" were very happy to be part of Zhukov's "People's Army.")

Ask the "Rusky" how he likes "American trucks," and he will say, "Studebakers." He is also familiar with the Aero-cobra fighter, and the Boeing bomber. He knows the Jeep, but can't speak for its performance. Staff officers and generals only have the "Jeeps."

The way to make a good impression on the "Rusky" is to borrow his tommy-gun, and shoot a German, or shoot up the inside of a German house until the rafters rattle like skeletons.

The Russian WAC

One will find "Rusky" girls in any unit of the Russian armies, as clerks, cooks, military police, drivers, soldiers and interpreters. They are just as rugged and tough as the males. Many smoke cigars, when the cigars are available. Through necessity, she eats, sleeps and works with the soldiers. There is no such thing as privacy. They are sweet, calm, carefree, and fatalistic - like their brother soldiers. Many of them are really beautiful, particularly among the officer corps. Lt. Siska, Capt. Maher and I got to know these girls at Wielan, Poland, where we stayed five days. They cooked and served us food and they were very good talkers, asking many questions about America. It was a pleasure for them to wait on us, and to read the Russian *Stars and Stripes* to Lt. Siska. When they moved forward, they stated that they regretted to leave, but that they had a big job to do on ahead. And don't think that Joe "Rusky" is not proud of his big "sisters." He is; I can assure you.

Lend-Lease

To the average American, it is known that so many millions of dollars worth of materials go to Russia annually under the heading of Lend-Lease. But how many realize how much of this or that, or how many tanks, planes, trucks, cans of meat, etc. actually find their way from America to Russian combat troops? I hardly saw how Mr. John Doe in America could possibly grasp the scope of this tremendous undertaking, or the ultimate effect of this Lend-Lease material. Seeing is believing. I saw.

"Amerikanski Studebaker"

For an escaped American prisoner of war who is walking down the Rogozno road, prior to contact with the "Ruskies," to suddenly see ten American trucks and one Russian truck pass by, that is something - especially in this part of the world! Hundreds of Generals Grant and Sherman tanks, all Lend-Lease vehicles, passed by us. The first ride in an American truck for over eighteen months was a thrill beyond expression. This was on January 27, 1945.

From Rogozno, I was carried to Wielan. The river divides this town, and the west part is in Germany. Hundreds of American trucks streamed past thousands upon thousands of foot infantry, pouring into Germany, down every cow-path and road. Swarms of them - is a better way of putting it. Lt. Siska asked many truck drivers how they liked the American trucks. Nine times out of ten it was the "Studebaker."

Another common American item was the 37mm cannon. The Red Army Infantry liked them and used them to a tactful advantage. The entire bank of the Netze River from Kreuz to Driesen and down to Landsberg was fortified (this was about January 30) with American and British anti-tank and anti-aircraft guns. Early one morning, three ME 109s made their appearance along the Netze near Driesen. In a few seconds, hundreds of anti-craft guns went into action, throwing up a perfect cloud of defense.

I saw many American and British tanks; however, none of them could stand up to the Russian "Voroschilovgrad" tank, which makes the Tiger look rather insignificant. The Russian tank destroyer is a vicious looking machine - a monster compared to any of

Hitler's "V" machines! As far as I could see, all of Russia's war weapons are very practical, adaptable and deadly. And so, let us Americans not claim too much credit in this slow process of grinding to death every single molecule of Nazi-ism. Take one look at the map; there is the story. Measure the distance from Stalingrad to the Odor River. Unfortunately, too few Americans will ever get to know the "Rusky" as a few of us have done. Too few of you can visualize the suffering and hardships the Russians have undergone at the gory, slimy hands of the Nazi. There are two things and two things only that the Germans failed to destroy: the land (or the soil), and the Russian will to fight until victory is won. Please enjoin with me, as an American, who has been, seen and believed. My contention is that Russia owes us nothing. If anything, our debt to her can never be paid.

Lend-Lease is an expedient to aid in the destruction of Nazi Germany; it should never be brought up after the war or used as a political football. "Chas prigot, time will tell, the hour will come," to paraphrase the "Rusky." Be patient and understanding!

Poland and Its People

Poland's flag flies once again after five years of Nazi tyranny. The church and school doors are opening - all since the Russians swept through Poland like a forest fire. Now there is a new fire burning; it is a fire of hope, happiness and rehabilitation. For five long years, the Poles were slaves to the "Master Race." For five years, they were not allowed any public assemblies, schools, church etc. - nothing at all.

There's Still a War Going On

I have previously explained that the Russian army lives on the land - by necessity. Consequently, there will be food famines for a long time to come. There is far more food west of the Vistula then there is east of the Vistula. To our great surprise, the Germans left plenty of food and livestock in the area liberated between January 12 and 28. Russia and Poland will continue to be hungry until families, horses, cattle and farm machinery are returned to the soil. The Ukraine, the Russian "bread basket," will produce those staple crops, wheat and barley, in abundance; but, this cannot be accomplished overnight. In Poland, there are many thousands of acres of wheat and barley already planted for this year's crop. The Poles did it under Nazi direction. There is much farm machinery, but - as in Russia - there is a shortage of horses and tractors.

Poland Needs Canned Milk and Clothing

Poland's most urgent need during the present phase is definitely not political "hot-shots," but loads of canned milk for the babies, clothing, and perhaps vitamins and medical supplies. Malnutrition is prevalent, particularly among Polish "slaves" who have been working for Hitler since 1939, 1940, and 1941. Perhaps UNRRA (United Nations Relief and Rehabilitation Administration) already has this problem under immediate consideration.

Polish Hospitality

I can say from personal experience, and listening to other Americans, that hospitality could not be more real and sincere than it is in Poland. This outward friendliness, in most instances, was warm and humble. I do know, however, that in some cases the show was for an ulterior motive or a personal reason. It was these individuals who were anti-Russian, slightly pro-German, or veterans of the 1939 Russian-Polish war and officers who believed the German propaganda during several years of imprisonment in Germany. Through this reactionary attitude, they tried to stir up resentment among young Americans against our Russian Allies. A surprising number of young Americans become gullible suckers and suddenly imagine themselves future heroes, political saviors of

Poland's so-called "plight." Several Poles tried their influence on me, but without any success. (I shall relate examples later under the heading of "Polish Politics.")

The first Polish citizen who gave me refuge from the Germans was H. Surowicka, whom I previously mentioned. During January 23, 24, 25, German stragglers came to his house for food. The fight was raging at this time for the Rogozno-Oberniki road. Each time the "Goons" came; he hid me under the bed! While staying here, Stanislaw (Joseph) Glowski, a neighbor boy, dropped in. He asked me, upon my return to America, to write his uncle Hendrich Glowski, a professor for twenty years - so Joseph says - at Notre Dame University.

At Kuna, Turek County, Poland (near Konin on the Varta River), Capt. Maher, Lt. Siska, three other Americans, an escaped Polish naval captain (one of those reactionaries), and I stayed for three days with Madame Emilia Delong, her three children and sister-in-law, in one room of the local school building. Before the Germans came, she and her husband had taught school in this little village of six hundred souls (now two hundred). In 1941, the Germans started their barbarous slaughter of educated people and Jews. The Gestapo came one night, got her husband out of bed and shot him, giving no explanation. She doesn't know where his body was taken, but she suspects to the "human soap" factory at Turek, twelve miles from here, where the Germans killed people, extracted their blood for serum, and threw their bodies into two big ovens. The fat was melted from the bodies and used for the manufacture of soap. Madame Delong showed us some pieces of this "human soap." I now possess a bar of it. If the weather had not been inclement, we would have visited this "soap" factory. The Russian press authorities have already written the history of this place and taken photographs of the melting pots. This brave little teacher told many tales of German atrocities, one more of which I shall relate:

The Turek area was under the brutal surveillance of one German Gestapo by the name of Kleibert, who was a pugilist before the war. Kleibert's method was that of the club and blacksnake. On the slightest provocation, he whipped Poles unmercifully; more often than not, the beating resulted in death. In 1943, a small boy in Kuna innocently killed a pig for his family. Kleibert lashed this boy to death.

When the "Ruskies" swept through this area in January, the Poles captured this "hind" Kleibert and held him until he was turned over to a Russian officer. Subsequently, this officer tied Kleibert to a post and sent out this message: 'All Poles who have been beaten by Kleibert come to Turek and beat Kleibert with his own whip.' Thus, Kleibert suffered for his cruel sins, until his own whip gave him a one-way ticket to hell. Lt. Siska and I talked with a young Pole and his two sisters who had walked to Turek to beat this criminal, but they found him hanging to a post, quite dead. An eye for an eye, a tooth for a tooth - yet a crime avenged.

We also heard about the Germans' largest concentration camp, Oswiecim, which was near Cracow. Here, some four million teachers, educated people, and Jews met their deaths in a gas chamber. Madame Delong read us a story from a February 9th copy of *Lodkze*, a Lodz newspaper. Some fifteen thousand prisoners in the Oswiecim concentration camp were annihilated by SS troops. When the Red Armies broke through the Cracow area, German troops guarding fifteen thousand prisoners, in order to lighten their responsibility, marched every single prisoner single-file into the forest, where machine-guns had been set up to defend the defile (a narrow passageway). The guards halted the prisoners in the defile, moved forward, gave the death signal, and fourteen thousand, seven hundred were slaughtered. Only three hundred escaped to tell the story.

Madame Delong, who for many months served as a house slave to the Germans, is now teaching Kuna children between the age of seven and fourteen, none of whom have ever been to school before. The school is opened daily with the children singing "Broze Gos Polske" (God Save Poland).

When the six of us left Kuna, Madame Delong and all of the students cried and tears rolled down their cheeks. God never made a more kind and simple-hearted people. And it is these reactionary upstarts who would throw away many more millions of Polish lives - for selfish reasons?

Polish Politics

Aristocracy, Plutocracy, So-called Democracy, Serfdom . . . Now what?

Was Poland a democracy before 1939? Webster's Dictionary defines democracy, aristocracy, serfdom, tyranny, etc., as being such and such. After listening to many Poles, in many walks of life, I still don't know what Poland was before 1939! "Frankly speaking," to quote a Polish school teacher, "When practically all the farm land in Poland was owned by ten land barons who lived in Warsaw - as was the case before 1939 - this is not a democracy but an aristocracy. When Hitler came, Poland was serfdom. Now what?"

Does anyone know what Poland was, is, or will be? A sore spot of Europe, I say.

London or Lublin

From the date the Lublin government was set up until after the results of the "Big Three" conference were made known, Poland was and still is a melting pot of muddled politics, of misunderstanding, distrust, and confusion. The reactionary groups, whether leaning on the London or the Lublin aide, did nothing but to add more confusion. Those who leaned the London way accused the Lublin boys of being a bunch of Jewish Communists; those who leaned the Lublin way accused the London boys of being a bunch of selfish aristocrats. Who is right?

Perhaps all accusations are biased, unfounded and unreasonable. X plus Y does not equal Z and will not until Nazi Germany is completely crushed. Until then, Poland will inevitably suffer from disorganization, poor communications, improper food distribution, food shortages and - certainly - political clashes.

To reiterate, the Russian soldier lives largely from the land. He must! Furthermore, many Poles can't seem to appreciate the fact that practically all supplies for the Red Army's fighting in Germany must necessarily come through Poland. My guess is that there are two million army service force troops in Poland. They are in the service of supplies. Those troops, quite naturally, eat much of Poland's food and billet (i.e., food left over or abandoned by the Germans) in Polish houses and homes. As the French would say, "C'est la Guerre." In the larger towns, the NKVD (some Poles call it the Russian Gestapo) is placed to keep law and order. From what I gathered, they are very patient and considerate toward the Poles. This is certainly a contrasting picture to "Goon" subjugation.

Poland, a Deficit

After seeing the Ukraine and southern Russia, I am convinced that it will require from ten to fifteen years to rebuild its homes, bridges, towns, etc.

The "Curzon Line" has been established and Russia has her slice. To take any more of Poland would not be feasible. Poland would be a deficit. The "Big Three" guaranteed Poland that she would be a free and independent nation. Then if we, as free thinkers, cannot believe the statements of the world's most powerful men, who are we to believe? Patience! Time will tell. "Cas prigets."

If Americans will use common sense in this Polish question, things will turn out for the betterment of Anglo-American-Russian relationships. This business about Americans being the food basket, the savior, the rehabilitator of the whole world is utterly fantastic! Surely, Poland is hungry (I have seen them eating potato peels from a garbage pile). Certainly, the Poles are fine people. The Russians are just as hungry and poor from this terrible conflict as the Poles.

Don't Believe It!

A certain young lieutenant colonel - we'll call him, Lt. Col. X, Academy educated but without any civilian experience, impressed thirty young Americans in Lublin, Poland on or about February 18, when he "blasted" a Russian major:

Scene 1 -

Lt. Col. X and thirty Americans, who for several days had been living in Warsaw with Polish families, walked into a Russian major's office. There was blood in the lieutenant colonel's eyes. He meets Major "Ruskie." Words are spoken (Incidentally, neither understood the other).

Scene 2 -

Lt. Col. X pounds on the table, growing angry (pretending, of course). Major "Rusky" looks puzzled. Lt. Col. X shouts at Major "Ruskie," "Goddamn it, America is feeding and supplying the whole world, (this sounded good to the thirty officers), and I have thirty Americans here who are starved and sleepy. I demand food and shelter for these officers immediately."

Major "Ruskie," not understanding, but guessing, goes and gets four bottles of vodka.

Scene 3 -

All is well. A toast is drunk for Roosevelt, Churchill and Stalin!

My congratulations to Lt. Col. X, he certainly impressed thirty Americans. One of the lieutenants, who had been in the army for a year and a POW for two years, stated to me:

"God; what a man this lieutenant colonel is! He's the smartest lieutenant colonel in the American Army."

As a matter of fact, this sort of shouting and demanding sometimes gets results. Using firm diplomacy, in my opinion, is a better system. Remember this; no "Rusky" is afraid of anybody, not even the devil himself. I haven't seen a "Rusky" panicky, excited or "rattled," which is more than you can say for a "Goon." A "Goon" reacts or responds like a machine. He doesn't think for himself. This is not true in the case of a "Rusky."

Self-Vindication

When an American makes statements as I have above, he has certainly laid himself open for criticism, which is also an American privilege and characteristic. I hope we will be rational in this Polish-Russian political situation. I don't know what it is all about; I do not want any part of it in America. What has worked in Russia will not work in America. One cannot compare Russia to the United States, using United States standards as a basis. If Poland cannot solve her own political problem without continual bickering and upheaval, then who is the likely neighbor to step in and solve it for her? It's Russia, of course. Civil revolutions after this war might mean another war. I don't believe Russia will permit such carryings-on. The "Big Three'" gave Poland liberal terms and opportunity. Now, how smoothly and capably can the Poles put those terms into execution? Time will tell. The United States certainly has a stake in maintaining peace in Europe for years to come. In my opinion, Poland is a sore spot that will need firm - but considerate - treatment, rendered jointly by the United States, Great Britain and Russia.

All the way from eastern Germany, through the Russian Ukraine to Odessa, I never once saw a "Rusky" who failed to appreciate American Lend-Lease Aid and the importance it has played.

On Going Home - Nice If You Can Get There

Fulfillment of Duty. Once upon a time I was told, as was every officer and soldier - that in event of capture it was my duty to escape from enemy hands. Escape I did. In fact, some ten thousand British and Americans did.

Take down a map of central Europe, glance at the area from the Vistula to the Odor. The Oflags and Stalags were generally concentrated around Bydgoszcz (Bromberg), Poznan (Posen), Poland and Keustrin, Germany. That is to say, most of those ten thousand escapees came from these areas, particularly the Americans. Oflag 64, Szubin (Altburgund): approximately five hundred out of fifteen hundred officers escaped. Oflag 64-Z, Skoki (Schokken), where I was sent to be the Senior American Officer, ninety-eight Americans either escaped or were liberated by the Russians. (Oflag 64-Z was for sixteen months an internee camp for two-hundred Italian generals and admirals, who were picked up by Hitler's Army at the Italian capitulation, September 1943.)

All of these were liberated (those who had not already escaped) with Col. Hurley E. Fuller, United States Army, from San Antonio, Texas, who had been captured on the West Front in the big German offensive in December 1944. At Stalag III - C, Keustrin, some nineteen-hundred American non-commissioned officers and men escaped. Keustrin is on the Odor River. On January 28, Russian columns thrust into this area, but withdrew the next day.

Puzzlement

With this orientation in mind, try to follow this "escape-to-freedom" business through curious, crazy, queer events until evacuation became a reality - not a horrid nightmare or dream. Some individuals or groups of individuals escaped from columns, which were under German Wehrmacht guards; some escaped by overpowering their guards; some were liberated when the Russians captured the columns or POW camps and slew the guards; some were left to their freedom when the local guards deserted their posts and fled from the "Ruskies."

Without repeating the story of the commotion and confusion at first contact with the Russian Allies, it might be stated that the great majority of the "Ruskies" were as puzzled at seeing the Americans as the Americans were at seeing the "Ruskies." Because Roosevelt, Churchill and Stalin had come to an agreement on the exchange of liberated soldiers, was no guarantee that the average "Joe Rusky" knew about it. Red tape in the front lines is a myth. At no time did I see a morning report or a casualty list. "Oh, well, so many 'Joe Ruskies' killed! So what?" Things just happen and solve themselves. The situation just takes care of itself.

So, it took about thirty days for things to work themselves out. Until official orders came down from Marshal Zhukov's headquarters and officers were dispatched for this Allied round-up, no one knew what the score was. Some were advised by "Rusky" soldiers to catch trains to Moscow! A few Americans did get to Moscow, I understand. Many others were attempting to, when picked up and sent to collecting points set up at Exin, Charnakau, Prague, Rembertow and Lublin. Many Americans - call them "big operators" - went AWOL from at least three different collecting points - to be picked up again and corralled. This irregular conduct - to the humiliation of American Senior Officers - may or may not be excused due to the most unusual circumstances, to such abnormal conditions, to the strain and tension of the whole "business," to the over-eagerness to get home and to downright stupidity on the part of many delinquents. (Strange, this nostalgia was more apparent among short term ex-"Kriegies" than old timers.)

There is one argument in their defense. Small groups fared much better, made faster time to the rear and ate better than did the larger groups. Repercussions of this AWOL business: Russian and American Senior

Officers at these various collecting points found the strength dwindling to only a handful of duty-bound officers; consequently, an orderly and systematic evacuation become almost impossible. Russian officers, though not too disturbed about it, were amazed at the show of American impatience. It was not until a sizeable collection of officers was achieved at Lublin and Rembertow (just outside of Prague - east Warsaw) that final evacuation got under way for about forty-five hundred American and British, who rated priority over the other nationalities.

This narrative from here on will deal with the human or inhuman side of the American, the "Rusky," and the British - for what it is worth - if anything - at these various places previously mentioned and until "God's Country" is reached.

January 28 - Kreuz, Germany

Here, Lt. John Siska, Lt. S.E. Selmer, and two Italian officers from Oflag 64-Z saw the little town cleared of the last two German soldiers. They were hidden in a house. A Russian officer shot them in their bellies with his pistol, then borrowed a soldier's rifle and shot their brains out. We saw one living German, a girl about sixteen. She was not being molested; on the contrary, some "Ruskies" were preparing a meal for her.

Lt. Franco Saba, a Sicilian from Catania, Sicily, under the influence of too much "spiritas," became numb and his foot froze. When he sobered up - after a siege of rubbing and thawing - he began to cry and shout. "Comrade, Rusky," and "Viva Stalin, Viva Bagdolio!" More yelps . . . A "Rusky," patting his tommy gun, said he would put him to sleep! He would have, permanently, if Lt. Siska, who speaks Russian, hadn't interceded.

January 29

Capt. James Maher, Jr., who had spent the night in Major Gen. Powel Firsov's headquarters, joined us. Gen. Firsov was a great admirer of Lt. Gen. George Patton. He stated that all Russian "Panzer" generals liked Patton's methods and tactics.

January 30 - Wielan (Filehne), Poland.

It was here that we met the cigar-smoking "Rusky" WACs. It was here that we heard the highest praise for the Aero-cobra, General Sherman tanks, and Studebaker. Here, a Russian major apologized for not being able to "furnish" us with girl companions!

Lt. S. B. Selmer wandered off down the street and found an abandoned car. He liked it and proceeded to place it in running order. Two curious "Ruskies" took him to be a German trying to escape and came near shooting him!

"Ruskies" kill their meat with tommy-guns. Standing by Hotel Hess, Lt. Siska was asked if he would like to have some fresh pig. Yes, he would; so, the "Rusky" pulled out his tommy-gun and sprayed the first stray pig that came by. We had meat all right, with plenty of holes in it.

All of the vacated houses in Wielan contained plenty of good food, such as canned cherries, pears, apples, blueberries, cheese, jam and potatoes. Great quantities of candy and chocolate cocoa were abandoned in a building adjacent to Hotel Hess. The Germans, from a food standpoint were far better off than we ever dreamed.

January 31 - Szubin, Poland - Oflag 64

Oflag 64 was evacuated on this date, as was Oflag 64-Z. Col. F. W. Drury and about sixty other Americans were permitted by the German doctors (in effect, they were "permitted" by Capt. Burgenson, Senior American Medico) to remain behind for "physical" reasons. Four officers hid out in my old abandoned tunnel at Oflag 64, which, after six months, still remained a mystery to the "Goons."

About two-hundred Red Cross food parcels were left for the sixty officers. Eight thousand food parcels were abandoned at Dietfort, thirty-five kilometers away. (These had been strictly under German control) It was learned later that the eight thousand parcels fed Poles, Germans - and later Russians. The "Ruskies" took out the cigarettes and chocolate and threw the other items by the roadside. Lt. Siska saw a wagonload of those parcels being stripped for cigarettes and chocolate near Charnakav, which is about 110 kilometers from Dietfort! "C'est la Guerre!"

By four in the afternoon on this date, no Germans remained in this area. The Poles and the sixty Americans celebrated the occasion. Many got drunk. The Poles thoroughly ransacked the living quarters, theater, etc. Some six thousand "Y" books and some ten thousand dollars worth of musical instruments were stolen, destroyed, scattered or trampled! Why, I wish to ask, didn't some sensible American officer turn those books and musical instruments over to the mayor of the town? The next day, the "Ruskies" came and completed this looting business. A Russian press representative took some pictures, passed out the "spiritas" and said, "Well boys, we have come to take you to Moscow!" It sounded good all right. The "Ruskies" always mean well.

"You just wait here," they would say, "You will be evacuated to Moscow very soon!" "Cas prigets," the hour will come . . .

On February 6, with six companions, I returned to Oflag 64 to find about one hundred Americans still there. Col. George Millet and about fifty others just left on American trucks for Warsaw, where an American mission was supposed to be!

Keustrin, Germany, Stalag III - C - January

The story of how nineteen hundred and eighty-five American non-commissioned officers and enlisted men were liberated from the German claws at Keustrin, under most unusual circumstances was told me by 1st Sgt. Leroy Coleman, Newton, Mass., and Staff Sgt. W.

A. Miller, Sewickly, PA. (Keustrin, on the Odor River, forty-five miles east of Berlin, was announced captured March 14 in the *Egyptian Mail*, the Cairo newspaper!)

On January 31, according to the two sergeants, Russian tank columns occupied Keustrin. Except for the Stalag III – C Guard Company, most all of the Germans fled across the Odor – at least those capable of fleeing. Subsequently, the Stalag came under fire from General Sherman tanks. The "Oberst," German Colonel, ordered the guard company to march the POWs out. The Oberst and his wife fled in an automobile but were both killed a few hundred yards from the Stalag. Once outside the lager, the tanks fired point-blank on the column, killing fifteen Americans, and one "Rusky" POW. (Some forty "Rusky" POWs were with the Americans.) The guards fled back to the barracks. A few "Ruskies" contacted the Red Army column of tanks. The other "Ruskies" over-powered the guards, taking their weapons. Then, the long awaited revenge commenced.

Every "Goon," except one German sergeant, who had previously befriended the Russian POWs, was hunted down, dragged out of the buildings and put to death. One German captain committed suicide. One "Goon" who had cruelly mistreated the "Ruskies," was forced to sit on a stump while his jugular veins were cut - slowly but surely - with a dull razor blade. By the time this gory operation had ended, another "Goon" was hanged by the big toes with wire and cut to pieces by knives and razor blades, and the tanks had arrived upon the scene. To the surprise of Sgt. Miller and the other Americans, half of the tank personnel were Russian WACs. A female captain, smart, good looking, smoking a cigar and driving a General Sherman tank, commanded the tank company.

By nightfall the infantry came. Many of them were also female. The next day, the Americans marched toward Driesen. Two days later, the Germans re-occupied Keustrin!

January 20 - Thorn, Poland, Stalag 20 - A (British)

The following bits of information of what took place in the Thorn area, which is east of Bromberg, were gathered from Capt. Geoffrey Allen, RAMC, Durham, England and Corp. George Forrester, Harper Road, London S.E.I.:

Peculiar things happened . . . the Volkdeutsche were ordered to defend. Some did, some didn't. Uprising Poles killed those who did. Those who didn't were later either captured or killed by the "Ruskies." Escape was a simple and easy matter; but to find a safe refuge was something else. Fighting inside Bromberg (Bydgoszcz) went on for several days during which time Poles hid British POWs. When the mopping up was complete, hardly a German or a Volkdeutsche remained alive. All of them, men, women, and children were "eliminated."

Capt. Allen says a few Germans tried to escape by putting on British or Russian uniforms. The majority of these were recognized by the Poles, who either shot them on the spot or turned them over to the "Ruskies." All of those carryings-on made it very difficult for the POWs. The Bromberg Poles rendered invaluable service by their vouching for the identity of the British.

Corp. George Forrester has had an unusual existence since February 23, 1943. On this date, the Gestapo removed him from Thorn. He was tried for a crime against the "Reich" and sentenced to five years hard labor. While awaiting transfer, he escaped and a few days later rejoined his comrades who were in a Kommando camp, without the Germans knowing about it. And for two years he lived with his buddies at Stalag 20-A, as a "ghost!" Now

he is a free man on his way home in one of
"His Majesty's Ships."

January 23 - Kcynia (Exin), Poland

Col. Edgar Gans and about one hundred and fifty
other Americans, escapees, congregated at a large farm
estate. Upon the advice of the Poles, they remained
hidden in a large barn until the Russians and the Poles
had "eliminated" the local "Goons." Then the "Ruskies"
contacted them in the barn.

"Gentlemen, I have come to take you to Moscow!"
promised a Lt. Max, Russian Interpreter, who,
incidentally, is a graduate of New York City College.

Everybody was happy, and the "spiritas" was passed
around; many got drunk. Lt. Max said he was one of
Zhukov's battalion commanders. Those drunk blinked
and believed him; those sober didn't, but knew he was a
counterintelligence officer.

Col. F. W. Drury, who had his picture taken,
proposed a toast, and quite glibly - but quite innocently -
made a mistake, according to Col. Gans.

"Here's to the 'Big Three', Stalin, Churchill, (a pause
- to drink, no doubt) and Hitler!"

Everything got very quiet. Lt. Max turned white,
then red. Finally, Col. Drury saw his unpardonable
social blunder and said, "Oh, I mean Hitler is Kaputt!"
to quote Col. Gans.

A West Pointer, quite "tight," added more tension to
the occasion by making this stupid toast:

"Here's to the sixty billion dollars of Lend-Lease
America has sent to Russia."

This toast was certainly unfit and unfitting. Lt.
Max, with a cold smirk on his face, retorted:

"Yes, and here's to the twenty million Russians who
have died to save America - and Russia!"

Col. Gans declared that he did everything in his
power to keep the Americans in and out of trouble. Two
young officers, who had been sleeping out with two
Polish girls, were ordered back to the barn. They came,
but under insubordinate protests. When asked why they
wanted to stay with the Poles, they explained that they

were doing it only to protect the "virtue" of two Polish girls against the "Ruskies;" and that the "Ruskies" were after all the young girls in town! This of course, was a gross false statement.

The Russians, anxious for harmony, became quite angry when they learned that a few reactionary Poles were inciting reactionary feelings among a few simple-minded Americans.

During the three weeks of waiting at Exin, Col. Gans command dwindled from one hundred and fifty to about sixty! All the rest had taken off for better hunting grounds. The fault with the American is his impatience and ungratefulness. I'm inclined to agree.

Why Did the Officers Go AWOL?

If Col. Gans should ask the delinquent why he went AWOL, he would probably say, "Sir, I have no excuse," or "Sir, I didn't know that I was violating any order."

If a disinterested party - say a lieutenant - should ask the delinquent why he did so, he would probably say, "Col. Gans just sat around and didn't force the Russians to evacuate us," or "The living conditions and the food situation were terrible and Col. Gans did nothing about it." Actually, Lt. Col. Lewis Gershenow, from Pennsylvania and Lt. Col. Gains Barron, from Waco, Texas, were there. They will tell you that Col. Gans' hands are clean; that he did everything he could to get everyone evacuated; and that at no time did any one of them go hungry or live under "terrible" conditions. Most important of all, he carried out the instructions of the Russian officers in the sense of cooperation.

Chapter Twenty Six
February 1945

February 14 - Konin, Poland (Wartaland)

Konin was the scene of bitter, suicidal rear guard defense on the part of Jerry. Konin was a key communication center on the Varta River. The OKW knew that the Varta was the last natural obstacle before the Odor River. Hence, according to Poles in Konin, the OKW left fifteen thousand troops to slow up Marshal Zhukov's mighty hordes. It took two days for Zhukov's "Ruskies" to destroy this force - to the last man. There is a forest between Konin and Kola. Many Germans fled into this forest. I saw thousands of German equipment, e.g., helmets, uniforms, broken up rifles, etc. along the Konin-Kola road. A Polish sergeant swore that this forest now contained the dead bodies of the eighteen thousand - to the last bone.

February 15 - Warsaw (The City That Used To Be)

Briefly speaking, Warsaw, particularly on the east side of the Vistula, is now a pile of rubble and dead bodies. Why waste words that wouldn't be believed? Only seeing is believing. Even if you have seen it, you wouldn't believe it.

The Vistula at Warsaw is about a kilometer wide. Jerry destroyed all four bridges. This didn't stop the "Rusky." After Warsaw was captured in January, the "Rusky" engineers, with the help of eight thousand Poles, built an all-wood railway bridge across the Vistula. According to Lt. Col. Tom Riggs, ex-POW, a former 106th Infantry Division engineer on the West Front, it's a masterpiece of bridge-work. Cantilever style arches are built in, as is an all steel design. The greatest marvel of this project, however, is the fact that ten days from the time the first plank was nailed up, military trains were rolling across the Vistula with vital supplies for Marshal Stalin's Red Armies! At each end of the bridges, railway and highway, stands an imposing color portrait of Marshal Stalin.

February 17, 1945 - Relocation and Dislocation

Now, there are millions of refugees, soldiers and civilians of all ages, who have been liberated by the Russians, moving back by every conceivable way to a new home, or to the old one if it was still there. Poverty and misery are ever present. Some are walking, some are riding in boxcars and still others are moving back in dilapidated wagons, sleds or carts. Congestion is terrific on the roads and in the towns. Many are hungry, and a few are starving; however, Poland is still far better off from a food standpoint than Russia. I know; I have been in both places. The hardest hit were milk-less mothers with nursing babies. In Kuna, Poland, Lt. Siska and I stopped a refugee wagon for information; on this wagon were a man, his wife and two baby girls - the smallest baby having died because the mother could not obtain milk.

The Poles are slowly taking hold of the situation and setting up Red Cross centers in every town to feed and care for the transients. In spite of all hardships, these people are rugged. They have always known hardships. They expect hardships. But there is a glow of light. Regardless of what you might hear, these people are happily regaining self-confidence and self-control.

February 26 - Rembertow, Poland

Before the war, Rembertow was the largest containment and training area in all Poland. As of this date, it's the largest international collecting point ("refugee mad-house" is a better name) in Poland. If I saw one pile of human feces, I saw a hundred thousand. To quote Col. Drury: "It's too damn bad these refugee camps couldn't have been located a mile apart, and then Poland wouldn't have needed any fertilizer for the next hundred years." There's one good thing about this Rembertow "manure" business; you had to be alert; if you weren't - well, you'd likely step on - or in - the wrong thing.

You will never understand the problem of the Russian authorities unless you have seen thousands of refugees, ex-prisoners of all nationalities, men, women and children in one place - under uncontrollable and impossible circumstances - all eating together (mainly potatoes and "kasha" rice) and sleeping together (on floors, on the ground etc.). It was no uncommon sight to see men, women and children side-by-side, unblushing, and unashamed, it was just taken for granted nothing else could be done about it.

What did we eat out of? Cans, buckets, anything with a bottom. Was there any griping? Naturally.

There was one thing worthy of praise for everybody: in spite of everything they were happy. Rembertow represented the first real phase of evacuation. Vera Friedman, one of fifty liberated Jewish refugee girls, told of her experience:

We are Czech Jews, most of us coming from Travala, Czechoslovakia (Slovensko). The Jews in Slovensko were not particularly persecuted until Marsh 19, at which time the Gestapo marched into this country. One afternoon, the Gestapo and SS troops came to Travala, rounded up all Jews and informed us that we were to leave in two hours for the Reich. We left, in two hours, in a prison train.

At a concentration camp near Cracow, SS troops threw two thousand of us into a large room and ordered every one of us - men, women and children - to strip naked. Then they sorted us into several groups, according to age, sex, size, physical fitness and looks. All of our heads were shaved to mark us. The SS troops sneered and laughed at those women who were unshapely, with sagging "tummies" and other things.

From here, we were sent to East Prussia. No child was allowed to see its mother. One afternoon, in an East Prussia lager, a female child saw her mother from across the street, and ran to meet her. An SS guard shot her full of holes with an automatic gun.

For eight months, we dug trenches, tank traps, and laid mines in Prussia. Many of us died of malnutrition and typhus. Our clothing consisted of a stiff heavy work dress. We had no underwear.

Then, in January, the Russians broke through the East Prussian defenses so rapidly, that the SS troops didn't take time to dispose of us. Now, here we are in Rembertow. We are not annoyed at Rembertow discomforts and filth. It's a pleasure to be here.

(Incidentally, the Jewish girl's hair was just beginning to grow out, at this date, February 16, 1945.)

February 19

A very handsome and distinguished captain arrived as a personal representative from Marshal Zhukov's HQ. This captain was the "Hero of the Soviet" order, which is one of the U.S.S.R.'s highest awards, the "Order of Victory" being the highest.

Lt. Max and Col. Drury were informed that on February 22, all Americans and British in Rembertow and Lublin must leave by train for the Port of Evacuation: Odessa, the great Russian Port on the Black Sea. Wine was brought out. Everybody celebrated - some got drunk - but everybody was happy. Especially Lt. Max, the Russian officer in charge of the Americans at Rembertow!

The food situation east of the Vistula was fair to bad! Congested areas suffer much more than small towns, villages and farms. In Rembertow, I saw those who having money or something to trade, ate fairly well. On the other hand, I saw others, having nothing but their freedom, eating potato-peelings from garbage piles. So, draw your own conclusions.

You have heard it said, no doubt, that wherever Americans go, price control machinery takes a tail-spin. How true! You have also heard it said that the American is the best-liked individual in the world. Take away the American's money, his extra cigarettes, clothing, and shoes, which he normally barters with - and he would be liked, individually, as the British, French and other nationalities are. Rembertow markets were swamped with GI clothing, Red Cross blankets, etc. The Americans did not fool Lt. Max when they told him that they needed more clothing and blankets to keep themselves warm. Max had been in the markets; and furthermore, he had seen his whole grain bread thrown away, after the Americans had stocked their private bags with this Polish white bread! Max didn't like this evacuation "business" a little bit. Who could blame him?

February 22

Some twelve hundred Americans and British on the train, at long last.

"You'll be in Odessa by February 27," said Lt. Max.

"Horosho, horosho." (Good, good)

"Da, da." (Yes, yes)

February 24 - 29 - Rembertow to Odessa

The train pulled out - two days late.

"Will we still arrive at Odessa on the 27th?" was the impatient question.

"Da, da," replied "Polkevnik" Baritshovske, distinguished thirty-one year old Russian colonel in charge of the train.

"Chas priget," time will tell; be patient!

The "Polkevnik" colonel was back from Marshal Zhukov's HQ. Among other things, this little colonel had been a division commander, until he was wounded. He bore the Medal of Honor, Order of the Red Banner, Order or the Red Star and the Order of Lenin. Russia's recognition of meritorious deeds in the form of decoration and orders is characteristically a great morale factor among her worthy Red Army officers and soldiers.

The "Polkevnik" had accompanying us on his staff, one doctor, two nurses, six other girls and twenty "Rusky" GIs. They were all great boys and girls, and were a lot of fun throughout the trip.

It is about 1,450 kilometers from Rembertow to Odessa, via Brest-Litovsk, Kovel-Rovne, Berditschev, Shmerinka, Brisula, and Rasdjelnaja. All personnel, except field officers and the Russian staff, rode in boxcars, provided with straw mattresses and stoves. The cold Russian winter made it pretty uncomfortable. Nevertheless, this train was better provided for than a similar train bearing Russian personnel. So, why should we complain?

February 25 - Brest-Litovsk

Not so many months ago, in the summer of 1944, it will be recalled that this place figured highly in world news. It changed hands several times and today Brest-Litovsk is like Warsaw - one ugly pile of rubble. German fashion! The Bug River is wide, formidable and ugly. The only activity in the destroyed city is hinged in the railway yards, up and down the tracks. Scores of Russian women are engaged in laying new tracks and repairing the old.

It will be remembered that Brest-Litovsk was the scene of the 1917 Armistice, ending the Russian-German conflict.

February 26

Between Brest-Litovsk and Kovel, a land of graveyards and desolation, it looks cold and bleak. Very little activity was observed, except right along the railway, where the Russians either lived in mud huts or in dug-outs. Every foot of the railway tracks had been plowed up by the gigantic German Wehrmacht tie-splitting plow. All was in working order, now, in spite of the methodic destruction.

The "Rusky" gals were a jolly lot, even though they "ne ponimaju," didn't understand a word we said. Among other things, Major Dobson taught a couple of them to sing - by sounds - "Pistol Packing Mama." Before the train reached Kevel, two "Rusky" GIs fell off the train. "It didn't hurt them," said the "Polkevnik," "they will catch up with us at Odessa." They did. Occasionally, the "Rusky" fired his tommy gun at various objects - dug-outs- posts, etc. - just to keep his gun in working order. It was O.K. with the "Polkevnik" as long as "Joe Rusky" didn't exceed his daily allowance of ammunition - fifteen rounds.

February 27 - Vissizn (South Bug River)

The further south we went into the fertile rolling Ukraine, the more activity we observed. Russian women and German POWs were doing construction of some sort.

This city, on the Bug that flows into the Black Sea, must have been a beautiful old city before the "Goons" came. Along the riverbanks, old steepled castles, some partially destroyed, silhouetted the morning sky-line.

War-correspondent Wright Bryan, ex-West Front (*Atlanta Journal*) correspondent who had gotten a radio from a Polish officer, kept us posted on world news. We ex-POWs wonder if people so far away from the battle-front know what it is like inside of Germany, when such high officials as Sir James Grigg, British Minister of War, makes the following statement released over BBC in London:

"Prisoners of war in the congested areas of Germany are likely to suffer food shortages, due to poor transport service." (True!) But, "Sir James Grigg has been informed by International Red Cross officials at Geneva that American trucks are standing by at I.R.C. headquarters to rush food parcels to POWs." (We heard this same story in November and December 1944, when we had no parcels) Sir James continues, "Food will be dropped to them by parachute if it becomes necessary." (A good cause - but most highly fantastic, Sir James.

You apparently don't know the "Goons," furthermore, you would have to drop the food all over central Germany.) The POWs would sardonically laugh at this "dream."

February 27 - Shmerinka 2:00 P.M.

For the first time, I saw a "Rusky" with his "feathers up." Yanks got tired of the Russian ration, as they began to trade off clothing, blankets, etc., for what food they could find (which was very little) at each stop. The "Polkevnik" hit the top when he caught a Yank trading a Russian-issue blanket for a dozen eggs! (Clothing in this part of Russia is scarcer than food.) You could get a pocket full of rubles for a pair of pants, or a pair of shoes or a blanket.) The staff was sympathetic to the "Polkevnik's" problem, but how to put an end to it was another thing,

From here, southward, there was a distinct climate change - climate more like that in "God's Country." Instead of two coats, you needed only one. Most of the snow had melted and there were signs of approaching spring weather. The plains as far down as Odessa, are fertile, flat and wet. The breeze from the sea is wonderful!

February 29 - Odessa 11:00 P.M.

Odessa was the first Russian town during the entire trip that was not destroyed - only part of it. The "Goons" were in a hurry when they left Odessa.

We were not the first Americans and British escapees to reach this port. The "AWOLs" (among them was Lt. Col. "Q", let's call him) from Exin, Lublin, and Rembertow, had beaten us to the port. "Home-in-a-hurry" boys! There were about fifty of these "jerks" in this category.

We were divided into four camp groups and housed in the pre-war Soviet Film colony. Being the senior lieutenant colonel at camp, I assumed command, while Lt. Col. "Q," who was relieved, made it a point to stay out of circulation. This "AWOL" had done a good job at Odessa. He saw to it that the other "AWOLs" got at least three complete "Rusky" uniforms! Why? God only knows. The Yanks certainly did not need them, but like children looking for a new toy - they wanted souvenirs and bartering goods. Besides, they ran a chance of getting the hometown paper to take a picture of them in this all "Rusky" attire! I stopped this "business" and naturally hurt a few feelings - dear, dear God.

As I've stated before, there's nobody like an "Amerikanski." The American mission minister, a Maj. Hall (a Cornell graduate), and the Russian staff went out of their way to be nice to us. American chow from the ships nicely supplemented the Russian ration. "Rusky" girls prepared the food - three whole meals a day. I drank grapefruit juice - from the Lower Rio Grande Valley - for the first time in twenty-two months. Oh, how wonderful it was!

Two charming Russian girls on "Polkevnik" Afanassi Ivan Stoev's staff, both interpreters, had just arrived from Moscow: Natasha Koroleva and Olga Politikina, language graduates of the University of Moscow. I've never talked with more cheerful girls. When she was a young girl, Natasha's father was an Ambassador to Tokyo. She started her language instruction under an American while there, and expects to leave for Mexico City shortly, to work for the Russian Ambassador.

Life in Odessa is pretty dull. Every ounce of Russian energy here - as well as everywhere else along the way - is put to the war effort. There are movies and operas for the people - some two hundred thousand (before the war, seven hundred thousand). There is no admission charged. Seats are filled well in advance of the performance. I was told the Germans left the Opera House intact. They were in too great a hurry.

A "Rusky" staff sergeant said that you have to pay twenty thousand rubles for a milk cow or a horse. The only trouble was that you couldn't find the cow or the horse. Either they were transported beyond the Urals or stolen by the Germans.

Chapter Twenty Seven
March 1945

March 7 - All Aboard!! H.M.S. Moreton Bay

Saying "Good-bye" to our Russian friends at the docks, some four thousand American and British ex-POWs boarded the Moreton Bay. Col. F. W. Drury and Wright Bryan, who hoped to fly to Moscow and then to the United States, and Lt. Col. "Q," who planned to hitch-hike his way back to his battalion "somewhere in France," remained in Odessa. On leaving Russia, I sincerely hope for them - what I believe the "Rusky" wants - many years of post war peace. It has been a pleasure knowing them.

An egg, bacon and good American coffee - that was the first breakfast. "Living the life of Riley!" Ah, yes, yes!

March 8 - The Bosporus and Istanbul

Turkey, the land of Kemel Antaturk, who tried to uncover that modest Moslem female face by banishing the veil - but couldn't. The Bosporus Strait, which separates two continents but not the people, with the ancient water that today sees as much of the Red Star as the Quarter Moon and Three Stars i.e., the Soviet and Turk flags, respectively.

Istanbul, once called Constantinople, is the ancient city of minarets and outmoded "Harem" Palaces of Turkish Sultans. I saw Istanbul from H.M.S. Moreton Bay. It is a place I'd like to see again. After "der Krieg is Kaputt."

March 9 - The Dardanelles

Ask the British Empire if they remember the Dardanelles. Most likely they will say, "Yes, by-jove: World War I!" One squint at the Dardanelles and you understand.

March 9 - 10 - The Aegean Sea

If you have ever seen one of the islands in the Aegean Sea, you have seen them all for they all look alike. It was in the Aegean that a rumor went around aboard the Moreton Bay, that all Yanks who don't have a sufficient amount of clothing to keep them warm (it must be at least sixty degrees warmer here than in Russia this time of the year) come to the ship's clothing storeroom - "D" Deck and "indent" for a British Battle suit.

Of course, practically every "lef-tenant" and captain - also a couple of majors - wanted one of these suits. But, Lt. Col. Kelsey, C.O. of the Americans, had made it plain that if they already had (and they did) a pair of trousers, a shirt and a pair of shoes (American or British) they wouldn't get anymore. Well, the way to get around that was to throw overboard all clothing - walk up to the supply office and look powerfully cold and naked! Believe it or not, Lt. Col. Lou Gershenow, Maj. Merle Meacham and I stood on the starboard side of the ship and saw all sorts of clothing, (pants, shirts and shoes) flying out of the portholes. The three of us went immediately to Lt. Col. Kelsey and reported the "foxy" old trick. Then, Lt. Col. Kelsey went smartly to the supply room. What did he find? Eighty Yanks in pajamas, shorts and stockings only, all lined up to draw a British Battle suit, so they wouldn't be cold when they hit Port Said, on the sunny shores of the Mediterranean. The C.O. "blew his top" and ordered all eighty back to their quarters, giving each individual fifteen minutes to turn out for personal inspection, in full dress! They passed the inspection, all right. Didn't breathe a word as to where they got the extra uniforms they had borrowed.

March 10 - Crete

We saw Crete at a safe distance. Some of the British on board had been captured there.

Before leaving H.M.S. Moreton Bay, I must say that the entire ship crew was extremely nice to us, in spite of the fact that we practically ate up all of their food.

March 14 - Port Said, Egypt

The dear old British Empire practically owns and controls the entire Suez Canal and Port Said, but Old John Bull - who is nobody's fool - manages it in such a subtle way as to make it appear to old King Farouk and his Egyptians that they do. It's an old trick, in an old land, but it works: Titles, plenty of brassy-bronze medals and decorations, arm-bands, plenty of fanfare and plenty of "you-are-it" publicity, which suits to a tee the ego of the Egyptian "class." The British are great colonizers. The "nobility" has held the Empire together, I believe. Take the power from them and give it to the Bevin Bureaucrats and Great Britain will fall apart, because this universal loyalty to one subject, the King, is and always has been the important thing that makes the U.K. work. What works in Britain will not work in the United States - and vice versa - but they both work. Most Americans care nothing for titles, and being a Texan, myself, I want no part of it. But I say "Let the British have them, if that is what they want."

It was nice to set foot on Africa once more. Middle East Service Command Yanks had things well organized. Brigadier Gen. Ritter, whom I formerly knew in North Africa, was there with his M.E.S.C. staff to take care of a few hundred American ex-POWs. They did it in good old American style. Two whole "B-rations" daily (we ate it all, too); all the Army GI clothing we wanted; the most recent American magazines; Red Cross girls with their smiles, and loads of kits, phonographs, recordings, and radios; Special service movies; and Mr. Charles Garvey's U.S.O. Unit #316. "Gentlemens," I'm here to tell you that there's no soldier in the entire world, who is better cared for than the American. There's nothing like it.

Let's not forget to thank the British M.E.S.C. authorities for the nice manner in which they treated us at Port Said.

March 16, 1945 - All Aboard H.M.S. Samaria

Once again we're in the Mediterranean - under very different circumstances from those in 1942-43. Food, conveniences, and conditions were even better aboard U.S.S. Samaria then H.M.S. Moreton Bay. This menu should prove my point:

Breakfast
Coffee, Cereal, Toast, 2 eggs

Lunch
Iced-tea, Salad, Steak, French Fries, Ice Cream

Dinner
Milk, Soup, Mutton Dinner, Cream Pie (and seconds if desired)

Just Plain Unadulterated "Crap" in American Magazines.

While breezing along at sixteen knots, with time for complete rest and relaxation, I found myself hungrily reading all sort of American magazines - the most recent and the old. Those articles dealing with or telling about Russia, I read and re-read. Some, in my opinion, were the truth, but some were unadulterated "crap." As I read them, I found myself enjoying some and underscoring others with what I call biased statements.

(1) Edgar Snow's "The Ukraine Pays the Bill," *Saturday Evening Post*, Jan. 27 1945 issue:

From what I saw of Russia and Europe, I agree with Snow 100% when he says, "The Ukraine has suffered more from Nazi pillaging and needs more reconstruction than any other part of Europe." I can't vouch for Snow's figures but I can vouch for the truthfulness of the above statement.

(2) William White's "Report on the Russians," Part II, *Reader's Digest* for January 1945. Being an American, I believe in being able to gripe about anything, anytime I so desire - but I do believe in being logical, unbiased and using common sense, in those characteristic American "gripes." Now after reading, "Report on Russian," Part II, I am convinced that Mr.

White was sure of the type of article he was going to write before he even went to Russia. How can he say that the Russian soldier is extremely well fed, particularly the front line soldier, when in the first place, he was several hundred kilometers from the front line soldier, and when in the second place, he seems to make all of his comparisons and criticisms with American standards? As a matter of fact, a bottle of "spiritas," a slab of fat meat, a loaf of black bread, and a little "Kasha" would be a good ration to the "Rusky." But - how about the American?

Mr. White quoted a Russian soldier as saying that the Jeep he was riding in was made in Russia. By citing this one case, Mr. White has given the American public a misleading fact, which is that all Russians believe that the Jeeps, Studebakers, etc. are made in Russia and are not part of Lend-Lease. It is not true. I was with thousands of Russian soldiers and not one case did I find where the "Rusky" did not appreciate or know the role that Lend-Lease is playing.

Mr. White says the Russian women are sallow and tired. He never mentioned seeing pretty, port ones. I saw many, many really beautiful "Rusky" WACs. How Mr. White could criticize the Russian for too much "Red Tape" I don't know. I was more amazed at the absence of "Red Tape" than at the presence of it. Is there any country that has as much "Red Tape" as America?

He complains about the Russians not giving American reporters freedom to roam about in Russia and write about anything to their heart's desire. I personally don't blame the Russian for this action since there are many who misrepresent the picture.

March 20 - Naples, Italy

A long, slow round trip is almost completed. It was at Avellino, forty miles east of Naples that I was taken prisoner September 15, 1943.

The place in Naples that I wanted to go first was the belching old volcano, Vesuvius. How bad had been the damage? How many civilians had it killed when it erupted in 1944? The German press had carried the story that the American "Terror-bombers" had bombed the crater intentionally to start this eruption, and that it was designed to terrorize the civilians of Naples. The press said that the lava had practically destroyed Naples.

The Replacement Depot MTOLISA gave us a fine reception, excellent chow, more clothing, late movies, and passes to see Naples. I was very much surprised to see so much of everything to sell, to see the population going about normally. After having read Archbishop Francis J. Spellman's "Report from Italy," *Colliers*, January 20, 1945, I expected to see the Italians starving to death by the thousands. I expected to see the Italians "crushed." I expected to see Italy in an almost unbelievable state of famine. I expected to find things deplorable. I guess the Bishop and I just don't see things alike. If he should see Poland and Russia, he would most likely die with anxiety before he could write the story up for the American public. Bishop, you could better serve by sticking to your job of preaching!

I just can't "sabe" the kind of war that is being fought in "Naples." I've been a doughboy (infantryman) too long I guess, to want to hang around.

Chapter Twenty Eight
April 1945

On a C-54, fifteen of us ex-POWs hopped off for Tunisia. The airport certainly didn't look like the bomb-torn field that I saw at the close of the Tunisia campaign. How much American dough has been sunk into this immaculate new modern airdrome, I could not venture to guess.

Casablanca

The Azores

New Foundland

Washington, D.C.

It's wonderful!!!!!

Epilogue

Back In The USA

Upon his return to the U.S., Col. Yardley sent a post card to his folks dated March 21, 1945, which states the following:

My, it's wonderful to be back - free with Uncle Sam's boys. You will never know my feelings, Darlings, I am awaiting transportation home. I will call you as soon as possible upon my arrival there. All my very best regards and love to all of you.

Your loving Son,

/s/ Doyle

Assignment in South America

On May 19, 1945, after a 90-day period of "rest and recuperation," the War Department sent Col. Yardley to Panama where he worked with the Military Mission Division under Gen. Jerome Waters, Sr. from Panama. He went on a goodwill tour through Central and South America to tell the Latins what he learned about the Germans while a prisoner of war. Being fluent in Spanish made this an easy and enjoyable assignment for him. In August 1945, he was returned to the United States once more.

Returning to Civilian Life

A collection of handwritten notes and letters give us further information about Doyle following his military discharge. On May 31, 1945, he wrote, "My Dearest Auntie and Uncle Al, I haven't heard from my wife since April 27 - I'm going to start divorce actions very soon if she doesn't write."

On December 1, 1945 he writes regarding his possible candidacy for United States Congressman:

Dearest Auntie and Uncle Al, I'm on my terminal leave. I go back to inactive status Feb. 4, 1946.

I have been down here going over District 15 to feel out possibilities for Congress. But Auntie, the vote is practically sewed up in a "machine." I think I'll sell my farm. I think I can get $150 per acre and put the money in bonds and get a job and forget all about this business of politics.

I'm going to work in Dallas, or Washington with the Standard Fruit Company in Central America. I know Mom is not going to approve of this Central American idea at all, but "I must live my own life, Mary."

On Feb. 4, 1946, he received his discharge, after serving over five years for his country, 37 months of this service being overseas.

Back Home

Doyle eventually left his south Texas farm to temporarily live with his parents. There he worked with his father on the family farm while pursuing several career opportunities. He became a representative to the American Legion, Texas Chapter, and was helping them formulate policies to help "veterans who want to become farmers." The week of April 16th, he spent three days working with an American Legion Committee in Washington, D.C. on this veterans' project. Minutes of that Washington meeting indicate that he and his colleagues met with and were briefed by top officials of the Department of Agriculture and a number of other federal agencies.

Upon returning home, he wrote friendly letters to the American Legion about his work (dated April 22, 1946). In that letter he detailed his enthusiasm for their work and planned to contribute actively in future meetings.

On April 23rd Doyle wrote Capt. and Mrs. Bailey, who he acknowledged as among his best friends, and chatted about coming to see them soon in San Antonio. This was the last letter Doyle ever wrote.

Doyle Yardley died that same day, April 23, 1946, at his parent's home near Lingleville, Texas. He had just celebrated his 33rd birthday. Both the letter to the Baileys and the letter to the American Legion were found in his military footlocker, in addressed envelopes, never mailed.

A local newspaper obituary tells of this tragic loss:

From Newspaper Clipping: "Paratroop Officer Fatally Shot While Cleaning Gun:"

DUBLIN, April 24 - Col. Doyle R. Yardley, 33, paratroop officer and former prisoner of war of the Germans, was accidentally shot to death Tuesday afternoon in the bathroom of his parents' home, four miles west of Lingleville.

He was the son of Mr. and Mrs. A. A. Yardley. His father said he had been rabbit hunting and was cleaning his rifle, when it was discharged. He was shot through the lung, near the heart.

Yardley, a member of the 509th Parachute Infantry Battalion, who had seen service in North Africa and Sicily, was wounded and captured September 15, 1943, two and one-half hours after jumping behind German lines at Salerno, Italy. He held the Purple Heart and the Bronze Star Medal.

During most of the 16 months he was held captive he was confined in Oflag 64, Szubin, Poland. He escaped from the camp in January 1945, while German guards were moving prisoners to another camp, and made his way to the Soviet lines. He was with the Russian 5th Army under Marshal Zhukov for two months and then

was sent to Odessa, where transportation
to the United States was arranged.

He returned home in April last year
and later was sent to South America on an
assignment. He was discharged last Feb. 6.

Funeral services will be held at the
Baptist Church in Lingleville Thursday
afternoon. Burial will be in charge of the
American Legion.

Colonel Yardley's Legacy

There is no greater way to honor my Uncle Doyle
than to publish the diaries that were left behind in that
olive green footlocker. His story is remarkable. It
portrays the very best - and the very worst - of the
human spirit.

May God bless America and its soldiers, who so
valiantly protect our freedom - our greatest treasure as
a Nation.

Charles A. Turnbo

Index

Symbols

A

E

F

G

T

Y

Z